Great Escapes
Around the World
Europe • Africa • Asia • South America • North America

Great Escapes
Around the World

Europe • Africa • Asia • South America • North America

Edited by Angelika Taschen

TASCHEN

HONG KONG KÖLN LONDON LOS ANGELES MADRID PARIS TOKYO

704 Sundance, US
696 Dunton Hot Springs, US

Roisheim Hotel, NO 024
Charlton House Hotel, UK 034
Château de Bagnols, FR 070
Les Sources de Caudalie, FR 080
La Mirande, FR 088

Emerald Lake Lodge, CA 564

580 The Seth Peterson Cottage, US

Amangani, US 710

572 Trout Point Lodge, CA
586 Land's End Inn, US

Auberge du Soleil, US 682

Finca Son Gener, ES 1

Reid's Palace Madeira, PT 136

Wilbur Hot Springs, US 676

Hotel Dar Cherait,
Amanjena, MA 148

Post Ranch Inn, US 668

620 Ten Thousand Waves, US

M.S. Kasr Ib

594 The Moorings Village, US

El Capitan Canyon, US 662

Hotel Le Kambary, ML 282

552 Hotel San Pedro de Majagua, CO

Hope Springs Resort, US 650

602 Hotel San José, US

Parker Palm Springs, US 656

608 The Hotel Paisano, US

544 Kapawi Ecolodge & Reserve, EC

Furnace Creek Inn, US 642

614 Thunderbird Motel, US

Ng

The Ahwahnee, US 688

626 Rancho de la Osa, US

536 Hotel Monasterio, PE

436 Txai Resort, BR
446 Pousada Etnia, BR
462 Vila Naiá – Paralelo 17°, BR
454 Ponta do Camarão, BR
Sossusvlei Wilderness

634 Shady Dell RV Park, US

528 Hotel de Sal, BO

Pirá Lodge, AR 484

476 Yacutinga Lodge, AR

470 La Posada del Faro, UY

Hotel Antumalal, CL 518

492 La Escondida, AR
500 Estancia Santa Rita, AR

explora en Patagonia, CL 510

016 Icehotel, SE

042 Hotel Kaiserin Elisabeth, DE
058 Hotel Alpenhof Kreuzberg Looshaus, AT
066 Badrutt's Palace, CH
054 Hotel Vila Bled, SI
100 Villa Fiordaliso, IT
108 Hotel Cipriani & Palazzo Vendramin, IT

114 Grand Hotel Parco dei Principi, IT

414 Commune by the Great Wall Kempinski, CN

Gôra Kadan, JP 420
Benesse House, JP 426

292 Ananda, IN

164 Adrere Amellal Desert Eco-Lodge, EG
1.S. Eugenie, EG 174
Devi Garh, IN 300

310 Udai Bilas Palace, IN
Bagan Hotel, MM 338
The Regent Chiang Mai Resort & Spa, TH 346

Angkor Village, KH 354
408 Ana Mandara Resort, VN
402 Amanpulo, PH

Houseboat, IN 318
332 Ulpotha, LK
Taprobane Island, LK 324
Cheong Fatt Tze Mansion, MY 362

Il N'gwesi, KE 190
184 Sarara Tented Camp, KE
Dodo's Tower, KE 196
e Giraffe Manor, KE 204
o Crater Lodge, TZ 210
220 Emerson & Green Hotel, TZ
228 Chumbe Island Coral Park, TZ

368 Amanjiwo, ID
376 Losari Coffee Plantation – Resort and Spa, ID

236 Sausage Tree Camp, ZM

384 Four Seasons Resort Bali, ID
392 Taman Selini, ID

240 Jao Camp, BW
A 274
248 Nxabega Okavango Safari Camp, BW
a Lodge, ZA 266
258 Singita Boulders Lodge, ZA

270 Bloomestate, ZA

Contents Sommaire Inhalt

Europe

Africa

Contents Sommaire Inhalt

Asia

South America

Contents Inhalt Sommaire

North America

Europe

Sweden • Norway • England • Germany
Slovenia • Austria • Switzerland
France • Italy • Spain • Portugal

Text by Shelley-Maree Cassidy   *Edited by* Angelika Taschen

"Life is a journey, the idea is the map."
Víctor Hugo

SCOTLAND

IRELAND

ENGLAND

Charlton House Hotel 034 ●

FRANC

Château de Bagnols 070 ●

Les Sources de Caudalie 080 ●

La Mirande 08

PORTUGAL

SPAIN

Finca Son Gener 126 ●

● 136 Reid's Palace Madeira

MOROCCO   ALGERIA

● 016 Icehotel

● 024 Roisheim Hotel

● 042 Hotel Kaiserin Elisabeth

● 058 Hotel Alpenhof Kreuzberg Looshaus

● 066 Badrutt's Palace Hotel

● 054 Hotel Vila Bled

● 100 Villa Fiordaliso

● 108 Hotel Cipriani & Palazzo Vendramin

● 114 Grand Hotel Parco dei Principi

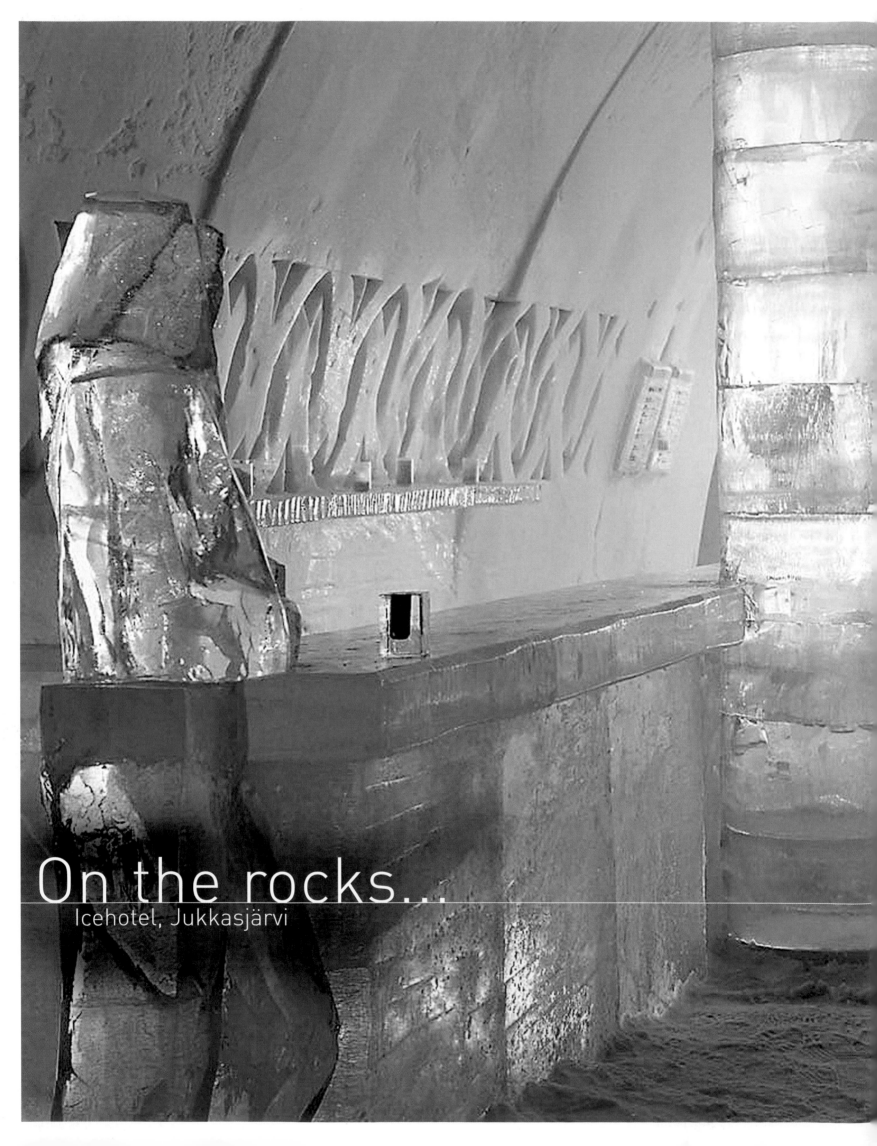

On the rocks...
Icehotel, Jukkasjärvi

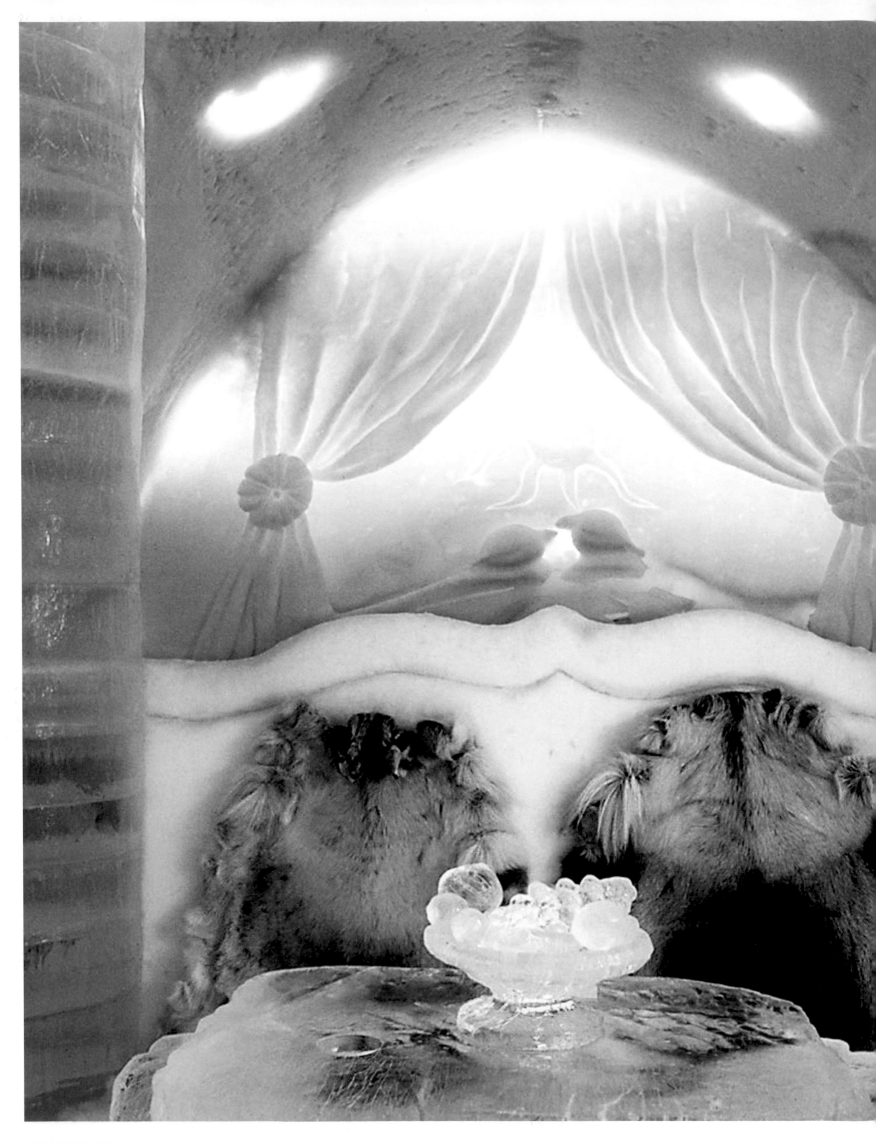

Icehotel, Jukkasjärvi

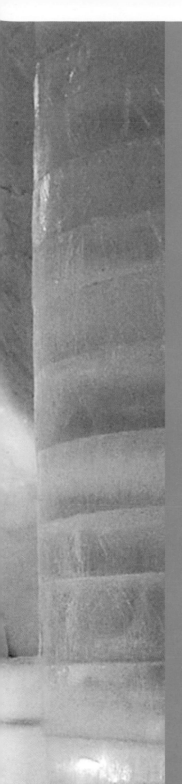

On the rocks

People flock to this icy place deliberately; experiencing life in an igloo is the magnet.

But this is of course not the usual sort of igloo. It is more of a frozen palace in the far north of Sweden. The Icehotel is proof of the saying that "all that glitters is not gold". Here, all that glitters shows that it is cold, very cold, or else the hotel would melt. And so it does. The arrival of summer sees it starting to thaw and then disappear. A new building is sculpted each year. Ice provides both the building blocks and the furnishings.

Inside, it is 3–5 °C below zero (23–24 °F), which is quite mild when compared to the climate outside. The thick ice is almost soundproof, so that even the noise of your teeth chattering will be muffled. But you'll be snug in an arctic sleeping bag, on your ice bed draped with reindeer skins. A hot drink comes with the wake-up call, and a sauna will bring you back up to room temperature.

Another of its attractions is the opportunity to see the stunning Northern Lights. Starry streaks of colour arch across the night sky in a painterly light show staged by Nature.

Books to pack: "Love in a Cold Climate" by Nancy Mitford
"Miss Smilla's Feeling for Snow" by Peter Høeg

Icehotel
SE – 981 91 Jukkasjärvi
Sweden
Tel· + 46 (0) 980 668 00
Fax: + 46 (0) 980 668 90
E-mail: info@icehotel.com
Website: www.icehotel.com
Booking: www.great-escapes-hotels.com

DIRECTIONS	200 km/124 m north of the Arctic Circle; 85-minute flight from Stockholm, 15 minutes from Kiruna
RATES	€ 189 to 299 for a night in the Icehotel; € 55 to 149 in the bungalows; open December to April
ROOMS	60 rooms, including 20 ice suites; in the Icehotel 30 bungalows and 12 rooms
FOOD	The local inn serves delicacies with a Laplandic touch
HISTORY	The Icehotel opened its doors for the first time in 1990 and is built anew every winter
X-FACTOR	The chill factor and Northern Lights

Auf Eis gelegt

Das Leben in einem Iglu scheint eine magische Anziehungskraft zu besitzen, denn die Menschen strömen in Scharen
an diesen eisigen Ort. Natürlich handelt es sich hier nicht
um einen gewöhnlichen Iglu, vielmehr um einen zu Eis
erstarrten Palast im höchsten Norden Schwedens. Das Icehotel ist der beste Beweis für das Sprichwort »Es ist nicht
alles Gold, was glänzt«. Denn alles, was hier glänzt, ist eisig
kalt, weil das Hotel sonst schmelzen würde. Und tatsächlich
beginnt das Hotel, wenn der Sommer naht, zu tauen und
verschwindet schließlich ganz. Jahr für Jahr wird es mitsamt
der kompletten Einrichtung neu gemeißelt.
Die Temperatur im Inneren des Hotels beträgt -3 bis -5 C°,
was verglichen mit der Außentemperatur geradezu mild
erscheint. Die mächtigen Eisblöcke sind nahezu schalldicht,
sodass nicht einmal das Klappern der Zähne zu hören ist.
Doch auf dem mit Rentierfell bezogenen Eisbett, einge-
mummelt in den Polarschlafsack, ist es schön mollig warm.
Mit dem morgendlichen Weckdienst wird ein heißes
Getränk serviert, und ein Besuch in der Sauna bringt den
Körper wieder auf Zimmertemperatur.
Eine weitere Attraktion ist die einmalige Gelegenheit, die
grandiosen Nordlichter zu beobachten: jene in allen Farben
erstrahlenden Lichtbögen am nächtlichen Himmel, die wie
eine von Künstlern erschaffene Lightshow anmuten.
Buchtipps: »Liebe unter kaltem Himmel« von Nancy Mitford
»Fräulein Smillas Gespür für Schnee« von Peter Høeg

Avec glaçon

Un endroit glacial, mais on y va de son plein gré, tant est
exaltante l'idée de séjourner dans un igloo.
Bien sûr, il ne s'agit pas de n'importe quel igloo. Parlons
plutôt d'un palais gelé, tout au nord de la Suède. L'Icehotel
est bien la preuve que « tout ce qui brille n'est pas or ».
Ici, tout ce qui brille est froid, glacé même, sinon l'hôtel
fondrait. Ce qui se produit régulièrement. L'arrivée de l'été,
en effet, le voit s'affaisser puis disparaître. Et chaque année,
un nouvel édifice est sculpté dans la glace, murs et mobilier
compris.
À l'intérieur, il fait -3 à -5° C, ce qui n'est rien comparé à la
température extérieure. Grâce à l'épaisseur de la glace, les
chambres sont quasiment insonorisées, et c'est à peine
si vous entendrez claquer vos dents tandis que vous vous
loverez dans un sac de couchage polaire, sur un lit de glace
recouvert de peaux de rennes. Une boisson chaude vous
sera servie dès votre réveil, et un sauna vous remettra à
température ambiante.
Parmi les autres attractions de l'hôtel figure la contemplation de l'aurore boréale : des arcs colorés illuminent la nuit
comme dans un spectacle de lumières mis en scène par la
Nature.
Livres à emporter : « L'Amour dans un climat froid » de Nancy
Mitford
« Smilla et l'amour de la neige » de Peter Høeg

ANREISE	200 km vom nördlichen Polarkreis entfernt, ca. 85 Minuten Flug von Stockholm, von Kiruna 15 Minuten Fahrt	ACCÈS	À 200 km au nord du cercle polaire arctique ; à 85 minutes d'avion de Stockholm, et à 15 minutes de Kiruna
PREIS	189–299 € pro Nacht im Icehotel, 55–149 € im Bungalow; geöffnet von Dezember bis April	PRIX	De 189 à 299 € pour une nuit à l'Icehotel ; de 55 à 149 € pour les bungalows ; ouvert de décembre à avril
ZIMMER	60 Zimmer, inklusive 20 Ice-Suites, im Icehotel 30 Bungalows und 12 Zimmer	CHAMBRES	60 chambres, dont 20 suites ; au Icehotel 30 bungalows et 12 chambres
KÜCHE	Das örtliche Gasthaus bietet Delikatessen mit leicht lappländischer Note	RESTAURATION	L'auberge locale sert des spécialités lapones
GESCHICHTE	Das Icehotel wurde 1990 eröffnet und wird jeden Winter neu aufgebaut	HISTOIRE	Inauguré en 1990, l'Icehotel est a nouveau sculpté chaque hiver
X-FAKTOR	Eisige Kälte und fantastische Nordlichter	LES « PLUS »	La glace, bien sûr, et l'aurore boréale

Norwegian wood...
Roisheim Hotel, Lom

Roisheim Hotel, Lom

Norwegian wood

Over the highest mountain pass of all in the "Land of the Midnight Sun"; through terrain that has been etched by great glaciers; with spectacular views of fjords far below, near the town of Lom, is this quaint old farmhouse. It has been here since the 17th century. Travellers who came this way have always stopped to rest here. After a short pause, they would resume their journey. Now, although it appears at first sight to still be an old farmhouse, it is a hotel.

Once you pass through the simple façade of this ancient building, you will find there is quite a plush interior. The charming style is one that respects its heritage, yet blends it with modern touches.

Roisheim Hotel is in the heart of one of the most superb parts of Norway. The greater part of this area is a national park. You can see why the wild and beautiful region is called the Home of the Giants. In this impressive landscape are two of the highest peaks in Europe. It seems apt that a museum of mountains is to be found in Lom.

Book to pack: "Dreamers" by Knut Hamsun

Roisheim Hotel		
2686 Lom	DIRECTIONS	350 km/220 m north-west of Oslo, 15 km/9 m from Lom
Norway	RATES	€ 134 to 175
Tel: + 47 61 21 20 31	ROOMS	24 rooms in 13 cottages
Fax: + 47 61 21 21 51	FOOD	The food is a combination of traditional ingredients and modern cuisine
E-mail: roisheim@dvgl.no	HISTORY	The oldest building was built about 1550, most of the others date from the 18th century. Roisheim has been receiving guests since 1858
Website: www.roisheim.no		
Booking: www.great-escapes-hotels.com	X-FACTOR	Fantastic landscape with breathtaking views

Norwegisches Holz

Jenseits des höchsten Gebirgspasses im »Land der Mitter-
nachtssonne«, eingebettet in eine von gewaltigen Gletschern
geprägte Landschaft mit einem atemberaubenden Blick auf
die Fjorde, befindet sich nahe der Stadt Lom dieses malerische alte Haus, in dem sich früher eine Poststation befand.
Es wurde im 16. Jahrhundert erbaut und bot seit jeher
Reisenden, die hier vorbeikamen, die Möglichkeit zu rasten,
bevor sie ihren Weg fortsetzten. Zwar wirkt es auch heute
noch auf den ersten Blick wie ein altes Bauernhaus, doch
verbirgt sich hinter der einfachen Fassade ein äußerst
elegantes Hotel. Die geschmackvolle Einrichtung legt Wert
auf Tradition, ohne auf einen Hauch von Modernität zu
verzichten.

Das Roisheim Hotel liegt in einer der herrlichsten Landschaften Norwegens, deren größter Teil Naturschutzgebiet
ist. Sie werden es sicher schnell verstehen, warum man
diese wilde, wunderschöne Gegend auch die »Heimat der
Riesen« nennt. In dieser eindrucksvollen Landschaft befinden sich zwei der höchsten Berge Europas. Womöglich aus
diesem Grund gibt es in Lom ein Bergmuseum.

Buchtipp: »Segen der Erde« von Knut Hamsun

Le bois norvégien

Au-delà du plus haut col montagneux du « Pays du soleil
de minuit », près de la ville de Lom, sur une terre sculptée
par les glaciers et entourée de vues spectaculaires sur les
fjords en contrebas, se dresse une vieille ferme datant du
XVIe siècle. Autrefois, les voyageurs sillonnant la région y
faisaient de courtes haltes avant de reprendre la route.
Aujourd'hui, un hôtel est installé dans la ferme qui a conservé
son aspect de jadis. La façade rustique cache un intérieur
aussi confortable que douillet. Le charme de l'aménagement
réside dans le respect du patrimoine mêlé à quelques touches
modernes.

Le Roisheim Hotel se trouve en plein cœur de l'une des plus
belles contrées de Norvège, dont la majeure partie est un
parc national. Surnommée le « pays des géants », cette
région compte deux des plus hauts sommets d'Europe. On
ne s'étonnera pas qu'un musée de la montagne ait élu
domicile à Lom.

Livre à emporter : « Rêveurs » de Knut Hamsun

ANREISE	350 km nordwestlich von Oslo, 15 km von Lom entfernt	ACCÈS	350 km au nord-ouest d'Oslo, 15 km de Lom
PREIS	Zwischen 134 und 175 €	PRIX	De 134 à 175 €
ZIMMER	24 Zimmer in 13 Häusern	CHAMBRES	24 chambres dans 13 maisons
KÜCHE	Eine Kombination aus einheimischen Zutaten und moderner Küche	RESTAURATION	Une combinaison d'ingrédients traditionnels et de cuisine moderne
GESCHICHTE	Das älteste Gebäude stammt von 1550, die meisten anderen wurden im 18. Jahrhundert erbaut. Seit 1858 empfängt Roisheim Gäste	HISTOIRE	Le bâtiment le plus vieux a été construit autour de 1550, la plupart des autres datent du XVIIIe siècle. Roisheim reçoit des hôtes depuis 1858
X-FAKTOR	Herrliche Landschaft mit atemberaubenden Aussichten	LES « PLUS »	Paysage merveilleux et vue à couper le souffle

Temptations of the countrysi
Charlton House Hotel, Somerset

Die Versuchungen des Landlebens

»Auf dem Lande kann jeder gut sein. Da gibt es keine Versuchungen.« Dies war Oscar Wildes Meinung – doch er kannte das verführerische Charlton House nicht. Gewiss hätte er es unwiderstehlich gefunden.

Der Stil des idyllisch gelegenen, luxuriösen Hotels ist durch und durch englisch. Dies ist in erster Linie auf die Einrichtung aus der Mulberry Collection, einer führenden britischen Marke für Lederwaren und Textilien, zurückzuführen. Eine große Verlockung stellt ferner das mehrfach vom Guide Michelin ausgezeichnete Restaurant dar. Egal ob Sie die traditionelle Küche lieben oder exotischen Speisen den Vorzug geben – das Restaurant hält kulinarische Genüsse für jeden bereit. Zu den vielen Reizen des Hauses zählt ebenso die angenehme Atmosphäre wie auch die herrliche Umgebung, die zum Entspannen einlädt. Im Übrigen ist Charlton House der ideale Ort, um Weihnachten zu feiern. Wer sich hierhin zurückzieht, geht dem alljährlichen Feiertagsstress auf äußerst elegante Weise aus dem Weg. Falls Ihnen dieser Gedanke verlockend erscheint, sollten Sie ihn unbedingt in die Tat umsetzen, denn »der einzige Weg, eine Versuchung loszuwerden, ist ihr nachzugeben«.

Buchtipps: »David Copperfield« von Charles Dickens
»Das Bildnis des Dorian Gray« von Oscar Wilde

Les tentations de la campagne

« Tout le monde peut être bon à la campagne. On n'y trouve aucune tentation. » Oscar Wilde n'a certainement jamais visité Charlton House où abondent les tentations. Il n'aurait certainement pas pu y résister.

Dans le silence de la campagne, ce splendide hôtel est la quintessence du plus pur style anglais. En effet, tous les éléments de l'aménagement intérieur proviennent de la Collection Mulberry, une marque renommée d'articles en cuir, de vêtements pour hommes et dames et de textiles pour la maison. L'hôtel possède d'autre part un restaurant doté d'une étoile au Michelin, proposant aussi bien une cuisine traditionnelle que des plats exotiques. Outre une agréable atmosphère, on y trouve de nombreux agréments, ne serait-ce que la contemplation du magnifique paysage environnant. Charlton House est une retraite rêvée pour passer Noël, loin du stress de la période des fêtes. Pourquoi ne pas vous l'offrir en cadeau? Si l'idée vous tente, n'hésitez pas un instant : « le meilleur moyen de se débarrasser d'une tentation, c'est d'y succomber. »

Livres à emporter : « David Copperfield » de Charles Dickens
« Le Portrait de Dorian Gray » d'Oscar Wilde

ANREISE	29 km südlich von Bath, 193 km südwestlich von London
PREIS	Zimmer zwischen 115 und 225 £, Suiten zwischen 250 und 355 £; Frühstück inklusive
ZIMMER	16 Zimmer
KÜCHE	Preisgekrönte und vom Guide Michelin ausgezeichnete Küche
GESCHICHTE	Das Gebäude wurde im 17. Jahrhundert erbaut und 1997 als Hotel eröffnet
X-FAKTOR	Klassisch englischer Landhausstil

ACCÈS	29 km au sud de Bath, 193 km au sud-ouest de Londres
PRIX	De 115 à 225 £ pour les chambres, de 250 à 355 £ pour les suites, petit déjeuner compris
CHAMBRES	16 chambres
RESTAURATION	Restaurant primé et des étoiles au Michelin
HISTOIRE	Construit au XVIIe siècle, l'hôtel a été ouvert en 1997
LES « PLUS »	Résidence à la campagne, dans la plus pure tradition anglaise

Royal antecedents...
Hotel Kaiserin Elisabeth, Bavaria

Menüs à la
Kaiserin Elisabeth
Kulinarisches und Lyrisches
Aufgekocht von
Sisi

FLASH

The red retreat...
Hotel Vila Bled, Bled

Hotel Vila Bled, Bled

The red retreat

In the northwest of Slovenia, nestled in the Julian Alps, is the breathtakingly lovely Lake Bled. Within this romantic fairytale setting, there is a residence with a real political story to tell. Once the summer home of the former Yugoslav royal family, and rebuilt to serve as the country villa of Marshal Tito, the Hotel Vila Bled now welcomes a more egalitarian range of guests within its walls. Despite its mid-1980s conversion to a prestigious hotel, the 1950s architecture and design has been left largely untouched. Much of the furniture, porcelain, and silverware are original, dating from its Eastern-Bloc days. The interior is an intriguing combination of austerity and ornamentation, with polished marble floors inset with colourful mosaics, plain chairs swathed in velvet, and patterned wall-coverings.

From the hotel's balconies and pavilion restaurant, you can look out at the picturesque island, where the little St. Marija Church has stood for centuries. Across the lake is the grim-looking medieval Castle Bled, imposingly sited on a huge rock. Summer or winter, this is a magical place with charismatic scenery and a powerful past.

Books to pack: "Black Lamb and Grey Falcon: A Journey through Yugoslavia" by Rebecca West
"The Radetzky March" by Joseph Roth

Hotel Vila Bled	
Cesta svobode 26	
Sl-4260 Bled	
Slovenia	
Tel: + 386 (0) 45 791 500	
Fax: + 386 (0) 45 741 320	
E-mail: hotel@vila-bled.com	
Website: www.vila-bled.com	
Booking: www.great-escapes-hotels.com	

DIRECTIONS	35 km/22 m north from Ljubljana Brnik International Airport, 35 km/22 m south from border crossings with Austria (Karawankentunnel) and 45 km/28 m from Italy (Ratece)
RATES	€ 95 to 360
ROOMS	30 rooms, including suites
FOOD	Slovenian cuisine
HISTORY	Built in 1947 for Marshal Tito, the Hotel Vila Bled opened in 1984
X-FACTOR	Fairytale setting and 1950s communist style

Die rote Zuflucht

Im Nordwesten Sloweniens, mitten in den Julianischen Alpen, liegt der atemberaubend schöne See von Bled. An diesem märchenhaft romantischen Fleckchen Erde befindet sich ein Domizil mit überaus spannender politischer Geschichte. Das Hotel Vila Bled diente früher der jugoslawischen Königsfamilie als Sommerresidenz und wurde später zum Landsitz von Präsident Tito umgebaut. Heute beherbergen seine Mauern jedoch Gäste aller Art. Beim Umbau des Gebäudes Mitte der 1980er-Jahre zu einem Luxushotel erhielt man zum größten Teil die Architektur und das Design aus den 1950er-Jahren. Auch zahlreiche Möbel sowie das Porzellan und das Silberbesteck stammen noch aus der Ostblock-Ära. Die Interieurs zeigen eine faszinierende Kombination aus Schlichtheit und Prunk, die in polierten Marmorböden mit farbigen Mosaiken ebenso zum Ausdruck kommt wie in gemusterten Tapeten und einfachen Stühlen, die mit luxuriösem Samt bezogen sind.

Von den Balkonen und dem Restaurantpavillon des Hotels aus blicken Sie auf eine malerische Insel, auf der die kleine, jahrhundertealte Kirche St. Marija steht. Am anderen Ufer des Sees thront die trutzige mittelalterliche Burg Bled auf einem hohen Felsen. Dieser magische Ort mit seiner eindrucksvollen Vergangenheit und faszinierenden Landschaft ist im Sommer wie im Winter ein besonderes Erlebnis.

Buchtipps: »Black Lamb and Grey Falcon. A Journey through Yugoslavia« von Rebecca West
»Radetzkymarsch« von Joseph Roth

Un refuge rouge

Au nord-ouest de la Slovénie, dans les Alpes Juliennes, s'étend le lac Bled, d'une beauté à couper le souffle. Ce cadre de conte de fées abrite une résidence dont les murs, s'ils parlaient, pourraient relater l'histoire politique des lieux. Villégiature d'été de la famille royale de Yougoslavie, reconstruit ensuite pour le maréchal Tito auquel il servit de maison de campagne, le Vila Bled fait désormais preuve d'un plus grand égalitarisme quant aux hôtes qu'il accueille. Transformé en un hôtel prestigieux au milieu des années 1980, il conserve toutefois son architecture et son style des années 1950. Le mobilier, la porcelaine et l'argenterie sont en bonne partie d'origine et datent de la période communiste. L'intérieur est un étonnant mélange d'austérité et d'ornementation : sols en marbre poli incrustés de mosaïques multicolores, sièges tout simples revêtus de velours et riches tentures murales.

Des balcons et du restaurant-pavillon de l'hôtel, on a vue sur une île pittoresque où la petite église Sainte-Marija se dresse depuis des siècles. Sur l'autre rive du lac, le château médiéval de Bled, d'aspect sinistre, couronne un énorme rocher. Été comme hiver, c'est un lieu magique empreint d'histoire, au paysage extraordinaire.

Livres à emporter : « Agneau noir et Faucon gris : un voyage à travers la Yougoslavie » de Rebecca West
« La Marche de Radetzky » de Joseph Roth

ANREISE	35 km nördlich vom internationalen Flughafen Brnik in Ljubljana, 35 km südlich von der österreichischen Grenze (Karawankentunnel) und 45 km von Italien (Grenzübergang Ratece)
PREIS	Zwischen 95 und 360 €
ZIMMER	30, einschließlich Suiten
KÜCHE	Slowenische Küche
GESCHICHTE	1947 für Präsident Tito erbaut, als Hotel Vila Bled 1984 eröffnet
X-FAKTOR	Märchenhafte Lage und sozialistisches Design der 1950er-Jahre

ACCÈS	À 35 km au nord de l'aéroport international Brnik de Ljubljana, à 35 km au sud de la frontière avec l'Autriche (Karawankentunnel) et à 45 km de l'Italie (Ratece)
PRIX	De 95 à 360 €
CHAMBRES	30 chambres et suites
RESTAURATION	Cuisine slovène
HISTOIRE	Construit en 1947 pour le maréchal Tito, le Vila Bled a ouvert ses portes en 1984
LES « PLUS »	Cadre de conte de fées et style des années 1950

Nature, no ornament.
Hotel Alpenhof Kreuzberg Looshaus, Payerbach

Hotel Alpenhof Kreuzberg
Looshaus, Payerbach

Nature, no ornament

"Design a country house for me; rustic, but with style", might have been the brief that Paul Khuner gave the famous architect Adolf Loos.

This is the house that was built for him in 1930. Loos was keen on design that was free of decoration, and explained his beliefs in an essay titled "Ornament and Crime". He argued that rich materials and good workmanship made up for a lack of decoration, and in fact far outshone it. The house may not be a decorative one, but it is not plain. Kept preserved much like it was when first built, it is now a hotel. The Alpenhof Kreuzberg Looshaus is perched high on a hillside in the Austrian Alps, encircled by fresh clean mountain air. While its function has altered, the present owners have guarded its original nature, which is as it should be for a building that has been recognized as a state treasure. Although some renovation has been carried out, it is in accord with the design. The colourful interior is proof of the architect's edict that planning should be done from the inside out, and his fondness for cubic shapes is obvious. The region is famed for its winter sports and spas, as well as being home to this design jewel.

Books to pack: "Ornament and Crime" by Adolf Loos
"Brother of Sleep" by Robert Schneider

Hotel Alpenhof Kreuzberg Looshaus	
Kreuzberg 60	
2650 Payerbach	
Austria	
Tel: + 43 (0) 2666 52911	
Fax: + 43 (0) 2666 5291134	
E-mail: steiner@looshaus.at	
Website: www.looshaus.at	
Booking: www.great-escapes-hotels.com	

DIRECTIONS	An hour's drive south of Vienna
RATES	€ 24 to 34, breakfast included
ROOMS	14 rooms
FOOD	Renowned home-style cooking with regional specialities
HISTORY	Built in 1930, the Looshaus was adapted as a holiday resort at the beginning of the 1950s
X-FACTOR	Design classic in a spectacular setting

Natur, keine Ornamente

»Entwerfen Sie mir ein Landhaus, rustikal, aber mit Stil«, so mag die Anweisung des Lebensmittelfabrikanten Paul Khuner an den berühmten Architekten Adolf Loos gelautet haben.

Das Ergebnis ist dieses 1930 erbaute Haus. Loos war Verfechter eines geradlinigen, schnörkellosen Stils, der seine Philosophie in einem Essay mit dem viel sagenden Titel »Ornament und Verbrechen« erläuterte. Seiner Meinung nach waren hochwertige Materialien und handwerkliches Können weitaus wichtiger als dekorative Elemente. Und so ist dieses zweigeschossige Blockhaus, das bei seiner Umgestaltung zu dem heutigen Hotel weitgehend im Originalzustand belassen wurde, auch nicht überschwänglich ausgeschmückt, dabei jedoch alles andere als schlicht.

Das Hotel Alpenhof Kreuzberg Looshaus liegt an einem Berghang hoch in den österreichischen Alpen, umgeben von frischer, reiner Bergluft. Obwohl es seine Funktion geändert hat, haben die heutigen Besitzern es originalgetreu renoviert, wie es einem Gebäude angemessen ist, das als nationales Baudenkmal anerkannt wurde. Notwendige Renovierungsarbeiten erfolgten in engem Einklang mit dem ursprünglichen Design. Die farbenfrohen Interieurs sind der beste Beweis dafür, dass ein Haus von innen nach außen geplant werden sollte, so wie es der Architekt forderte, und zeugen von seiner Liebe zu kubischen Formen.

Abgesehen von diesem architektonischen Juwel ist die Region berühmt für ihr Wintersportangebot und ihre Kurorte.

Buchtipps: »Ornament und Verbrechen« von Adolf Loos »Schlafes Bruder« von Robert Schneider

Nature sans ornements

« Dessinez-moi une maison de campagne, rustique, mais qui ait du style ! » Telle aurait pu être la commande passée par Paul Khuner au célèbre architecte Adolf Loos, et telle est la maison construite pour lui en 1930.

Loos préconisait une architecture dépouillée et a exposé ses principes dans un manifeste intitulé « Ornement et Crime ». Il affirmait que la richesse des matériaux et la qualité du travail compensaient l'absence de décoration, qu'en fait, ces deux facteurs jouaient un rôle bien plus important. Si la maison n'est pas décorative, elle sort cependant de l'ordinaire. Transformée en hôtel, elle conserve en grande partie son état d'origine.

L'Alpenhof Kreuzberg Looshaus, perché à flanc de montagne dans les Alpes autrichiennes, respire l'air frais alpin. Bien qu'il ait changé de fonction, devenant hôtel, ses propriétaires actuels ont veillé à lui garder son aspect original, comme il se doit pour un bâtiment classé. Les quelques rénovations effectuées s'accordent avec la conception d'origine. L'aménagement aux couleurs vives illustre parfaitement la prédilection de l'architecte pour les formes cubiques et son principe selon lequel la conception devait se faire de l'intérieur.

Outre pour ce bijou d'architecture, la région est réputée pour ses stations de sports d'hiver et ses villes d'eau.

Livre à emporter : « Frère sommeil » de Robert Schneider

ANREISE	Eine Fahrstunde mit dem Auto südlich von Wien	ACCÈS	À une heure de route au sud de Vienne
PREIS	Zwischen 24 und 34 €, Frühstück inklusive	PRIX	De 24 à 34 €, petit déjeuner compris
ZIMMER	14 Zimmer	CHAMBRES	14 chambres
KÜCHE	Berühmte Hausmannskost mit regionalen Spezialitäten	RESTAURATION	Cuisine familiale réputée avec spécialités régionales
GESCHICHTE	1930 erbaut und Anfang der 1950er-Jahre zum Hotel umgebaut	HISTOIRE	Construit en 1930, le Looshaus a été transformé en hôtel au début des années 1950
X-FAKTOR	Design-Klassiker in spektakulärer Umgebung	LES « PLUS »	Design classique dans un cadre spectaculaire

Auf Berges Spitze

Dieses wunderbare alte Grandhotel ist ein Symbol für
St. Moritz genauso wie die Berge und der See. Den ersten
Besitzern wird zugeschrieben, im ausgehenden 19. Jahrhundert den damals völlig neuen Wintersport eingeführt zu
haben. Vorher kamen die Reisenden eher im Sommer in die
Alpen, wanderten, suchten nach wild wachsenden Blumen
und genossen den Anblick der riesigen Bergspitzen. Durch
den Bau der ersten Rodelbahn und einer Curlinganlage ge-
lang es, die Gäste auch im tiefsten Winter und bei niedrigs-
ten Temperaturen zu einem Aufenthalt zu verführen. Heute
ist das Palace Hotel mit seinem Turm und seiner denkwür-
digen Silhouette zu einem Wahrzeichen geworden. In einer
atemberaubenden und bis heute unzerstörten Idylle liegend,
eingesäumt von Privatgärten, ist das Hotel eine Institution,
hinter deren Mauern man sich gerne verstecken mag. Im
Gegensatz zum Trubel von St. Moritz verläuft das Leben hier
friedlich. Skifahren, Polospielen und Pferderennen
im Schnee sind die Hauptattraktionen, vom Klima ganz
abgesehen. Denn St. Moritz ist mit durchschnittlich 322
Sonnentagen im Jahr gesegnet. Stil und Name des Ortes
sind so bekannt und beliebt, dass es mittlerweile ein einge-
tragenes Markenzeichen gibt. Die Marke »St. Moritz – Top
of the World« bezieht sich dabei nicht nur auf die geogra-
fische Lage, sondern auch auf den Status dieses Ortes.
**Buchtipp: »In eisige Höhen. Das Drama am Mount Everest«
von Jon Krakauer**

Au sommet du monde

Ce vieil hôtel magnifique est un symbole de Saint-Moritz
autant que le lac et les montagnes qui entourent la localité.
À la fin du XIXe siècle, ses premiers propriétaires jouèrent
un rôle primordial dans la création des sports d'hiver.
Jusqu'alors, on villégiaturait surtout en été dans les Alpes,
pour y faire de la randonnée, admirer les fleurs sauvages et
les imposants sommets. En construisant la première piste
de luge du monde, ainsi qu'un terrain de curling, l'hôtelier
attira des clients en plein cœur de l'hiver. Le Palace Hotel,
avec sa tour et sa silhouette unique, est devenu un véritable
monument. Situé dans un cadre aussi splendide qu'intact,
et entouré de jardins privés, l'hôtel est une véritable institution, au sens noble du terme. La vie y est paisible, malgré sa
situation en plein centre de cette station très courue. Ski,
polo et courses de chevaux sur la neige font partie de ses
atouts, sans oublier le climat : Saint-Moritz bénéficierait de
322 jours de soleil par an. La station est si renommée que
son nom est devenu une marque déposée. « Saint-Moritz, top
of the world » résume à la fois sa situation et son standing.
Livre à emporter : « Tragédie à l'Everest » de Jon Krakauer

ANREISE	220 km südöstlich von Zürich entfernt. Die Fahrt durch Graubünden und das Engadin gehört zu den malerischsten und interessanten Routen Europas
PREIS	Zwischen 234 und 2892 €, Frühstück inklusive
ZIMMER	248 Zimmer, Suiten eingeschlossen. Vom 29. September bis zum 6. Dezember ist das Hotel geschlossen
KÜCHE	Das Hotel verfügt über drei Restaurants, darunter einen berühmten Dinersaal im französischen Stil
GESCHICHTE	Das Hotel aus dem 19. Jahrhundert eröffnete 1896
X-FAKTOR	Das Angebot an Aktivitäten. Für den Cresta-Run auf der gleichnamigen Bob-Bahn muss man etwas Mut aufbringen

ACCÈS	À 220 km au sud-est de Zurich. La ligne de chemin de fer à destination d'Engadine, qui traverse les Grisons, est l'un des trajets les plus pittoresques d'Europe
PRIX	De 234 à 2892 €, petit déjeuner compris
CHAMBRES	248 chambres, dont plusieurs suites. Fermeture annuelle du 29 septembre au 6 décembre
RESTAURATION	L'hôtel compte trois restaurants, dont le restaurant français, très réputé
HISTOIRE	Construit au XIXe siècle, l'hôtel a ouvert ses portes en 1896
LES « PLUS »	Les activités proposées, notamment le Cresta Run, célèbre course de bobsleigh

Majestic seclusion…

Château de Bagnols, Bourgogne

Château de Bagnols,
Bourgogne

Majestic seclusion

Lord of all you can see – at least this could be your dream,
as you look out from the ramparts of what was once a fortress,
and now is a secluded retreat.

Complete with moat and drawbridge, the Château de Bagnols
stands on a high vantage point in the lovely Burgundy coun-
try-side, guarding its guests from the public gaze and cares
of the outside world. Hidden behind massive stone but-
tresses and towers are a fabulous hotel and garden, a haven
for the fortunate few. First built in 1221 as a medieval strong-
hold, the Chateau is now one of France's historic monuments, restored to its rightful splendour. Its portcullis opens
to reveal peaceful gardens and terraces, sheltered by yew
hedges and encircled by a stone wall. After entering the castle's courtyard, the arriving guests step into an atmosphere
of history and grandeur. Many of the rooms have striking
Renaissance wall paintings, uncovered during recent restoration. Antique beds are hung with period silk velvets and
embroideries; rich tapestries adorn walls, and great elabor-
ately carved fireplaces blaze out warmth in the winter.

The famous vineyards of Beaujolais and the charming towns
and villages in the rolling green hills and valleys beyond may
well tempt you out from your castle realm.

Book to pack: "The Red and the Black" by Stendhal

Château de Bagnols	
69620 Bagnols	
France	
Tel: + 33 (0) 474 71 4000	
Fax: + 33 (0) 474 71 4049	
E-mail: info@bagnols.com	
Website: www.bagnols.com	
Booking: www.great-escapes-hotels.com	

DIRECTIONS	24 km/15 m north of Lyon
RATES	€ 397 to 1145; open April to January, or by arrangement
ROOMS	20 rooms, including 8 apartments
FOOD	Beaujolais cuisine, regional specialities
HISTORY	Built in 1221, the château has been transformed several times over the centuries. The hotel was opened in 1991
X-FACTOR	Regal rural retreat, privacy assured

Majestätische Ruhe

Wenn Sie vom Schutzwall dieser ehemaligen Festung um sich schauen, werden Sie sich wie der Herr über die Ihnen zu Füßen liegenden Ländereien fühlen. Denn das Château de Bagnols, umgeben von einem Graben mit einer Ziehbrücke, überragt majestätisch die liebliche Landschaft des Burgund. Heute birgt es ein abgeschiedenes Plätzchen, das Schutz vor der Außenwelt bietet.

Versteckt hinter massiven steinernen Pfeilern und Türmen befindet sich ein Hotel mit einem wunderschönen Garten, in dem Sie sich herrlich entspannen können. Das im Jahr 1221 errichtete mittelalterliche Château gehört heute zu Frankreichs Baudenkmälern. Hinter seinem Falltor erstrecken sich friedliche Gärten und Terrassen, geschützt durch Eibenhecken und eine steinerne Mauer. Sobald Sie den Burghof betreten, werden Sie von der ganz besonderen Atmosphäre verzaubert. Viele der Zimmer bestechen durch eindrucksvolle Wandgemälde aus der Renaissance, die erst vor kurzem freigelegt wurden. Seidensamtvorhänge und Stickereien zieren die antiken Betten; die Wände sind mit üppigen Gobelins behängt, und große Kamine mit kunstvollen Einfassungen verbreiten im Winter wohlige Wärme.

Doch die berühmten Weinberge des Beaujolais sowie die reizenden Städte und Dörfer, die verstreut über die umgebenden Hügel und Täler liegen, sind geschaffen dafür, Sie auch gelegentlich hinter Ihren Burgmauern hervorzulocken.

Buchtipp: »Rot und Schwarz« von Stendhal

Une retraite majestueuse

Montez sur les remparts de cet ancien château fort, aujourd'hui paisible retraite, et imaginez-vous seigneur des lieux qui s'étendent sous votre regard.

Avec ses douves et son pont-levis, le Château de Bagnols, érigé dans une situation admirable, domine la ravissante campagne bourguignonne. Derrière ses tours et contreforts massifs se cachent un hôtel fabuleux et un charmant parc, paradis pour les happy few. Forteresse médiévale dont la construction débute en 1221, ce château classé monument historique a retrouvé sa splendeur d'antan. La herse se lève pour révéler des jardins et terrasses paisibles, abrités derrière des haies d'ifs et entourés d'un mur en pierre. Histoire et splendeur accueillent les hôtes dès leur arrivée dans la cour du château. Un grand nombre des salles sont revêtues de magnifiques fresques Renaissance, découvertes durant la récente restauration. Les lits anciens sont fermés par des rideaux de velours de soie et de dentelles d'époque ; de riches tapisseries ornent les murs et, en hiver, les grandes cheminées sculptées avec art font rayonner leur chaleur.

Les célèbres vignobles du Beaujolais ainsi que les jolis bourgs et villages qui émaillent ce paysage de collines et vallées verdoyantes vous inciteront certainement à quitter les murs de votre château de rêve.

Livre à emporter : « Le Rouge et le Noir » de Stendhal

ANREISE	24 km nördlich von Lyon
PREIS	Zwischen 397 und 1145 €; Öffnungszeiten April bis Januar oder nach Vereinbarung
ZIMMER	20 Zimmer, einschließlich 8 Apartments
KÜCHE	Regionale Spezialitäten aus dem Beaujolais
GESCHICHTE	Das Gebäude wurde 1221 errichtet und über die Jahrhunderte mehrfach umgebaut. Als Hotel wurde es 1991 eröffnet
X-FAKTOR	Königliches, ländliches Refugium mit garantiertem Schutz der Privatsphäre

ACCÈS	À 24 km au nord de Lyon
PRIX	De 397 à 1145 €, ouvert d'avril à janvier, ou sur demande
CHAMBRES	20 chambres, dont 8 suites
RESTAURATION	Cuisine du Beaujolais, spécialités régionales
HISTOIRE	Construit en 1221, le bâtiment a été transformé plusieurs fois au cours des siècles. L'hôtel a ouvert en 1991
LES « PLUS »	Retraite rurale royale, tranquillité garantie

Im Wein liegt Wahrheit

Ein Gläschen Wein, so sagt der Hausarzt, sei gut für die Gesundheit. Nun, hier können Sie nicht nur einen guten Rot- oder Weißwein trinken, Sie können auch in ihm baden. Les Sources de Caudalie ist ein Hotel, das rundherum dem Gaumen schmeichelt. Nicht nur, dass dieses Hotel eine außergewöhnliche Wellnessanlage besitzt, es liegt zudem zufälligerweise mitten in einem Weinberg.

Wer sich mit der einzigartigen »Vinotherapie« verwöhnen lassen möchte, kann einen Merlotwickel versuchen, eine Sauvignonmassage oder ein Körperpeeling mit zerstoßenen Cabernettraubenkernen. Einige der Behandlungen, ob Anti-Age oder Abnehmkur, basieren auf Weinprodukten und schmecken so gut, wie sie aussehen. Überdies werden dem Feinschmecker gleich zwei Restaurants und ein Weinkeller mit über 15 000 Flaschen geboten. Hartnäckige Raucher dürfen sich nach dem Dinner in die Bibliothek des Turmzimmers zurückziehen und Mitglied des Zigarrenverkostungsclubs werden. Andere verwöhnen in der Bar French Paradox ihre Geschmacksnerven mit Kostproben besonderer Jahrgänge.

Und wenn Sie nicht gerade das Restaurant oder den Wellnessbereich genießen, können Sie zum Beispiel Touren per Fahrrad oder Limousine zu den nahe gelegenen bedeutenden Weingütern der Regionen des Médoc, Sauternes, Pomerol und Saint-Émilion unternehmen. Der Abschied schließlich lässt sich nicht nur durch Mitbringsel der örtlichen Weinproduktion versüßen, sondern auch durch Caudalies Hautpflegeserie auf Traubenbasis.

Buchtipp: »Der große Meaulnes« von Alain-Fournier

La vérité est dans le vin

On sait fort bien que le vin est excellent pour la santé. Ici, non seulement on le consomme, mais on peut également se baigner dedans.

Les Sources de Caudalie est un hôtel délicieux, dans tous les sens du terme. Il offre une remise en forme très particulière et ce au beau milieu d'un vignoble.

Pendant votre séance de vinothérapie, unique en son genre, vous aurez le choix entre un enveloppement Merlot, un massage Sauvignon ou une exfoliation Cabernet ; à moins que vous ne préfériez un traitement anti-âge et minceur fondé sur des dérivés du raisin, qui vous mettrait presque l'eau à la bouche.

Les gastronomes trouveront deux restaurants, ainsi qu'une cave de 15 000 bouteilles. Après le dîner, les fumeurs pourront se retirer dans la tour-bibliothèque, fief du club des amateurs de cigares. Les autres choieront leurs papilles gustatives en dégustant des grands crus dans le bar French Paradox.

Après avoir goûté aux plaisirs de la table et des soins de beauté, vous irez découvrir les châteaux viticoles environnants, à bicyclette ou en limousine, et les grands domaines des régions de Médoc, Sauternes, Pomerol et Saint-Émilion. En souvenir, vous emporterez quelques bouteilles de vin local et les fameux produits de beauté Caudalie.

Livres à emporter : « Le grand Meaulnes » d'Alain-Fournier « Les Cent plus beaux textes sur le vin » de Louis et Jean Orizet

ANREISE	15 Minuten südlich von Bordeaux
PREIS	Zimmer zwischen 175 und 240 €, Suiten zwischen 290 und 425 €, je nach Saison
ZIMMER	49 Zimmer und Suiten
KÜCHE	Ein wahres Fest für die Sinne
GESCHICHTE	Erbaut und eröffnet 1999
X-FAKTOR	Wein für Gaumen, Sinne und Körper

ACCÈS	À 15 minutes au sud de Bordeaux
PRIX	Chambres de 175 à 240 €, suites de 290 à 425 €, selon la saison
CHAMBRES	49 chambres et suites
RESTAURATION	Le nec plus ultra pour les sens
HISTOIRE	Construit et ouvert en 1999
LES « PLUS »	Du vin pour le goût, la santé, la beauté

inner sanctum...
La Mirande, Avignon

La Mirande, Avignon

Inner sanctum

In medieval times, Avignon was the residence of several popes. Conflicts within the Catholic Church as well as between the Pope and the worldly powers are to be held responsible for this relocation.

The Pope's temporary displacement to Avignon resulted in a building fervour, as cardinals and prelates of the church strove to construct worthy earthly palaces and houses to dwell in. Originally the site of a 14th-century cardinal's residence, La Mirande is blessed with an ideal position. It is in the heart of the city, in a tranquil cobbled square, at the very foot of the Popes' Palace. Behind the hotel's original stone façade is an exquisite interior; one that bears testament to a real quest to attain a near faultless authenticity. Its success is such that even though it is relatively new, the interior seems to have evolved over generations and time.

Meticulously restored, using the style and materials of the 17th and 18th century, La Mirande has all the splendour of an aristocratic residence of the era, together with the best of contemporary cuisine. Under the coffered ceiling of the restaurant, inventive fare that makes you truly grateful is served.

**Books to pack: "All Men are Mortal" by Simone de Beauvoir
"Tartarin de Tarascon" by Alphonse Daudet**

La Mirande		
4, Place de la Mirande	DIRECTIONS	2.5 hours south from Paris by TGV; in the centre of Avignon
84000 Avignon	RATES	€ 260 to 640
France	ROOMS	19 rooms and 1 suite
Tel: + 33 (0) 490 859 393	FOOD	Michelin-starred restaurant, Provencal and French cuisine, with a cooking school for disciples
Fax: + 33 (0) 490 862 685		
E-mail: mirande@la-mirande.fr	HISTORY	Originally built in the 14th century, La Mirande was trans-formed several times over the centuries. The hotel was opened in 1990
Website: www.la-mirande.fr		
Booking: www.great-escapes-hotels.com	X-FACTOR	Aristocratic interior and heavenly food

Im Allerheiligsten

Im Mittelalter war Avignon mehrfach für kurze Zeit Sitz des Papstes. Konflikte innerhalb der Kurie sowie zwischen Päpsten und weltlichen Mächten führten zu diesen unfreiwilligen Ortswechseln.

Begleitet wurde dieser kurzzeitige Umzug nach Avignon von einem wahren Bauboom, denn Kardinäle und Prälaten der Kirche machten es sich zur Aufgabe, schon auf Erden Paläste und Häuser zu errichten, die ihrer würdig waren. Wo heute das Hotel La Mirande steht, befand sich im 14. Jahrhundert die Residenz eines Kardinals. Auch strategisch liegt das Hotel himmlisch, mitten im Herzen der Stadt nämlich, an einem verträumten Platz mit Kopfsteinpflaster, direkt am Fuß des Papstpalastes. Hinter der Originalfassade des Hotels versteckt sich ein herrliches Interieur, das auf Schritt und Tritt das Bestreben erkennen lässt, so viel Authentizität wie möglich herzustellen. Obwohl noch gar nicht alt, wirkt die Innengestaltung, als hätten an ihr ganze Generationen und Zeitläufte gewirkt.

Im Stil des 17. und 18. Jahrhunderts bis ins Detail restauriert, strahlt La Mirande die Pracht einer aristokratischen Residenz aus und bietet gleichzeitig das Beste aus der heutigen Küche. Unter der Kassettendecke des Restaurants wird kreative Kochkunst geboten, die zu wahren Dankesgebeten verleitet.

Buchtipps: »Alle Menschen sind sterblich« von Simone de Beauvoir

»Die Abenteuer des Herrn Tartarin aus Tarascon« von Alphonse Daudet

Inner sanctum

Au Moyen Âge, Avignon devint pendant plusieurs courtes périodes la ville des Papes, lorsque des conflits au sein de la curie et entre la papauté et les pouvoirs temporels conduisirent à ce changement de résidence involontaire.

L'installation du Pape en Avignon entraîna un boom dans la construction, les cardinaux et prélats rivalisant dans l'édification de palais et demeures luxueuses. Autrefois résidence d'un cardinal du XIVe siècle, l'hôtel La Mirande jouit d'une situation privilégiée. En plein cœur de la ville, sur une paisible place pavée, il se dresse au pied du Palais des Papes. Derrière la façade d'origine, se cache un ravissant intérieur qui se targue de rechercher une authenticité quasi parfaite. Cela avec grand succès, car bien qu'il soit relativement récent, l'intérieur de La Mirande semble avoir évolué au fil des générations et du temps.

Méticuleusement restauré, dans le style et les matériaux des XVIIe et XVIIIe siècles, l'hôtel possède toute la splendeur d'une résidence aristocratique d'époque. S'y ajoute une cuisine contemporaine de grand chef ; sous le plafond à caissons du restaurant, de superbes plats originaux vous seront servis.

Livres à emporter : « Tous les hommes sont mortels » de Simone de Beauvoir

« Aventures prodigieuses de Tartarin de Tarascon » d'Alphonse Daudet

ANREISE	2,5 Stunden Fahrt südlich von Paris mit dem TGV. Im Zentrum von Avignon gelegen
PREIS	Zwischen 260 und 640 €
ZIMMER	19 Zimmer und 1 Suite
KÜCHE	Vom Guide Michelin ausgezeichnetes Restaurant mit provenzalischer und französischer Küche. Eine Kochschule ist dem Restaurant angeschlossen
GESCHICHTE	Erbaut im 14. Jahrhundert, mehrfach über die Jahrhunderte umgebaut und 1990 als Hotel eröffnet
X-FAKTOR	Aristokratisches Interieur und himmlisches Essen

ACCÈS	À 2 heures 30 au sud de Paris en TGV ; en plein centre-ville d'Avignon
PRIX	De 260 à 640 €
CHAMBRES	19 chambres et 1 suite
RESTAURATION	2 étoiles au Michelin, cuisine française et provençale. Cours de cuisine pour les adeptes
HISTOIRE	Construit au XIVe siècle, le bâtiment a été transformé plusieurs fois au cours des siècles. L'hôtel a ouvert en 1990
LES « PLUS »	Intérieur aristocratique et cuisine succulente

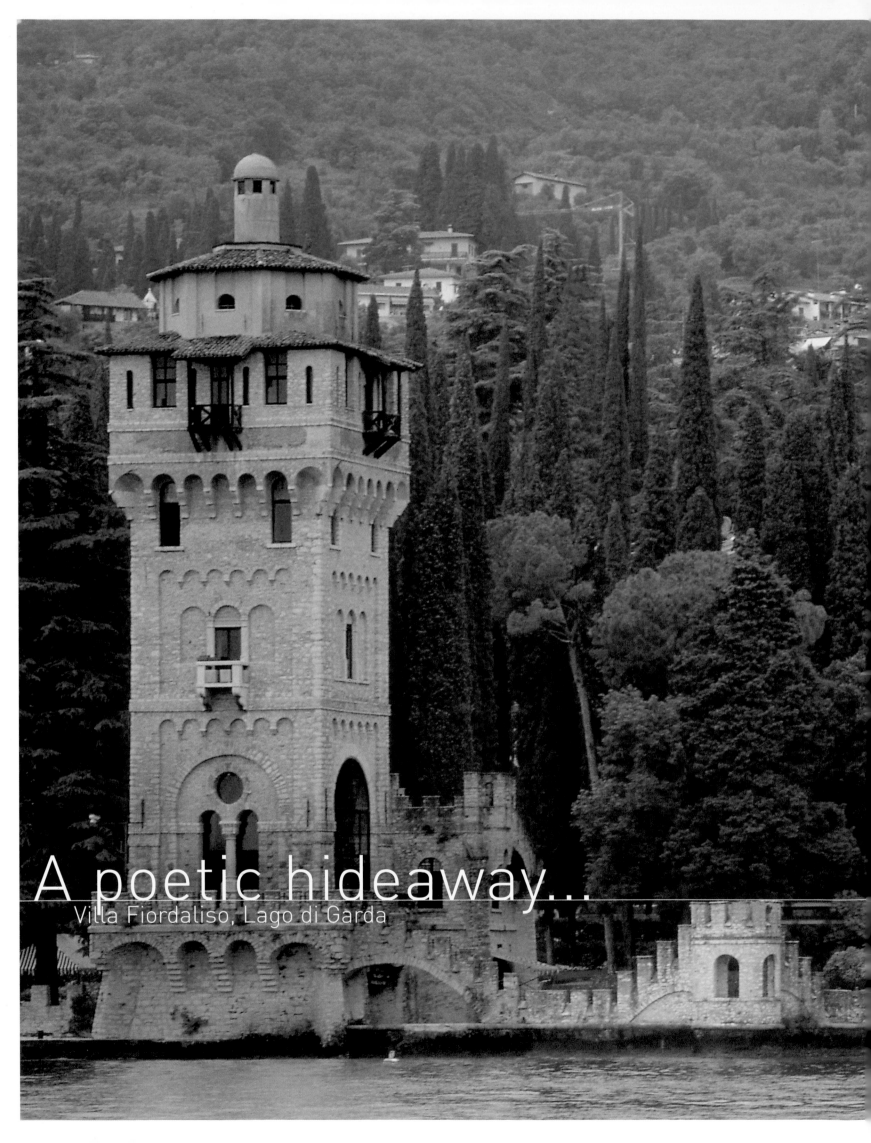

A poetic hideaway...
Villa Fiordaliso, Lago di Garda

Villa Fiordaliso, Lago di Garda

A poetic hideaway

There is a romantic air of time gone by here. The view is much the same across the lake as it was when the poet Gabriele D'Annunzio looked out from his window. Perhaps he had writer's block and was hoping to be inspired as he gazed at the tranquil waters.

Villa Fiordaliso is an ideal place to hide away, whether or not you are prone to poetry or prose. The setting is poetic in itself. Framed by cypresses, pine, and olive trees; and on the edge of Lake Garda, the elegant old villa has a sense of absolute calm. No doubt, if the walls of the classic interior could speak, many anecdotes might be told of those who have stayed here, from poets to dictators. For utter romantics, there is a most enticing place close by; the city of Verona, famed for being the source of the tragic love story of Romeo and Juliet. Walking through the streets and underneath the balconies of the "pair of star-crossed lovers", you believe the tale to be true.

You will very likely become lyrical over the cuisine, since the menu may not have been written by a poet, but is certainly cooked by artists. Parting from Villa Fiordaliso will indeed be an occasion for "sweet sorrow".

Books to pack: "Romeo and Juliet" by William Shakespeare "The Flame" by Gabriele D'Annunzio

Villa Fiordaliso
Via Zanardelli 150
25083 Gardone Riviera
Italy
Tel: + 39 (0) 365 201 58
Fax: + 39 (0) 365 290 011
E-mail: fiordaliso@relaischateaux.com
Website: www.relaischateaux.com
Booking: www.great-escapes-hotels.com

DIRECTIONS	40 km/25 m north-west of Verona
RATES	€ 181 to 491
ROOMS	7 rooms
FOOD	A Michelin-starred restaurant
X-FACTOR	Utterly romantic

Ein malerisches Versteck

An diesem Ort spürt man den Zauber vergangener Zeiten.
Der Blick über den See ist noch derselbe wie damals, als der
Dichter Gabriele D'Annunzio aus seinem Fenster schaute.
Vielleicht hatte er einen Schreibblock dabei und ließ sich
von dem ruhigen Gewässer vor seinen Augen inspirieren.
Die Villa Fiordaliso ist ein idealer Ort, um sich zurückzu-
ziehen. Allein die Landschaft ist reinste Poesie! In der von
Zypressen, Pinien und Olivenbäumen eingerahmten alten
Villa am Ufer des Gardasees herrscht absolute Stille. Wenn
die Wände des klassischen Interieurs reden könnten, wür-
den sie zweifellos hübsche kleine Anekdoten über die vielen
berühmten Persönlichkeiten – ob Dichter oder Diktatoren –
erzählen, die hier genächtigt haben. Romantiker finden ganz
in der Nähe einen besonders reizvollen Ort, nämlich die Stadt
Verona, die durch die tragische Liebesgeschichte von Romeo
und Julia weltberühmt wurde. Wenn man durch die Straßen
und unter den Balkonen entlangpromeniert, könnte man fast
glauben, die Geschichte habe sich wirklich zugetragen.
Die Küche der Villa Fiordaliso ist ein wahres Gedicht, und
auch wenn die Speisekarte vielleicht nicht von Dichterhand
geschrieben wurde, sind es doch Künstler, die hier wirken.

**Buchtipps: »Romeo und Julia« von William Shakespeare
»Das Feuer« von Gabriele D'Annunzio**

Un refuge romantique

Il flotte ici un air de nostalgie romantique. La vue sur le lac
est sûrement très semblable à celle dont jouissait le poète
Gabriele D'Annunzio depuis sa fenêtre. Devant une page
blanche, peut-être recherchait-il l'inspiration en contemplant
ces eaux paisibles...
La Villa Fiordaliso est un refuge idéal, même pour ceux qui
ne taquinent pas la plume. Le cadre est un poème à lui seul :
cernée de cyprès, de pins et d'oliviers, solitaire sur une rive
du lac de Garde, l'élégante villa ancienne respire le calme
absolu. Si les murs de l'édifice néoclassique pouvaient parler,
ils ne tariraient pas d'anecdotes sur ses résidents – des poètes
aux dictateurs. Pour les esprits romantiques, la ville de
Vérone, théâtre des tragiques amours de Roméo et Juliette,
se trouve à proximité. Une promenade dans les ruelles et
sous les balcons vous fera peut-être croire à l'histoire des
malheureux amants.
Mais réservez plutôt votre lyrisme pour la table : si la carte
n'a pas été rédigée par un poète, les mets sont certainement
cuisinés par de véritables artistes.

**Livres à emporter : « Le Feu » de Gabriele D'Annunzio
« Roméo et Juliette » de William Shakespeare**

ANREISE	40 km nordwestlich von Verona
PREIS	Zwischen 181 und 491 €
ZIMMER	7 Zimmer
KÜCHE	Ein mit mehreren Michelin-Sternen ausgezeichnetes Restaurant
X-FAKTOR	Romantik pur

ACCÈS	À 40 km au nord-est de Vérone
PRIX	De 181 à 491 €
CHAMBRES	7 chambres
RESTAURATION	Plusieurs étoiles au Michelin
LES « PLUS »	Le summum du romantisme

A world afloat...
Hotel Cipriani & Palazzo Vendramin, Venezia

Hotel Cipriani & Palazzo Vendramin, Venezia

A world afloat

"Streets flooded. Please advise." So said a telegram once sent from here by a humorous writer. But seriously, there is not much that can match the first sight of Venice. You should choose to arrive by boat; the ride along the Grand Canal, past palaces and churches, then turning into the lagoon of San Marco to see the sunlight glinting on the domes of the Doge's Palace, is a memorable one. The boat will bring you to Palazzo Vendramin. The 15th-century residence is on one of the many islands that make up this ancient city. The Palazzo's beautiful arched windows frame one of the most romantic and famous views in the world: the front-row view of St. Mark's Square. With only a few suites, it is more akin to an elegant private home; but it is part of the famed Hotel Cipriani, which is a short stroll away across a courtyard. Guests may share in all of that hotel's wealth of resources. Just a few minutes from its calm cloisters is a busier, noisier place. This special city of the past is quite like a magnet. Yet, off the main sightseer trail, there is a quieter, slower Venice still to be glimpsed.

Books to pack: "Death In Venice" by Thomas Mann
"A Venetian Reckoning" by Donna Leon

Hotel Cipriani & Palazzo Vendramin		
Isola della Giudecca, 10	DIRECTIONS	30 minutes by boat from Marco Polo Airport
30133 Venezia	RATES	From € 1,558 to 3,723, including breakfast
Italy	ROOMS	15 suites and junior suites in the Palazzo Vendramin and the Palazzetto Nani Barbaro
Tel: +39 (0) 41 5207744		
Fax: +39 (0) 41 5207745	FOOD	The cuisine of the Cipriani and the Cip's Club is worth being marooned on an island for
E-mail: info@hotelcipriani.it	HISTORY	The Palazzo Vendramin was built in the 15th century and opened as a hotel in 1991, the Palazzetto Nani Barbaro opened in 1998
Website: www.hotelcipriani.it		
Booking: www.great-escapes-hotels.com	X-FACTOR	One of the ultimate locations.

Eine Welt im Fluss

»Alle Straßen unter Wasser. Was ist zu tun?«, lautete das Telegramm, das ein Schriftsteller mit Humor hier einst aufgab. Doch im Ernst: Der erste Anblick von Venedig lässt sich mit nichts vergleichen.

Wenn es geht, sollte man in der Stadt mit dem Boot ankommen. Die Fahrt auf dem Canal Grande vorbei an Palazzi und Kirchen, der Blick in die Lagune von San Marco, wenn die Sonne über den Dogenpalast dahingleitet, ist unvergesslich. Mit dem Boot gelangen Sie auch zum Palazzo Vendramin, einem Anwesen aus dem 15. Jahrhundert, das auf einer der vielen Inseln Venedigs liegt. Von hier aus bietet sich – gerahmt durch die Bogenfenster des Palazzo – ein fantastischer Blick auf den Markusplatz – einer der schönsten, berühmtesten und romantischsten Ausblicke der Welt. Der Palazzo erinnert mit seinen wenigen Suiten eher an ein elegantes Privathaus als an ein Hotel. Doch ist er Teil des berühmten Hotel Cipriani, das sich in einem wenige Minuten dauernden Spaziergang quer über einen Innenhof erreichen lässt. Den Gästen des Palazzo stehen die vielfältigen Angebote des Cipriani ebenfalls zur Verfügung. Nur wenige Minuten von der fast klösterlichen Ruhe und Beschaulichkeit entfernt, können sie in ein bunteres und lauteres Leben eintauchen.

Venedig scheint eine Stadt aus der Vergangenheit zu sein, doch ihre Anziehungskraft ist bis heute ungebrochen. Wie schön, dass es neben den typischen Touristenattraktionen noch ein leiseres und ruhigeres Venedig zu entdecken gibt.

Buchtipps: »Der Tod in Venedig« von Thomas Mann
»Venezianische Scharade« von Donna Leon

Entre terre et eau

« Rues inondées. Que faire ? ». Tel est le message télégraphique qu'envoya un visiteur de Venise qui ne manquait pas d'humour! Trêve de plaisanteries; rien ou presque n'égale l'impact de la première vision de Venise.

Arrivez de préférence à Venise par bateau. Le trajet le long du Grand Canal et de ses palais et églises, puis l'entrée dans la lagune de Saint-Marc pour voir le soleil scintiller sur les toits du Palais des Doges, est tout à fait mémorable. Le bateau vous amènera au Palazzo Vendramin. Cette résidence du XVe siècle se dresse sur l'une des nombreuses îles qui forment la ville ancienne. Le Palazzo donne sur la place Saint-Marc; ses superbes fenêtres en plein cintre encadrent l'une des places les plus romantiques et célèbres du monde. N'abritant que quelques suites, il évoque une élégante résidence privée, bien qu'il fasse partie de l'illustre hôtel Cipriani, situé seulement à quelques pas, de l'autre côté de la cour. Ses hôtes peuvent profiter de tout ce que le Cipriani a à offrir. À quelques minutes à peine de la tranquillité de ses murs, s'étend une place bruyante et fort animée.

Cette ville d'un autre temps est en effet un véritable aimant touristique. Néanmoins, au-delà des sentiers battus, se cache une Venise plus nonchalante et sereine .

Livres à emporter : « La Mort à Venise » de Thomas Mann
« Un Vénitien anonyme » de Donna Leon

ANREISE	30 Minuten Anfahrt mit dem Boot vom Marco Polo Flughafen
PREIS	Zwischen 1558 und 3723 €, Frühstück inklusive
ZIMMER	15 Suiten und Juniorsuiten im Palazzo Vendramin und dem Palazzetto Nani Barbaro
KÜCHE	Für die Küche des Cipriani und des Cip's Club kann man schon freiwillig zum Schiffbrüchigen werden ...
GESCHICHTE	Der Palazzo Vendramin wurde im 15. Jahrhundert erbaut. Er öffnete als Hotel im Jahr 1991, der Palazzetto Nani Barbaro 1998
X-FAKTOR	Einer der unvergleichlichsten Orte der Welt

ACCÈS	À 30 minutes de bateau de l'aéroport Marco Polo
PRIX	De 1558 à 3723 €, petit déjeuner compris
CHAMBRES	Le Palazzo Vendramin et le Palazzetto Nani Barbaro comptent 15 suites et junior suites
RESTAURATION	Se retrouver sur une île loin de tout, mais avec la table du Cipriani et du Cip's Club ...
HISTOIRE	Le Palazzo Vendramin a été construit au XVe siècle. Il ouvrait ses portes en 1991, le Palazzetto Nani Barbaro en 1998
LES « PLUS »	Un nec plus ultra à Venise

In a blue mood...
Grand Hotel Parco dei Principi, Sorrento

Grand Hotel Parco dei Principi, Sorrento

In a blue mood

According to the legend, the mermaids who tempted Ulysses
with their enchanting songs lived in the Sorrentine Sea.
In the real world, the charms of the Grand Hotel Parco dei
Principi has lured other travellers to that same coastline.
Built on a cliff in one of the most famous gardens in Italy,
the hotel's clean lines and cool blue and white decor seem
to reflect the colour of the sea below. Master architect Gio
Ponti created the hotel in the 1960s, applying his one-colour
theory of interior design to striking effect, from the tiled
floors to the window blinds.

The spacious terraces offer a dazzling view of the blue Bay
of Naples and the volcano of Mount Vesuvius. An elevator or
stairway built into an ancient cave takes the guests down to
the hotel's private jetty and beach. Or bathers may prefer the
swimming pool, secluded in the historic park that was once
the property of various noble families.

Nearby is the picturesque town of Sorrento that crowns the
rocky cliffs close to the end of the peninsula. In the cafés
you can taste delicious cakes, ice cream, and a glass of
"Limoncello", the local lemon liqueur, just some of the many
attractions of this much-celebrated place.

**Books to pack: "The Island of the Day Before" by Umberto Eco
"Thus Spoke Bellavista: Naples, Love and Liberty" by Luciano
De Crescenzo**

Grand Hotel Parco dei Principi	DIRECTIONS	On the outskirts of Sorrento, 48 km/30 m south from Naples
Via Rota 1		
80067 Sorrento	RATES	€ 180 to 350
Italy	ROOMS	173 rooms, open from April to October; ask for a room with sea view
Tel: + 39 (0) 81 878 46 44		
Fax: + 39 (0) 81 878 37 86	FOOD	Neapolitan cuisine and local specialties in a beautiful restaurant
E-mail: info@grandhotelparcodeiprincipi.it	HISTORY	Built and opened in 1962
Website: www.grandhotelparcodeiprincipi.it	X-FACTOR	Enduring style in a stunning location
Booking: www.great-escapes-hotels.com		

Blaue Stunde

Der Legende zufolge war es vor Sorrent, wo Odysseus und seine Gefährten von den Gesängen der Sirenen betört wurden. In der realen Welt werden indes andere Reisende vom Zauber des Grand Hotels Parco dei Principi an diese Küste gelockt. Die klaren Linien und das kühle Blau und Weiß dieses auf einer Steilküste aus Tuffstein erbauten Hotels, welches inmitten eines der berühmtesten Gärten Italiens liegt, scheinen das Farbenspiel des Meeres widerzuspiegeln. Der Meisterarchitekt Gio Ponti, der das Hotel in den 1960er-Jahren entwarf, hat hier seine Philosophie von einer mono-chromen Innenraumgestaltung mit spektakulärem Erfolg umgesetzt: von den gekachelten Fußböden bis hin zu den Jalousien.

Die großzügigen Terrassen bieten fantastische Ausblicke auf die blaue Bucht von Neapel und den Vesuv. Über einen Auf-zug oder eine Treppe, die durch das Innere des Tuffsteins führt, gelangen Gäste zu dem Privatstrand des Hotels, der auch über einen eigenen Steg verfügt. Wassernixen können sich natürlich auch im Pool tummeln. Dieser liegt versteckt in dem historischen Park, der sich früher im Besitz verschie-dener Adelsfamilien befand.

In der Nähe liegt die malerische Stadt Sorrent auf den Fels-klippen am Ende der Halbinsel. Hier können Sie sich in den Cafés an köstlichem Kuchen, Eis-Spezialitäten und einem Glas Limoncello, dem in der Region produzierten Zitronen-likör, erbauen, um dann eine der zahlreichen Sehens-würdigkeiten dieses viel gepriesenen Ortes zu erkunden.

Buchtipps: »Die Insel des vorigen Tages« von Umberto Eco »Also sprach Bellavista. Neapel, Liebe und Freiheit« von Luciano De Crescenzo

Conte bleu

Selon la légende, les sirènes qui séduisirent Ulysse et ses compagnons par leur chant trompeur vivaient dans la mer de Sorrente.

Dans le monde réel, les charmes du Grand Hôtel Parco dei Principi ont attiré d'autres voyageurs vers ce littoral. Les lignes pures et le décor bleu et blanc de l'hôtel, construit sur une falaise dans l'un des jardins les plus célèbres d'Italie, semblent refléter les couleurs de la mer qui danse à ses pieds. Du carrelage aux stores, le célèbre architecte Gio Ponti, qui a créé l'hôtel dans les années 1960, a appliqué avec bonheur sa théorie selon laquelle la décoration d'in-térieur se doit d'être monochrome.

Depuis les terrasses spacieuses, on découvre une vue éblouissante sur la mer bleue de la baie de Naples et sur le Vésuve. Les clients de l'hôtel descendent à la jetée et à la plage privées par un ascenseur ou un escalier qui traverse une grotte ancienne. On peut aussi se baigner dans la piscine, cachée dans le parc historique qui a appartenu autrefois à diverses familles nobles.

Tout près, la ville pittoresque de Sorrente couronne les falaises rocheuses proches de l'extrémité de la péninsule. Dans les salons de thé, on peut goûter aux gâteaux délicieux, aux glaces ou au limoncello, la liqueur de citron locale, quelques-uns seulement des nombreux attraits de cet endroit si célèbre.

Livres à emporter: « L'Ile du jour d'avant » d'Umberto Eco « Ainsi parlait Bellavista » de Luciano De Crescenzo

ANREISE	Am Stadtrand von Sorrent, 48 km südlich von Neapel
PREIS	Zwischen 180 und 350 €
ZIMMER	173 Zimmer, Öffnungszeiten April bis Oktober; fragen Sie nach einem Zimmer mit Meerblick
KÜCHE	Neapolitanische Küche und lokale Spezialitäten in einem wunderschönen, eleganten Restaurant
GESCHICHTE	Erbaut und geöffnet 1962
X-FAKTOR	Zeitloser Stil in atemberaubender Umgebung

ACCÈS	Dans les environs de Sorrente, à 48 km au sud de Naple
PRIX	De 180 à 350 €
CHAMBRES	173 chambres ; demandez une chambre avec vue sur la mer. Ouvert d'avril à octobre
RESTAURATION	Cuisine napolitaine et spécialités locales servies dans un restaurant splendide
HISTOIRE	Construit et ouvert en 1962
LES « PLUS »	Style intemporel, dans un cadre éblouissant

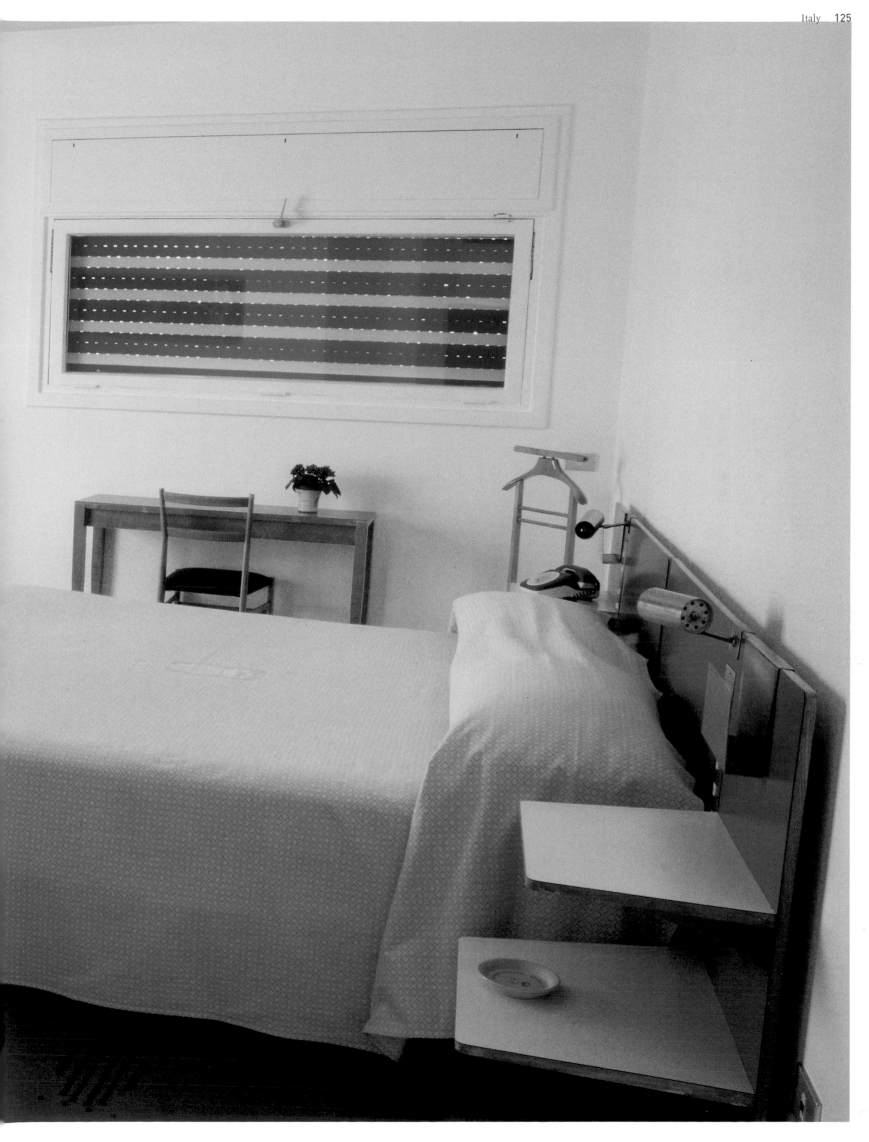

Silence is golden...
Finca Son Gener, Mallorca

Finca Son Gener, Mallorca

Silence is golden

Rural life has many rewards; one of the best is silence. And although the crowing of a rooster or the bleating of sheep may break that silence now and then, the peace and quiet that rules here is a treat in our noisy world.

On the island of Majorca, there is the chance to lead a simple country life for a few days. Some of the most beautiful places here are set in idyllic landscapes just near the coast, and often hidden behind thick natural stone walls. The country estate of Son Gener is one of these havens. Built in the 18th century, and used for making oils and grains, it has been totally restored. The classic finca – farm – is on the eastern side of the island, on the brow of a small hill, with a view of the village, sea, and mountains. Surrounded by green fields, olive and almond trees, this is a dream domain to bask in. While the estate's simple style is in keeping with its tranquil backdrop, it has been refurbished with skill. The soft rich colours that make up the interiors are in themselves conducive to a sense of calm. The elegant house calls to mind the patrician life of past days. Those who are privileged to be guests here will be content with their choice for a pastoral interlude.

Book to pack: "Goya" by Lion Feuchtwanger

Finca Son Gener	
Apartat de Correus, 136	
07550 Son Servera	
Majorca	
Spain	
Tel: + 34 971 183612	
Fax: + 34 971 183591	
E-mail: hotel@songener.com	
Website: www.songener.com	
Booking: www.great-escapes-hotels.com	

DIRECTIONS	Between the towns of Son Servera and Artà, 70 km/44 m east from Palma de Mallorca, 20 km/12 m northeast from Manacor
RATES	Each suite from € 222, including breakfast
ROOMS	10 suites
FOOD	On request, Majorcan dishes made with homegrown organic produce are served
HISTORY	Built in the 18th century, the finca was turned into a hotel in 1998
X-FACTOR	Outdoor and indoor serenity

Himmlische Ruhe

Das Landleben hat viele Vorzüge, aber einer der größten ist die Stille. Und auch wenn sie gelegentlich durch das Krähen eines Hahns oder das Blöken eines Schafs unterbrochen wird, herrscht doch meist Ruhe und Frieden – ein Luxus in unserer lauten Welt.

Auf der Insel Mallorca haben Sie Gelegenheit, für einige Tage dem einfachen Landleben zu frönen. Einige der schönsten Unterkünfte finden sich hier inmitten idyllischer Landschaften nahe der Küste, oft versteckt hinter dicken Mauern aus Naturstein. Unter ihnen ist auch der Landsitz von Son Gener, eine klassische Finca, wie hier die Bauern-höfe genannt werden, die auf der Ostseite der Insel auf der Kuppe eines kleinen Hügels liegt. Umgeben von grünen Feldern, Olivenhainen und Mandelbäumen finden Sie hier ein traumhaftes Urlaubsziel. Das im 18. Jahrhundert ursprünglich für die Öl- und Getreideproduktion gebaute Haus wurde komplett und mit großem Können renoviert. Davon zeugt der einfache Stil des Hauses, welcher sich harmonisch in die Umgebung einpasst. Zur allgemeinen Atmosphäre der Ruhe tragen die sanften, satten Farben im Hausinneren bei. Das elegante Haus weckt Erinnerungen an das Leben des gehobenen Bürgertums in früheren Zeiten. Wer das Privileg genießt, an diesem Ort Gast zu sein, wird mit seiner Wahl dieser ländlichen Oase der Ruhe mehr als zufrieden sein.

Buchtipp: »Goya oder der arge Weg der Erkenntnis« von Lion Feuchtwanger

Le silence est d'or

La vie à la campagne a de nombreux avantages, en particulier le silence. Dans notre monde bruyant, cette paix et cette tranquillité, seulement interrompues de temps à autre par le cri d'un coq ou le bêlement d'un mouton, constituent un plaisir authentique.

Dans l'île de Majorque, on peut, le temps d'un séjour, goûter à la vie campagnarde simple. Ici, certaines des plus belles villégiatures se cachent souvent derrière d'épais murs de pierre, dans des cadres idylliques, à proximité du littoral. Le domaine de Son Gener est l'un de ces havres de paix. Construit au XVIIIe siècle, à l'origine destiné au pressage de l'huile et à la culture des céréales, il a été entièrement restauré. Cette finca (ferme) traditionnelle est située dans la partie orientale de l'île, au sommet d'une petite colline. Entourée de champs verdoyants, d'oliviers et d'amandiers, c'est un lieu de détente rêvé. Si le style simple du domaine s'harmonise avec son cadre rustique, celui-ci a été rénové avec goût. Les couleurs riches et douces des intérieurs favo-risent l'impression de sérénité. L'élégante maison principale évoque la vie patricienne d'antan.

Les privilégiés qui auront la chance de séjourner à Son Gener seront ravis du choix de leur interlude champêtre.

Livre à emporter : « Goya » de Lion Feuchtwanger

ANREISE	Zwischen den Städten Son Servera und Artà, 70 km östlich von Palma, 20 km nordöstlich von Manacor
PREIS	Suiten inklusive Frühstück ab 222 €
ZIMMER	10 Suiten
KÜCHE	Auf Anfrage werden inseltypische Gerichte mit Zutaten aus eigenem biologischem Anbau serviert
GESCHICHTE	Das Gebäude stammt aus dem 18. Jahrhundert und ist seit 1998 Hotel
X-FAKTOR	Entspannte Atmosphäre in Haus und Umgebung

ACCÈS	Entre les villes de Son Servera et Artà, à 70 km à l'est de Palma, à 20 km au nord-est de Manacor
PRIX	Chaque suite, petit déjeuner compris, à partir de 222 €
CHAMBRES	10 suites
RESTAURATION	Sur demande, plats majorquins préparés avec des produits bio cultivés sur place
HISTOIRE	Construit au XVIIIe siècle, le bâtiment est un hôtel depuis 1998
LES « PLUS »	Sérénité intérieure et extérieure

Grace and favour...
Reid's Palace, Madeira

Reid's Palace, Madeira

Grace and favour

For generations this grand old hotel has been the byword of grace. Reid's Palace has served as a home away from home to many of the most well-known people of the last century. The guest book is a roll call of celebrities. Anybody who was, or is still, somebody has stayed here at one time. So little seems to have changed that you can picture Winston Churchill taking afternoon tea on the terrace; Elisabeth, the Empress of Austria, gazing out to sea from her veranda; and imagine watching George Bernard Shaw being taught the tango on the lawn. The old-fashioned charm continues to draw the rich and famous, as well as the not yet renowned. Part of the attraction is the setting on the island of Madeira. High up on the cliff tops overlooking the Bay of Funchal and the Atlantic, the hotel's site adds to the privacy of its guests. Staying here is almost like being on the "grand tour"; but the days of luxury travel are not re-created here, in fact it has always been like this.

Reid's Palace evokes eras that were more gracious and less hurried than the one we live in now. Time has been kind to this lovely old landmark.

Book to pack: "Pygmalion and My Fair Lady" by George Bernard Shaw

Reid's Palace
Estrada Monumental 139
9000-098 Funchal
Madeira
Portugal
Tel: + 351 291 71 71 71
Fax: + 351 291 71 71 77
E-mail: reservations@reidspalace.com
Website: www.reidspalace.orient-express.com
Booking: www.great-escapes-hotels.com

DIRECTIONS	22 km/14 m from Madeira International Airport
RATES	Rooms from € 259 to 496, suites from € 616 to 2619, inclusive of breakfast
ROOMS	130 rooms and 34 suites
FOOD	5 restaurants to choose from
HISTORY	The original hotel was built and opened in 1891. In 1967 an extension was built
X-FACTOR	A destination in itself

Ruhm und Ehre

Seit Generationen war dieses große alte Hotel der Inbegriff von Eleganz.

In Reid's Palace fanden viele berühmte Persönlichkeiten des letzten Jahrhunderts eine zweite Heimat. Alle Berühmtheiten haben – so scheint es – schon einmal hier gewohnt. Und so wenig scheinen sich die Zeiten verändert zu haben, dass man sich noch jetzt Winston Churchill beim Nachmittagstee auf der Terrasse vorstellen kann oder die österreichische Kaiserin Elisabeth, berühmt als Sisi, die von ihrer Veranda aus auf das Meer blickt, oder George Bernard Shaw, der auf dem Rasen Tango lernt. Ungebrochen scheint der altmodische Charme des Hotels wie ein Magnet auf die Reichen und Schönen zu wirken, aber ebenso auf die nicht wirklich oder noch nicht Berühmten. Ein weiterer Anziehungspunkt ist die Lage des Hotels. Hoch über den Klippen errichtet, bietet es einen Blick über die Bucht von Funchal auf den Atlantik und schützt durch seine exponierte Lage die Privatsphäre der Gäste.

Wer hier zu Gast ist, wird sich fühlen wie damals die reichen jungen Leute, die durch die Welt reisen, um ihren Horizont zu erweitern. Aber hier muss die Vergangenheit nicht künstlich wiedererweckt werden, hier ist es einfach so, wie es schon immer gewesen ist. An diesem Ort, zu dem die Zeit so freundlich war, darf man noch einmal teilhaben am Charme und der Ruhe früherer Zeiten.

Buchtipps: »Pygmalion and My Fair Lady« von George Bernard Shaw

»Churchill« von Sebastian Haffner

Retraite des célébrités

Symbole d'élégance depuis des générations, le Reid's Palace a accueilli maintes célébrités du siècle passé, comme en témoigne son livre d'or. Tous les grands personnages ont séjourné au moins une fois en ces lieux. Le cadre a si peu changé que l'on imagine sans peine Winston Churchill prendre le thé sur la terrasse, Sissi, impératrice d'Autriche, scruter la mer depuis sa véranda, ou George Bernard Shaw prendre des cours de tango sur la pelouse. Le charme désuet continue d'attirer les grands et les moins grands de ce monde. L'un des atouts de l'hôtel est sa situation sur l'île de Madère. Perché sur les falaises dominant la baie de Funchal et l'Atlantique, il offre la retraite discrète recherchée par la clientèle.

Un séjour dans ce palace évoque les somptueux voyages de la haute société d'autrefois; mais le luxe n'a pas été recréé. Ici, il existe depuis toujours. Le Reid's Palace rappelle une époque plus raffinée et moins agitée que celle d'aujourd'hui. Le temps a su épargner cet endroit plein de charme et de chic.

Livre à emporter : « L'Homme et les armes » de George Bernard Shaw

ANREISE	22 km vom Flughafen Madeira International
PREIS	Zimmer zwischen 259 und 496 €, Suiten zwischen 616 und 2619 €, Frühstück inklusive
ZIMMER	130 Zimmer und 34 Suiten
KÜCHE	5 Restaurants stehen zur Auswahl
GESCHICHTE	Das ursprüngliche Hotel wurde 1891 gebaut und eröffnet; 1967 kam ein Anbau hinzu
X-FAKTOR	Ein Ziel an sich

ACCÈS	À 22 km de l'aéroport Madeira International
PRIX	Chambres de 259 à 496 €, suites de 616 à 2619 €, petit déjeuner compris
CHAMBRES	130 chambres et 34 suites
RESTAURATION	5 restaurants au choix
HISTOIRE	L'hôtel a été construit et a ouvert en 1891. Une annexe a été ajoutée en 1967
LES « PLUS »	Une destination en soi

Africa

Morocco • Tunisia • Egypt • Kenya
Tanzania • Zambia • Botswana
South Africa • Namibia • Mali

Text by Shelley-Maree Cassidy   *Edited by* Angelika Taschen

Amanjena 148 ●

MOROCCO

WESTERN
SAHARA

MAURITANIA

MAL

Hotel Le Kambary 282 ●

SENEGAL

GAMBIA

GUINEA BISSAU

GUINEA

BURKINA

SIERRA
LEONE

IVORY
COAST

GHA

LIBERIA

"All I wanted to do now was get back to Africa. We had not left it, yet, but when I would wake in the night I would lie, listening, homesick for it already."

Ernest Hemingway, *Green Hills of Africa*, 1935

● 156 Hotel Dar Cherait

● 164 Adrere Amellal Desert Eco-Lodge

M.S. Kasr Ibrim & M.S. Eugenie 174 ●

Il N'gwesi 190 ●   ● 184 Sarara Tented Camp

Dodo's Tower 196 ●

The Giraffe Manor 204 ●

Ngorongoro Crater Lodge 210 ●

● 220 Emerson & Green Hotel
228 Chumbe Island Coral Park

● 236 Sausage Tree Camp

● 240 Jao Camp
248 Nxabega Okavango Safari Camp

Sossusvlei Wilderness Camp 274 ●

Garonga Lodge 266 ●

● 258 Singita Boulders Lodge

Bloomestate 270 ●

A star is born...
Amanjena, near Marrakech

Amanjena, near Marrakech

A star is born

Can there be a mirage in an oasis? Such a stunning scene in the desert is more often than not a mere vision. This could be a film set: a Hollywood dream of a Moorish palace. But the glamorous scene is real, not an illusion.

This serene place is the sumptuous Moroccan resort of Amanjena; framed by pink tinged walls, set among palms and olive trees, with a dramatic backdrop of snow-capped mountains that glitter in the sun and turn roseate at day's end. Though it is new, it has a timeless feel. The pictures of this lavish location need few words; they show that luxury is on offer here. There is the luxury of space; of calm; of rest; and privacy. You can stay secluded within the walls of your own domain, shutting out the rest of the world, if you so choose. Each pavilion has a courtyard and dining room of its own; some have private pools.

The focal point is a great pool, sixty square metres in size. Termed a basin, it was traditionally used to collect water from the mountains. Here its purpose is just a decorative one. Its tranquil surface reflects the sky by day; by night, it mirrors the lights of lanterns, candles and the stars.

All the vigour of Marrakech is just a short drive away, as are Berber villages and beaches. Some will give thanks that two of the best golf courses are near this peaceful paradise.

Book to pack: "The Sheltering Sky" by Paul Bowles

Amanjena	
Route de Ouarzazate, km 12	
Marrakech	
Morocco	
Tel: + 212 (44) 403 353	
Fax: + 212 (44) 403 477	
E-mail: amanjena@amanresorts.com	
Website: www.amanresorts.com	
Booking: www.great-escapes-hotels.com	

DIRECTIONS	A 20-minute drive north from Marrakech's Menara airport
RATES	US$800 to US$2,200 per pavilion per night
ROOMS	6 two storey maisons, 34 pavilions
FOOD	Moroccan, European and Thai tastes opulently catered
HISTORY	Opened in 2000, the first Aman resort on the African continent
X-FACTOR	A fabulous fantasy retreat. Back to the real world at the end

A star is born

Kann es in einer Oase eine Fata Morgana geben? Denn man könnte meinen, dass ein solch überwältigender Anblick eigentlich nichts als bloße Einbildung sein kann. Dieser Ort könnte Drehort für einen Film sein: ein Traum von einem maurischen Palast à la Hollywood. Doch dieser zauberhafte Schauplatz ist keine Illusion, sondern Wirklichkeit.

Die Rede ist von dem opulenten marokkanischen Amanjena-Resort, – mit rosé-mellierten Wänden befindet er sich zwischen Palmen und Olivenbäumen vor einer spektakulären Kulisse von schneebedeckten Bergen, die in der Sonne glitzern und sich blutrot färben, wenn der Tag zur Neige geht. Obwohl die Anlage neu ist, scheint sie zeitlos zu sein. Die Bilder dieser üppigen Anlage sprechen für sich, sie zeigen, dass hier der Luxus zu Hause ist. Sei es der Luxus, viel Platz zu haben, der Luxus der Ruhe, der Entspannung oder der Ungestörtheit. Wer möchte, kann zurückgezogen in seinem privaten Bereich bleiben und sich vom Rest der Welt abschotten. Jeder Pavillon hat einen eigenen Hof und ein eigenes Speisezimmer, manche verfügen über Privatpools. Mittelpunkt bildet ein großartiges Wasserbecken mit einer Fläche von vierundsechzig Quadratmetern. Seine Bezeichnung Bassin deutet an, dass derartige Becken traditionellerweise genutzt wurden, um das Wasser zu speichern das aus den Bergen kam. In diesem Falle dient es jedoch ausschließlich dekorativen Zwecken. Am Tage spiegelt seine ruhige Oberfläche den Himmel wider, in der Nacht wirft es das Licht von Laternen, Kerzen und Sternen zurück.

Das pulsierende Leben in Marrakesch, Berberdörfer und Strände sind nur eine kurze Autofahrt weit entfernt. So mancher wird sich freuen, dass auch zwei der besten Golfplätze ganz in der Nähe dieses friedlichen Paradieses liegen.

Buchtipp: »Himmel über der Wüste« von Paul Bowles

Une étoile est née

Les mirages existent-ils aussi dans les oasis ?

Car on pourrait penser qu'une vue aussi grandiose est l'effet d'une illusion. Un tel lieu pourrait servir de décor de cinéma : un palais maure comme on en rêve à Hollywood. Non, le cadre grandiose qui s'offre à vos yeux est bien réel.

Ce lieu serein, c'est la somptueuse station touristique marocaine d'Amanjena. Encadrée de murs aux tons roses, située au milieu de palmiers et d'oliviers, elle a pour spectaculaire toile de fond des montagnes enneigées qui resplendissent au soleil et se teintent de rouge sang le soir venu. L'hôtel est récent, mais il inspire un sentiment d'éternité. Les photos de cet endroit fastueux parlent d'elles-mêmes : le mot-clé est ici le luxe, un luxe d'espace, de calme, de repos et d'intimité. Chaque pavillon ayant sa propre cour et sa propre salle à manger, et certains disposant même d'une piscine privée, vous pouvez rester à l'abri des murs de votre domaine et oublier le monde extérieur si vous le souhaitez.

Le point central d'Amanjena est un grand bassin de soixante mètres carrés, traditionnellement utilisé pour recueillir l'eau des montagnes. Sa fonction est aujourd'hui décorative. Le jour, sa surface tranquille réfléchit le ciel et la nuit, elle reflète la lumière des étoiles et celle des bougies brûlant dans les lanternes.

L'effervescence et l'énergie de Marrakech ne sont qu'à quelques minutes en voiture, tout comme les villages berbères et les plages. Certains seront ravis d'apprendre que deux des meilleurs terrains de golf du monde sont à proximité de ce paisible paradis.

Livre à emporter : « Un Thé au Sahara » de Paul Bowles

ANREISE	20-minütige Fahrt nördlich vom Flughafen Marrakesch
PREIS	800 US$ bis 2.200 US$ pro Nacht für ein Pavillon
ZIMMER	6 Häuser, 34 Pavillons
KÜCHE	Aufwändig zubereitete marokkanische, europäische und thailändische Gerichte
GESCHICHTE	Der erste Aman-Resort auf dem afrikanischen Kontinent, eröffnet im Jahr 2000
X-FAKTOR	Märchenhafter Zufluchtsort mit anschließender Rückkehr in die Wirklichkeit

ACCÈS	À 20 minutes au nord de l'aéroport de Marrakech en voiture
PRIX	800 à 2.200 $ US par pavillon et par nuit
CHAMBRES	6 maisons, 34 pavillons
RESTAURATION	Succulents menus marocains, européens et thaïlandais
HISTOIRE	Ouvert en 2000, il s'agit du premier hôtel Aman du continent africain
LES « PLUS »	Retraite de rêve. Le retour à la réalité est difficile

Sesam, öffne Dich

Hier können Sie den Zauber arabischer Nächte erleben, und zwar in weniger als tausend und einer Nacht. Am Rande der Sahara, in der Stadt Tozeur, liegt ein ganzer Park, in dem sich alles um diese berühmten Erzählungen dreht. Die magischen Worte, die Ali Baba einst aussprach, benötigen Sie nicht, um sich Zutritt zu diesem vornehmen Palast zu verschaffen. In der wirklichen Welt dient eine Kreditkarte als »Sesam, öffne Dich«.

In seiner prachtvollen Ausstattung kann das Hotel Dar Cherait leicht mit dem Märchen mithalten, obwohl es mit »Überbleibseln« eingerichtet wurde. Die Familie Cherait hatte nämlich zunächst ein Museum gebaut – es liegt ganz in der Nähe – um dort ihre umfangreiche Sammlung tunesischer Kunstwerke zu zeigen. Anschließend errichteten sie das Hotel und alle Möbel, Gemälde und Kunstgegenstände, die in dem Museum keinen Platz mehr fanden, wurden hier zur Schau gestellt. Reich verzierte Teppiche und bunte Kacheln tragen zu dem üppigen, maurischen Stil bei.

Dass Dar Cherait im Herzen eines großen Palmenhaines liegt, verdankt es einem arabischen Mathematiker, der erstmals eine geeignete Methode entwickelte, mit der die von der glühenden Sonne ausgetrockneten Gärten bewässert werden konnte. Ibn Shabbat entwickelte ein komplexes System von Bewässerungskanälen, das die gesamte Stadt durchzieht. All dies geschah im 13. Jahrhundert; immer noch verdankt Tozeur heute sein saftiges Grün den außergewöhnlichen Fähigkeiten dieses Mannes. Tausende und Abertausende von Palmen konnten seitdem in der Oase, die er einst begründete, sowie in vielen ähnlichen anderen, wachsen.

Buchtipp: »Die Nacht der Tausend Nächte« von Naguib Mahfouz

Sésame, ouvre-toi

Cet endroit vous permettra de connaître un peu la magie des Mille et Une Nuits, à ceci près que votre séjour ne durera pas aussi longtemps. Dans la ville de Tozeur, située en bordure du Sahara, se trouve un parc entièrement consacré à cette fable extraordinaire. Nul besoin de prononcer la formule magique d'Ali Baba pour se faire ouvrir les portes de ce somptueux palace. Dans le monde réel, c'est la carte de crédit qui fait office de « Sésame, ouvre-toi ».

Bien que l'hôtel Dar Cherait ait été meublé avec des « restes », son luxe est à la hauteur de celui décrit dans le conte. Avant de l'édifier, la famille Cherait fit construire un musée (aujourd'hui voisin de l'hôtel) afin d'y abriter sa vaste collection d'objets d'art tunisiens. Dar Cherait a donc hérité de tous les meubles, peintures et objets qui, faute de place, ne pouvaient pas être exposés dans le musée. Des tapis richement ornés et des carreaux de faïence d'une beauté éblouissante mettent en valeur le splendide style maure de l'hôtel. L'hôtel est installé au cœur d'une superbe palmeraie qui n'existerait pas sans un mathématicien arabe, Ibn Shabbat, inventeur d'une solution judicieuse pour amener l'eau jusqu'à un jardin desséché par un soleil implacable.

Ce savant mit au point un système complexe de canaux d'irrigation que l'on peut encore aujourd'hui voir serpenter dans toute la ville. Cette invention date du XIIIe siècle, et Tozeur doit sa luxuriance actuelle à ce savoir-faire du passé. La technique de Shabbat a en effet permis à des dizaines de milliers de palmiers de pousser dans l'oasis qu'il fit naître, et dans bien d'autres semblables.

Livre à emporter : « Les mille et une nuits » de Naguib Mahfouz

ANREISE	500 km südlich von Tunis, 5 Minuten vom Flughafen Tozeur/Nefta entfernt
PREIS	Ab 130 US$ für ein Doppelzimmer
ZIMMER	73 Doppelzimmer, 12 Suiten
KÜCHE	Tunesische und westliche Gerichte, berühmt für seine Datteln
GESCHICHTE	Eröffnet im Jahr 1995
X-FAKTOR	Die märchenhaft schöne natürliche Landschaft, welche die Oase umgibt, und die großartige Ziegelarchitektur

ACCÈS	À 500 km au sud de Tunis, à 5 minutes de l'aéroport Tozeur/Nefta.
PRIX	Chambre double à partir de 130 $ US
CHAMBRES	73 chambres doubles, 12 suites
RESTAURATION	Cuisine tunisienne et occidentale, célèbre pour ses plats à base de dattes
HISTOIRE	Ouvert en 1995
LES « PLUS »	Magnifique paysage autour de l'oasis et superbe architecture à base de briquetage

In einem Meer aus Sand

Tief im Innern der westlichen Wüste Ägyptens liegt eine Oase in einer Oase. Die Adrere Amellal Lodge, ein Bauwerk aus Palmstämmen, Salzgestein und Lehm – eine für diese Gegend typische Bautechnik, die auch als Kershaf bezeichnet wird – schmiegt sich an den Fuß des windgegerbten White Mountain, von dem die Lodge auch ihren Namen hat. Da ihre helle Farbe der des Sandes gleicht, sind ihre Gebäude in der Landschaft beinahe nicht auszumachen. Die einfache und gleichzeitig luxuriöse »Öko-Lodge«, die inmitten eines riesigen Wüstengebietes am Rande des Siwa Sees liegt, hat ihren eigenen Dattel- und Olivengarten und ein großartiges Schwimmbecken wurde um eine alte römische Quelle gebaut. Damit kein elektrisches Licht die Mond- und Sternennächte erhellt, sorgen ausschließlich handgemachte Kerzen für Beleuchtung und an kalten Winterabenden erwärmen glühende Kohlebecken die Luft. Auf der anderen Seite des Sees wellt sich das große Sandmeer, eine der größten Dünenlandschaften der Erde, dem Horizont entgegen.

Nahegelegene alte Grabstätten und Tempel zeugen von Siwas langer und glänzender Geschichte. Im Jahre 331 v. Chr. geschah es, dass der griechische Feldherr Alexander der Große hierher zum Orakeltempel kam um sich bestätigen zu lassen, dass er nicht nur ein außergewöhnlicher Mann, sondern gar ein Gott sei. Dieser abgeschiedene und schöne Ort bietet Normalsterblichen die Gelegenheit durch eine der am wenigsten erforschten Wüsten der Welt zu reisen.

Buchtipp: »Das Alexandria-Quartett« von Lawrence Durrell

Dans une mer de sable

Il existe, au cœur du désert occidental égyptien, une oasis au milieu d'une oasis. Niché au pied de la Montagne Blanche sculptée par le vent dont il tire son nom, Adrere Amellal Lodge a été érigé à partir de madriers de palmier, de roche saline et d'argile salifère, selon une technique de construction locale appelée *kershaf*. Les bâtiments sont ainsi presque invisibles, leur nuance pâle se fondant dans le sable.

Situé au centre d'un immense désert, au bord du lac Siouah, cet hôtel écologique simple mais luxueux dispose d'un verger de dattes et d'olives mais également d'une superbe piscine construite autour d'une ancienne source romaine. Afin que l'électricité ne fasse pas d'ombre à la lune et aux étoiles, des bougies faites à la main sont utilisées en guise d'éclairage et, durant les froides nuits d'hiver, des braseros réchauffent l'atmosphère. De l'autre côté du lac, l'immense mer de sable, l'un des champs de dunes les plus grands du monde, s'étend en ondulations jusqu'à l'horizon.

Les tombeaux et les temples antiques voisins témoignent de la longue et glorieuse histoire de Siouah : c'est ici, dans le Temple de l'oracle, que le guerrier grec Alexandre le Grand vint chercher confirmation en 331 av. J.-C. qu'il était non pas un homme extraordinaire hors du commun mais bien un dieu. Ce site isolé et majestueux est l'occasion pour les simples mortels de découvrir l'un des déserts les moins explorés de la planète.

Livre à emporter : « Le quatuor d'Alexandrie » de Lawrence Durrell

ANREISE	Momentan 8-10-stündige Fahrt in einem klimatisiertem Jeep westlich von Kairo oder Alexandria aus, eine Flugverbindung ist geplant
PREIS	Ab 400 US$ pro Doppelzimmer. In diesem Preis inbegriffen sind alle Mahlzeiten, Getränke und Tagesausflüge in die Wüste
ZIMMER	27 Doppelzimmer
KÜCHE	Ägyptische und europäische Küche für Feinschmecker; ein Großteil des Gemüses stammt aus biologischem Anbau aus dem hauseigenen Garten
GESCHICHTE	Ägyptens erste Öko-Lodge, eröffnet im Jahre 1997
X-FAKTOR	Landschaft wie in »Der englische Patient«

ACCÈS	À 8-10 heures à l'ouest du Caire ou d'Alexandrie en jeep climatisée. L'accès par avion est en projet
PRIX	Chambre double à partir de 400 $ US. Le prix comprend les repas, les boissons et les excursions de jour dans le désert
CHAMBRES	27 chambres doubles
RESTAURATION	Cuisine gastronomique égyptienne et européenne. La plupart des produits sont cultivés biologiquement dans le jardin de l'hôtel
HISTOIRE	Ouvert en 1997, il s'agit du premier hôtel écologique de l'Égypte
LES « PLUS »	Cadre du « Patient anglais »

Time travel on the Nile...
M.S. Kasr Ibrim & M.S. Eugenie, Lake Nasser

M.S. Kasr Ibrim & M.S. Eugenie, Lake Nasser

Time travel on the Nile

In Egyptian belief, and in daily life, boats have played a dual part, being borth a means of transport and a symbol of hope. The sun god Ra was thought to travel across the sky in a solar ship; and it was held that those who were worthy might join Osiris, the god of the dead, in his divine bark after death. That would be the infinite cruise.

But why wait for the next world? You can take this trip now. Aboard the M.S. Kasr Ibrim and M.S. Eugenie, you can bridge the age of the Pharaohs and the Flappers. The great monuments of the former are before you on the banks of the Nile; these splendid steamers on Lake Nasser call to mind the latter, with their Art Deco style.

One boat is named after the citadel of Kasr Ibrim, a relic of Nubia, the 'land of gold', one of ancient Egypt's richest states. The once mighty fortress has stood here for aeons; other temples were moved here, to higher ground, when the Aswan Dam was built. Sailing here, you will see what is left of a once fabulous past. The journey takes you from wonders such as the Avenue of the Sphinxes to the grand finale, the Great Temples of Ramses II at Abu Simbel. Time and nature may have worn down their glory, but they are still amazing to see.

On board the glamour has not faded. There is grandness on a scale that suits the location it sails in. What better way to see the splendour of Egypt than from the decks of these deluxe ships?

Book to pack: "Death on the Nile" by Agatha Christie

M.S. Kasr Ibrim & M.S. Eugenie		
Lake Nasser		
Nubia		
Egypt		
Tel: + 202 516 9653/4/6; 516 9763/9649		
Fax: + 202 516 9646		
E-mail: eugenie@soficom.co.eg		
Website: www.kasribrim.com.eg		
Booking: www.great-escapes-hotels.com		

DIRECTIONS	Departs from Aswan or Abu Simbel
RATES	From US$150 per person in a double room, including full-board accommodation, afternoon tea, sightseeing and transfers
ROOMS	55 cabins, 10 suites
FOOD	In keeping with the lavish surroundings
HISTORY	Launched in September 1997
X-FACTOR	Cruising the Nile in style, from era to era

Eine Zeitreise auf dem Nil

Sowohl dem ägyptischen Glauben nach, als auch im alltäglichen Leben, haben Schiffe dort stets eine Doppelrolle gespielt: sie stellten nicht nur ein Transportmittel dar, sondern auch ein Symbol der Hoffnung. Man glaubte, dass der Sonnengott Ra in einem Sonnensschiff quer über den Himmel reiste und es hieß, dass diejenigen, die sich verdient gemacht hatten, den Totengott Osiris nach dem Tode in seiner göttlichen Barke begleiten durften, um ihre unendliche Fahrt anzutreten.

Doch warum auf die nächste Welt warten, wenn Sie solch eine Reise schon heute unternehmen können? An Bord der M.S. Kasr Ibrim oder M.S. Eugenie kann man das Zeitalter der Pharaonen mit dem der Flappers verbinden. Die großartigen Monumente der ersteren breiten sich vor Ihnen am Nilufer aus, während diese prächtigen Dampfschiffe auf dem Nasser-Stausee mit ihren Art Deco Stil an letztere erinnert.

Ein Boot wurde nach der Zitadelle von Kasr Ibrim benannt, einem Relikt aus Nubien, dem Land des Goldes, einem der reichsten Staaten im alten Ägypten. Die einst mächtige Festung steht hier seit ewigen Zeiten. Als man den Assuan Staudamm erbaute, wurden die Tempel von Assuan hierher auf eine höhere Ebene versetzt. Wer hier segelt, sieht die Überreste einer einstmals sagenhaften Vergangenheit. Die Reise führt vorbei an Wundern wie der Straße der Sphinxen bis hin zum großen Höhepunkt, den großen Tempeln von Ramses II in Abu Simbel. Zwar mögen Zeit und Witterung an ihrer Pracht genagt haben, doch ihr Anblick ist unverändert beeindruckend.

An Bord sind Glanz und Gloria noch nicht verblasst. Die prachtvolle Ausstattung der Schiffe ist der Umgebung die sie durchsegelten, angemessen. Von wo aus ließe sich die Großartigkeit Ägyptens besser betrachten, als vom Deck dieser Luxusschiffe?

Buchtipp: »Der Tod auf dem Nil« von Agatha Christie

Un voyage sur le Nil à travers le temps

À la fois moyens de transport et symboles d'espoir, les bateaux jouaient un double rôle dans la croyance et la vie quotidienne des Égyptiens. Leur conviction était que Râ, le dieu soleil, sillonnait le ciel à bord d'un vaisseau solaire et qu'après leur mort, ceux qui en étaient dignes rejoignaient Osiris, le dieu des morts, pour une croisière sans fin sur sa barque divine.

Mais pourquoi attendre d'être dans l'autre monde pour profiter de ce voyage ? Une fois à bord du navire M.S. Kasr Ibrim ou M.S. Eugénie, il est possible de faire le lien entre l'époque des pharaons et celle des garçonnes, ces jeunes filles émancipées des années 20. Les grands monuments des premiers s'offrent au regard sur les rives du Nil et ce splendide bateau à vapeur de style Art Déco qui navigue sur le lac Nasser rappelle les secondes.

L'un des deux bateaux tire son nom de la citadelle de Kasr Ibrim, un vestige de la Nubie, « pays de l'or » et l'un des États les plus riches de l'Égypte antique. La forteresse, autrefois imposante, se dresse ici depuis des milliers d'années. Par la suite, lors de la construction du barrage d'Assouan, d'autres temples furent déplacés sur le site, où le terrain est plus élevé. Ce voyage sur l'eau vous permettra d'admirer ce qui reste de ce fabuleux passé et vous mènera de merveilles telles que l'Allée des sphinx jusqu'aux grands temples de Ramsès II à Abou Simbel, apothéose de votre périple.

Malgré les effets du temps et de la nature qui ont quelque peu terni leur splendeur, ces monuments restent stupéfiants. Votre bateau, lui, a conservé tout son éclat, et sa noblesse est à la hauteur de son environnement. Quel meilleur endroit que le pont de ce luxueux navire pour admirer la magnificence de l'Égypte ?

Livre à emporter : « Mort sur le Nil » d'Agatha Christie

ANREISE	Abfahrt in Assuan oder Abu Simbel
PREIS	Ab 150 US$ pro Person im Doppelzimmer inklusive Vollpension, Nachmittagstee, Führungen und Transfer
ZIMMER	55 Kabinen, 10 Suiten
KÜCHE	So erlesen wie die prächtige Umgebung
GESCHICHTE	1997 vom Stapel gelaufen
X-FAKTOR	Kreuzfahrt entlang des Nils, von einer Ära in die nächste

ACCÈS	Départ d'Assouan ou d'Abou Simbel
PRIX	Chambre double à partir de 150 $ US par personne. Les prix comprennent la pension complète, le thé de l'après-midi, les visites guidées et les transferts
CHAMBRES	55 cabines, 10 suites
RESTAURATION	Harmonie avec l'environnement somptueux
HISTOIRE	Ouvert en septembre 1997
LES « PLUS »	Une luxueuse croisière sur le Nil pour découvrir les diverses époques de l'Égypte

Natural habitat...
Sarara Tented Camp, Namunyak Wildlife Conservancy

Sarara Tented Camp, Namunyak Wildlife Conservancy

Natural habitat

By night, the sounds of Africa are not like those of other places. A whole range of sounds fills the night here and adds to its mystery. Noises you have not heard before can keep you awake, in the dark. Maybe the raspy breath of some 'thing' nearby, an odd rustle and snap of twigs, or a sudden harsh cry. It is the bush orchestra tuning up – the roar of a lion, a hyena's laugh, or the shrill call of a jackal. In spite of the noise, you will nod off, and wake to early morning birdsong; and perhaps the squeal of a monkey, or the cry of the fish eagle.

A spell in an African bush camp, with the sound of nature around you, and canvas walls, has an effect on all of our senses. Free from the clatter of our normal life, our hearing goes on alert. We are not used to the trumpeting of an elephant; or to the deep silence that can fall here, in such dark nights. The luxury sleeping tents at the Sarara Camp are equipped such that there is no need to go out into that night. Deep in the bush, the camp is in a vast wilderness. Yet herds still come here; of elephants, that is. Sarara is a haven for them too. Lions are locals, along with wild dogs, zebra, giraffe and antelope. They will be at a safe distance; armed guards keep them from being too curious about you. Although difficult to spot, leopards are common; you may hear one near the camp at night. That dry cough just after you dozed off...

Book to pack: "Green City in the Sun" by Barbara Wood

Sarara Tented Camp	
Namunyak	
Kenya	
Tel: + 254 (20) 44 62 61	
Fax + 254 (20) 44 62 61	
Email: acacia@swiftkenya.com;	
2NWCT@bushmail.net	
Website: www.lewa.org	
Booking: www.great-escapes-hotels.com	

DIRECTIONS	A 7-hour drive north of Nairobi, or 2 hours from Samburu; or by private air charter from Wilson airport, Nairobi, to Namunyak airstrip
RATES	From US$190 per person per night fully catered
ROOMS	5 tents for up to 10 people
FOOD	Chefs, not boy scouts, in charge, everything cooked over an open campfire – even the bread
HISTORY	Sarara is part of the Namunyak Wildlife Conservation Trust, working with the tribal community to protect the land and the animals
X-FACTOR	Bush walking and bathing in the waterfalls or pool

Natürlich wohnen

Die Nacht klingt anders in Afrika. Sie ist erfüllt von einer ganzen Reihe von Geräuschen, die ihr etwas geheimnisvoll Mystisches verleihen. Fremde und neuartige Töne werden Sie in der Dunkelheit wach halten. Womöglich das heisere Atmen eines unbekannten Etwas, hier und da das Rascheln und Knacken von Zweigen oder ein plötzlicher rauer Schrei: Der Choral des afrikanischen Busch hebt an – das Brüllen eines Löwen, das Lachen einer Hyäne, oder der schrille Schrei des Schakals. Trotz der Geräuschkulisse werden Sie einschlafen und früh am Morgen vom Gesang der Vögel, dem Quietschen eines Affen oder dem Schrei des Fischadlers erwachen.

Schlafend zwischen Segeltuchwänden und umgeben vom Klang der Natur, berührt ein Aufenthalt in einem afrikanischen Buschcamp all unsere Sinne. Befreit vom Alltagslärm wird unser Gehör wachsam. Weder sind wir an das Trompeten der Elefanten gewohnt, noch an die tiefe Stille, die sich in solchen dunklen Nächten über das Camp breiten kann. Die Luxuszelte sind so ausgelegt, dass Sie sie in der Nacht nicht verlassen müssen. Das Camp befindet sich tief im Innern des Busches in weiter Wildnis. Hierher kommen auch Elefantenherden, denn Sarara ist auch für sie eine sicherer Hafen. Auch Löwen, wilde Hunde, Zebras, Giraffen und Antilopen leben hier. Doch sie werden in sicherer Entfernung bleiben, während bewaffnete Wächter aufpassen, dass sie Ihnen in ihrer Neugier nicht zu nahe kommen. Auch Leoparden sind hier zu Hause. Zwar ist es schwer, sie zu entdecken, aber möglicherweise werden Sie nachts, kurz vor dem Einschlummern, seinen kratzigen Husten hören.

Buchtipps: »Die weiße Massai« von Corinne Hofmann
»Rote Sonne, schwarzes Land« von Barbara Wood

L'état de nature

Les bruits qui s'élèvent de la nuit africaine sont uniques. Toute une gamme de sons résonne dans la nuit, ajoutant au mystère. Des bruits jusque-là inconnus peuvent vous tenir éveillé : la respiration rauque et proche d'un animal mysté-rieux, le bruissement et le craquement des brindilles ou un cri strident et soudain. Ce sont les instruments de l'orchestre de la brousse qui se mettent au diapason : le rugissement du lion, le rire de la hyène ou le cri perçant du chacal. Malgré tout, vous vous laisserez gagner par le sommeil, et c'est le chant matinal des oiseaux qui vous réveillera, peut-être suivi des vociférations des singes ou du cri des aigles pêcheurs. Séjourner dans un camp de brousse africain, entouré des bruits de la nature et de parois en toile, voilà qui met tous les sens en éveil. Libérée de la cacophonie de la vie quoti-dienne, notre ouïe est en alerte. Elle n'est pas habituée au barrissement des éléphants ou au profond silence qui règne ici une fois la nuit noire tombée.

Les tentes luxueuses de Sarara Camp sont, de toute façon, si bien équipées qu'il n'est nul besoin de s'aventurer dans l'obscurité. Le camp est situé en pleine brousse, au cœur d'une vaste étendue sauvage. Pourtant, les troupeaux – d'éléphants – y viennent en masse. Pour eux aussi Sarara est un havre. Les animaux qui vivent ici en permanence, à savoir les lions, les chiens sauvages, les zèbres, les girafes et les antilopes, sont tenus à distance. Des gardes armés les empêchent de se montrer trop curieux à votre égard. Même s'il est difficile de les apercevoir, les léopards sont ici courants. Peut-être en entendrez-vous un rôder autour du camp, la nuit, et émettre cette toux sèche caractéristique juste au moment où vous vous assoupirez…

Livre à emporter : « La Massaï blanche » de Corinne Hofmann

ANREISE	Etwa 7-stündige Fahrt nördlich von Nairobi, oder 2-stündig von Samburu; oder vom Wilson Airport, Nairobi, mit einer privaten Chartermaschine nach Namunyak fliegen
PREIS	Ab 190 US$ pro Person und pro Nacht Vollpension
ZIMMER	5 Zelte für bis zu 10 Personen
KÜCHE	Hier sind echte Köche am Werk – keine Pfadfinder. Alles wird über einem offenen Lagerfeuer zubereitet, sogar das Brot
GESCHICHTE	Sarara gehört zum Namunyak Wildlife Conservation Trust und arbeitet mit der Stammesgemeinschaft zusammen, um das Land und die Tiere zu schützen
X-FAKTOR	Wanderungen durch die Buschlandschaft und Baden in Wasserfälle

ACCÈS	À 7 heures en voiture au nord de Nairobi ou à 2 heures de Samburu. Possibilité d'emprunter un avion-charter privé jusqu'à la piste d'atterrissage de Namunyak
PRIX	À partir de 190 $ US par personne et nuit en pension complète
CHAMBRES	5 tentes pouvant accueillir jusqu'à 10 personnes
RESTAURATION	Les plats sont élaborés par des chefs cuisiniers et non par des boys scouts. Tout est cuit au feu de camp
HISTOIRE	Sarara fait partie du Namunyak Wildlife Conservation Trust et collabore avec la communauté tribale pour protéger l'environnement et les animaux
LES « PLUS »	Promenades en brousse et baignades en piscine ou sous les chutes d'eau

A bush wilderness...
Il N'gwesi, Northern District

Il N'gwesi, Northern District

A bush wilderness

For most animals, a key factor for their survival is that they learn, and learn fast, how best to fit in to their surroundings. Those who are adept at this have a better chance of a longer life.

Blending in so well that it is almost camouflaged, Il N'gwesi Lodge looks out over a vast and varied bush landscape. Sweeping views of Northern Kenya are to be seen from its hillside hiding place. At night no other lights shine out; the only sound is the deep chorus of the African bush. The lodge is an example of a modern style of tourism, one in which the local people play a major part in the preservation of wildlife. Both the wildlife and the people benefit from this. Profits are put back into the local community: Il N'gwesi's success has been such that it now helps support five hundred families and a school. The Lodge is also eco-friendly; only local materials have been used to build it; water is brought in by camels and heated by the sun. Elephant, lion, leopard and antelope turn up to drink at a waterhole of their own nearby; they can be watched, at a discreet distance, from a viewing platform.

A visit to a nearby Maasai manyatta – village – can be arranged, where not only their cultural practices and rituals of daily living are presented, but the hunting skills, traditional rites, and dancing of these proud people are also shared with their guests.

Book to pack: "Green Hills of Africa" by Ernest Hemingway

Il N'gwesi

Northern District

Kenya

Tel: + 254 (20) 44 71 51

Fax: + 254 (20) 44 16 90

E-mail: info@letsgosafari.com

Website: www.kenyanportfolio.com/
ilngwesi2.htm

Booking: www.great-escapes-hotels.com

DIRECTIONS	A 6-hour drive from Nairobi with access through Lewa or Borana. By private charter direct to Il N'gwesi airstrip. By scheduled service (Air Kenya) daily from Nairobi to Lewa, then a 1.5-hour road transfer
RATES	From US$190 per person per night, including full board accommodation, game drives and guided walks
ROOMS	6 rooms for up to three persons, one of them with a deck where the bed can be rolled out for a night under the stars
FOOD	There is a resident chef, but you need to bring your own food. A shop on site that stocks non-perishable items and drinks
HISTORY	Officially opened in December 1996
X-FACTOR	Choose your guests and contribute to the local community

In tiefster Buschwildnis

Für die meisten Tiere ist es eine überlebensnotwendige Eigenschaft, zu lernen – und zwar schnell zu lernen, wie sie sich am besten ihrer Umgebung anpassen können. Wer am geschicktesten darin ist, hat die größte Chance zu überleben. Die Il N'gwesi Lodge fügt sich so perfekt in ihren Hintergrund ein, dass sie beinahe wie getarnt wirkt.

Von diesem Versteck in den Hügeln eröffnet sich ein umwerfender Blick auf das nördliche Kenia. Das Dunkel der Nacht wird von keiner anderen Lichtquelle gestört; das einzige Geräusch ist der Chor der tiefen Stimmen des afrikanischen Buschs.

Die Lodge ist ein Beispiel für eine moderne Form des Tourismus, in welcher den Einheimischen eine Hauptrolle beim Schutz des Wildparks zukommt. Davon profitieren sowohl Mensch als auch Natur und die Gewinne fließen zurück in die Gemeinschaft. Il N'gwesi ist bisher ein so erfolgreiches Projekt, dass es mittlerweile fünfhundert Familien und eine Schule unterstützt. Außerdem ist die Lodge umweltfreundlich; bei ihrem Bau wurden ausschließlich Materialien aus der Gegend verwendet. Wasser wird von Kamelen gebracht und von der Sonne erwärmt. Elefanten, Löwen, Leoparden und Antilopen kommen zu einem nahegelegenen Wasserloch um ihren Durst zu löschen, wobei man sie von einer Aussichtsplattform aus angemessener Entfernung beobachten kann.

Es ist möglich, einen Besuch in einem benachbarten Massai-Dorf – manyatta – zu organisieren, wo sie ihre Kultur, die Rituale des täglichen Lebens, zur Schau stellen, und wo dieses stolze Volk seine Jagdmethoden, traditionellen Riten und Tänze mit seinen Gästen teilt.

Buchtipp: »Die grünen Hügel Afrikas« von Ernest Hemingway

Au coeur de la brousse

Pour la plupart des animaux, l'élément clé de la survie est d'apprendre rapidement à s'adapter à son environnement. Les plus habiles sont ceux qui ont le plus de chances de vivre plus longtemps.

Se fondant si parfaitement dans son environnement à flanc de coteau qu'il s'en trouve presque camouflé, Il N'gwesi Lodge domine un paysage de brousse vaste et varié et offre une vue panoramique du Nord du Kenya. La nuit, la seule source de lumière alentour est l'éclairage de l'hôtel, et l'unique son, celui de l'intense mélopée de la brousse africaine.

L'hôtel est à l'image du tourisme d'aujourd'hui, dans lequel les autochtones jouent un rôle essentiel en matière de préservation de la faune et de la flore et dont tirent parti tant les animaux que les individus grâce au réinvestissement des bénéfices dans la communauté locale. Le succès d'Il N'gwesi est tel qu'il fait aujourd'hui vivre cinq cent familles et subventionne une école. Il est également respectueux de l'environnement puisque seuls des matériaux locaux ont été utilisés pour sa construction, et l'eau est amenée par chameau et chauffée par les rayons du soleil. Les éléphants, les lions, les léopards et les antilopes viennent se désaltérer à un point d'eau situé à proximité de l'hôtel, et il est possible de les observer à distance respectueuse, depuis une plate-forme prévue à cet effet.

Une visite à un manyatta (village) massaï peut être organisée. Vous y découvrirez les pratiques culturelles et les rituels quotidiens de ce peuple fier, qui partagera avec vous ses techniques de chasse, ses rites traditionnels et ses danses.

Livre à emporter : « Les vertes collines d'Afrique » d'Ernest Hemingway

ANREISE	6-stündige Fahrt von Nairobi über Lewa oder Borana. Sie können mit einer privaten Chartermaschine direkt nach Il N'gwesi oder mit einem Linienflug täglich von Nairobi nach Lewa fliegen, anschließend 1,5-stündige Fahrt zum Anwesen
PREIS	Ab 190 US$ pro Person und pro Nacht, Verpflegung, Wildbeobachtungs-Fahrten und -wanderungen inbegriffen
ZIMMER	6 Zimmer für bis zu drei Personen
KÜCHE	Es gibt einen Koch, aber die Zutaten müssen Sie selbst besorgen. Vor Ort ist ein kleiner Laden
GESCHICHTE	Offiziell eröffnet im Jahre 1996
X-FAKTOR	Die Mitbewohner selbst aussuchen und etwas zur lokalen Gemeinschaft beitragen

ACCÈS	À 6 heures en voiture de Nairobi en passant par Lewa ou Borana. Liaison aérienne directe en charter privé entre Nairobi et la piste d'atterrissage d'Il N'gwesi
PRIX	À partir de 190 $ US par personne et par nuit en pension complète. Le prix comprend les safaris et les promenades guidées
CHAMBRES	6 chambres pouvant accueillir jusqu'à trois personnes, l'une d'entre elles étant équipée d'une terrasse
RESTAURATION	L'hôtel a son propre chef cuisinier, mais vous devrez apporter les ingrédients.
HISTOIRE	Officiellement ouvert en 1996
LES « PLUS »	Choisissez vos compagnons et contribuez à l'esprit collectif local

Towering aspirations...
Dodo's Tower, Lake Naivasha

Dodo's Tower, Lake Naivasha

Towering aspirations

Once upon a time, when I was a child, the tale of a girl kept in a tower was one of my favourites. "Rapunzel, Rapunzel, let down your golden hair"; the words the witch, and the prince, called to make her send her lengthy locks down to the ground was a line I loved. However, the tower in the Brothers Grimm story was as bleak as the fable. It had neither door nor staircase, and only one very high window. This is much more like a fairytale tower, and it's a real one. Dodo's Tower is a whimsical formation on the shores of an enchanting lake; it is one of the most fanciful places to stay in all of Africa. Just its tip can be seen above a forest of acacia trees, yet the rest of it blends quite naturally into the background. At some times of the morning and night, it can trick the eye, morphing more into a tree-trunk than a building. A closer look reveals that a playful yet sure hand, one that loves luxury as much as fantasy, has shaped it. The stylish pagoda is the happy ending to a dream that others can share. It seems to cast a benign spell over all who come here.

Having a wooden spire in the middle of the landscape does not seem to phase the creatures that share this setting. Hippos and giraffes, or pelicans and flamingos seldom play a part in fables; yet they can be seen far below from the verandas of this imaginative place.

Books to pack: Several, so that you need not come down...
"The Lord of the Rings. The Two Towers" by J.R.R. Tolkien
"The Seven Story Tower" by Curtiss Hoffman
"The Ebony Tower" by John Fowles
"Child of Happy Valley" by Juanita Carberry

Dodo's Tower	DIRECTIONS	A 20-minute charter flight from Nairobi to Naivasha airstrip and then a 40-minute drive to the estate. By road, the estate is a 1.5-hour drive north west from Nairobi
P.O. Box 24397		
Nairobi	RATES	US$500 per person, per night, including food
Kenya	ROOMS	5, on four floors, with a meditation room at the very top
Tel: + 254 (20) 57 46 89	FOOD	Magical menus conjured up by a French wizard
Fax: + 254 (20) 57 73 81	HISTORY	Built in the early 1990s on the same estate as Hippo Point House
E-mail: mellifera@swiftkenya.com		
Booking: www.great-escapes-hotels.com	X-FACTOR	The chance to be in a fairytale of your own

The Giraffe Manor, near Nairobi

Visits from giraffes

This elegant house was here before the giraffes; but luckily, it was constructed as a two-storey building, so that now the statuesque creatures can be fed at a height that best suits them. There are some benefits in being so tall. Gazing through the upper windows as they stroll by is a usual bent for them, though it might be surprising for guests.

The Giraffe Manor is home to several of these bizarre yet beautiful animals. The ones that live here in the acres of forest are rare Rothschild giraffes, descendants of what were once an endangered species. In the 1970s, the house owners set up the African Fund for Endangered Wildlife: a name that was soon and aptly shortened to AFEW. They transferred five baby giraffes to their property, with the result that they are on record as being the only people to have successfully brought up wild giraffes. Those are now grown-up with babies of their own.

There is a human story here too. One of the bedrooms is furnished with pieces that Tania Blixen, author of "Out of Africa", gave to the owners when she left Kenya. And upstairs, in the hall, are the bookcases that the love of her life, Denys Finch-Hatton, made for her.

The world's tallest animal does not have the sole advantage of height here; the snow capped peak of Kilimanjaro, the highest mountain in Africa, can be seen in the distance. "African legend insists that man arrived on earth by sliding down the giraffe's neck from Heaven"... Betty Leslie Melville, co-founder with Jock Leslie-Melville of AFEW.

Book to pack: "Zarafa" by Michael Allin

The Giraffe Manor
P.O. Box 15004
Langata, Nairobi
Kenya
Tel: + 254 (20) 89 10 78
Fax: + 254 (20) 89 09 49
E-mail: giraffem@kenyaweb.com
Website: www.giraffemanor.com
Booking: www.great-escapes-hotels.com

DIRECTIONS	20 km/12 m south west of Nairobi; 20 minutes from the airport
RATES	From US$595 per double room full board, including meals and drinks
ROOMS	6 bedrooms with bathrooms
FOOD	The chef focuses on providing for the guests, not the giraffes
HISTORY	Built in 1932
X-FACTOR	Feeding the giraffes from your upper-storey window, or at even closer quarters

Giraffen zu Besuch

Dieses elegante Haus stand bereits hier, bevor die Giraffen da waren; doch glücklicherweise wurde es zweistöckig konstruiert, so dass die stattlich hohen Tiere aus optimaler Höhe gefüttert werden können. So groß zu sein, hat einige Vorteile. Und während es für die Hotelgäste durchaus überraschend sein mag, ist es für die Giraffen ganz normal, dass sie einen Blick durch die oberen Fenster werfen, wenn Sie draußen vorbeistolzieren. Giraffe Manor beheimatet gleich mehrere dieser bizarren und doch gleichzeitig so schönen Kreaturen. Die Tiere, die in diesem mehrere Morgen großen Waldgebiet leben, gehören zur Spezies der seltenen Rothschild Giraffe, und sind somit Nachkommen einer einst vom Aussterben bedrohten Art.

In den 1970er Jahren riefen die Besitzer des Hauses den Afrikanischen Fond Existenzbedrohter Wildtierarten ins Leben (»African Fund for Endangered Wildlife«), ein Name, der bald darauf kurz und prägnant zu AFEW abgekürzt wurde. Sie siedelten fünf Babygiraffen auf ihrem Grundstück an und sind seither bekannt dafür, die einzigen Menschen zu sein, die es jemals geschafft haben, wilde Giraffen großzuziehen.

Hier gibt es jedoch auch eine Geschichte von Menschen zu erzählen. Eines der Schafzimmer wurde mit Möbeln ausgestattet, die Tania Blixen, die Autorin von »Out of Africa«, den Besitzern schenkte, als sie Kenia verließ. Und oben, in der Halle, stehen die Bücherregale, die Denys Finch-Hatton, die Liebe ihres Lebens, für sie gezimmert hatte.

Das größte Tier der Welt ist nicht das einzige, was hier einen Anspruch auf die Bezeichnung groß oder hoch erheben kann: in der Ferne kann man die schneebedeckte Kuppe des höchsten Berges in Afrika erkennen – die Spitze des Kilimandscharo.

»Die afrikanische Welterschaffungslegende besagt, dass der Mensch vom Himmel auf die Erde kam, indem er einen Giraffenhals hinabrutschte.« Betty Leslie-Melville, Mitbegründerin von AFEW gemeinsam mit Jock Leslie-Melville.

Buchtipp: »Zarafa« von Michael Allin

Visites amicales des girafes

Cet élégant édifice existait avant l'arrivée des girafes. Fort heureusement, l'architecte avait prévu deux étages, et l'on peut aujourd'hui nourrir ces créatures sculpturales depuis une hauteur appropriée. Il y a des avantages à être grand. Les girafes sont curieuses et ont tendance à venir regarder longuement au travers des fenêtres les plus hautes lors de leurs déambulations, même si cela peut prendre au dépourvu les clients de l'hôtel.

Giraffe Manor abrite plusieurs de ces étranges et magnifiques animaux. Les girafes qui vivent ici, dans l'immense forêt, sont des animaux rares, les girafes Rothschild, descendantes d'une espèce autrefois en voie d'extinction. Dans les années 70, les propriétaires fondèrent l'African Fund for Endangered Wildlife (Fonds africain pour les espèces menacées), rapidement abrégé en AFEW, et transférèrent cinq girafons dans leur propriété. C'est la seule expérience réussie au monde d'un élevage de girafes sauvages, aujourd'hui adultes et à leur tour mamans.

L'homme a aussi apporté sa pierre à l'histoire de ce lieu. L'une des chambres est en effet garnie d'objets donnés par Tania Blixen, l'auteur de « La ferme africaine » (« Out of Africa ») avant son départ du Kenya. En outre, dans le hall du premier étage se trouvent les bibliothèques fabriquées pour elle par l'amour de sa vie, Denys Finch-Hatton. L'animal le plus grand du monde n'a pas le monopole de la hauteur : vous apercevrez à l'horizon les sommets enneigés du Kilimandjaro, la montagne la plus haute d'Afrique.

« La légende africaine veut que l'Homme soit arrivé du paradis sur la terre en glissant le long du cou d'une girafe... » Betty Leslie Melville, cofondatrice de l'AFEW avec Jock Leslie-Melville.

Livre à emporter : « La girafe de Charles X » de Michael Allin

ANREISE	20 km südwestlich von Nairobi entfernt; 20 Minuten vom Flughafen	ACCÈS	À 20 km au sud-ouest de Nairobi et à 20 minutes de l'aéroport
PREIS	Ab 595 US$ pro Doppelzimmer, inklusive Speisen und Getränke	PRIX	Chambre double en pension complète à partir de 595 $ US, repas et boissons compris
ZIMMER	6 Zimmer mit Bad	CHAMBRES	6 chambres avec salle de bain
KÜCHE	Der Koch konzentriert sich darauf, die Gäste zu verwöhnen, nicht die Giraffen	RESTAURATION	Le chef cuisinier se consacre aux clients et non aux girafes !
GESCHICHTE	Erbaut im Jahre 1932	HISTOIRE	Construit en 1932
X-FAKTOR	Füttern Sie Giraffen vom Fenster Ihres Zimmers im ersten Stock aus, oder kommen Sie Ihnen sogar noch näher	LES « PLUS »	Vous nourrirez les girafes depuis votre chambre à l'étage ou depuis la terre ferme si vous le souhaitez

A heaven here on earth...
Ngorongoro Crater Lodge, Ngorongoro Conservation Area

Ngorongoro Crater Lodge, Ngorongoro Conservation Area

A heaven here on earth

Stand on the edge of the most impressive crater on earth and look down. Far below you is all that is left of what was once a great volcano. Three million years ago, when the giant mountain collapsed, it formed a deep and perfectly shaped basin. Steep walls ring the huge caldera of Ngorongoro.

Within there is a remarkable assortment of wildlife, like Noah's Ark in its selection. And perched on stilts on the rim of the crater is an exceptional place to stay for the human species that visit here. From the outside, the Ngorongoro Crater Lodge looks like a Maasai village. One built on the best possible site. Each suite has stunning views of the crater. But from the inside, you could picture yourself to be in Paris. The interior has a grandeur that is in accord with the dramatic landscape that can be seen from the windows. Outside is a real African Eden, teeming with thousands of animals. Black rhinos, elephants, lions, leopards, buffaloes, and cheetahs roam free and wild, all around the renowned safari lodge. Maasai warriors accompany you to and from your room at night, making sure that you are out of harm's way. Here, great wilderness and luxury are placed side by side.

Book to pack: "The African Queen" by Cecil Scott Forester

Ngorongoro Crater Lodge		
Ngorongoro Conservation Area		
Tanzania		
Tel: + 255 (27) 253 70 38		
Fax: + 255 (27) 254 82 86		
E-mail: information@ccafrica.com		
Website: www.ccafrica.com		
Booking: www.great-escapes-hotels.com		

DIRECTIONS	Ngorongoro Crater Lodge is accessible by scheduled flight from Arusha Airport, followed by a 2.5-hour road transfer
RATES	US$400 to US$535, including all meals and scheduled safari activities
ROOMS	3 adjacent camps with 30 Maasai-inspired suites
FOOD	Pan-African
HISTORY	Built in 1997
X-FACTOR	The location, the decoration and diverse inhabitants

Ein Himmel hier auf Erden

Stehen Sie an der Kante des atemberaubendsten Kraters der Welt und blicken Sie in die Tiefe hinab. Weit, weit unter Ihnen liegt all das, was davon übrig ist, was einst ein großer Vulkan gewesen ist. Vor drei Millionen Jahren brach der gigantische Berg in sich zusammen und schuf dabei ein tiefes und perfekt geformtes Becken. Steile Hänge bilden den kreisförmigen Kraterkessel von Ngorongoro.

Und in ihm lebt eine unglaubliche Anzahl wilder Tiere, so vielfältig in ihrer Art, wie einst auf Noahs Arche. Und auf Stelzen gebaut, oben am Kraterrand befindet sich ein ganz außergewöhnlicher Ort, an dem Besucher der menschlichen Spezies verweilen können: Von außen sieht die Ngorongoro Crater Lodge wie ein Massai Dorf aus – eines, das an der denkbar besten Stelle errichtet wurde. Doch betrachtet man sie von innen, so könnte man sich glatt vorstellen, man sei in Paris. Die Pracht der Inneneinrichtung steht im Einklang mit der dramatisch schönen Landschaft, die sich einem beim Blick durch die Fenster eröffnet.

Draußen liegt ein wahrer afrikanischer Garten Eden, in welchem sich Tausende von Tieren tummeln: Schwarze Nashörner, Elefanten, Löwen, Leoparden, Büffel und Geparden streifen wild und frei in der Nähe der renommierten Safari Lodge umher. Abends begleiten Sie Massai Krieger zu Ihrer Hütte und stellen sicher, dass Ihnen auch nichts passiert. Großartige Wildnis und Luxus gehen hier Hand in Hand miteinander einher.

Buchtipp: »Die African Queen« von Cecil Scott Forester

Le paradis sur terre

Approchez-vous du bord du cratère le plus impressionnant du monde et penchez-vous. Tout en bas, vous apercevez tout ce qui reste de ce qui fut un jour un immense volcan. Il y a trois millions d'années, la montagne gigantesque qui se dressait à cet endroit s'est effondrée et a laissé la place à une cuvette profonde de forme parfaite entourée de parois abruptes : l'énorme caldeira du Ngorongoro.

À l'intérieur vit une faune dont la remarquable diversité n'est pas sans rappeler l'Arche de Noé. Au bord du cratère, perché sur des pilotis, un refuge extraordinaire attend les visiteurs. Vu de l'extérieur, Ngorongoro Crater Lodge a tout d'un village massaï, un village érigé sur le meilleur site qui soit. Chaque suite offre en effet une vue sensationnelle sur le cratère. Toutefois, une fois à l'intérieur, on pourrait se croire dans l'un des hôtels les plus chics de Paris étant donnée l'harmonie entre la splendeur du décor et le spectaculaire paysage que l'on peut apercevoir à travers les fenêtres. Ce dernier est un véritable éden peuplé de milliers d'animaux : rhinocéros noirs, éléphants, lions, léopards, buffles et guépards sillonnent en toute liberté les alentours de cet hôtel célèbre pour ses safaris. La nuit venue, les guerriers massaï veillent sur votre sécurité en vous accompagnant dans vos allées et venues hors de votre chambre.

Ici, les grandes étendues sauvages et le luxe se côtoient.

Livre à emporter : « Aventure africaine » de Cecil Scott Forester

ANREISE	Die Ngorongoro Crater Lodge kann per Flugzeug vom Flughafen Arusha und einem anschließenden 2,5-stündigen Autotransfer erreicht werden
PREIS	Von 400 US$ bis 535 US$, inklusive aller Mahlzeiten, sowie planmäßig organisierten Safaris
ZIMMER	3 nebeneinander liegende Camps mit 30 Suiten im Stil der Massai-Hütten
KÜCHE	Panafrikanisch
GESCHICHTE	Erbaut im Jahre 1997
X-FAKTOR	Die Lage, die Ausstattung und diverse Bewohner

ACCÈS	On accède à Ngorongoro Crater Lodge par vol régulier depuis l'aéroport d'Arusha, suivi d'un transfert en voiture de 2H30
PRIX	De 400 à 535 $ US. Le prix comprend les repas et les activités programmées de safari
CHAMBRES	3 camps contigus avec 30 suites d'inspiration massaï
RESTAURATION	Panafricaine
HISTOIRE	Construit en 1997
LES « PLUS »	Le cadre, la décoration et les divers habitants du lieu

Spice of life...
Emerson & Green Hotel, Zanzibar

Emerson & Green Hotel, Zanzibar

Spice of life

When the Sultan of Oman came to visit this island, he was so smitten by it that he at once moved here to live. That was more than a century ago, but this is still an addictive place. And its name is one of the most captivating. Standing tall in the heart of Zanzibar's Stone Town is the Emerson & Green Hotel. It was the residence of one of the richest men in the Swahili Empire, who, due to his close ties to the Sultan of the time, was allowed to build his house as the second highest in the town, the highest being the Sultan's own palace. From the hotel roof, the view stretches over mosque minarets, Hindu temples, and church spires to the ocean beyond. The narrow, crooked streets below are lined with whitewashed houses, famous for their intricately carved doors. A stroll through the colourful market, artisans' workshops, mosques, an historic fort and sultans' palaces makes for vibrant sights, and sounds.

And exotic aromas carried by the sea breeze scent the air. Zanzibar was once the world's main source of cloves, and in the fragrant spice gardens, most of the known tropical spices, from cardamom to vanilla, can be seen growing in their natural state.

Book to pack: "Memoirs of an Arabian Princess from Zanzibar" by Emily Ruete

Emerson & Green Hotel	
236 Hurumzi Street	
P.O. Box 3417	
Stone Town	
Zanzibar, Tanzania	
Tel: + 255 (24) 223 01 71	
Fax: + 255 (24) 223 10 38	
E-mail: emegre@zanzibar.org	
Website: www.zanzibar.org/emegre	
Booking: www.great-escapes-hotels.com	

DIRECTIONS	A short drive from Zanzibar airport
RATES	US$150 per double room, including breakfast
ROOMS	10 double rooms
FOOD	Roof top restaurant serves up stunning views and sumptuous Arabian food
HISTORY	Built in the 19th century, it was restored to its former glory in the manner of a hotel in 1994
X-FACTOR	Opulent interior and exotic exterior

Die Würze des Lebens

Als der Sultan von Oman einst gekommen war, um diese Insel zu besuchen, war er gleich so von ihr hingerissen, dass er sofort zurückkehrte, um hier zu leben. Das ist nun mehr als hundert Jahre her, doch auch heute noch ist diese Insel ein Ort, der einen nicht mehr loslässt. Schon ihr Name ist so verheißungsvoll wie bei wenigen anderen.

Stolz ragt das Emerson & Green Hotel im Herzen von Stone Town in Sansibar in den Himmel. Einst war es der Wohnsitz eines der reichsten Männer im Königreich der Swahili. Da er eng mit dem damaligen Sultan befreundet war, gewährte man ihm das Recht, das zweithöchste Haus in der Stadt zu erbauen; das höchste Haus war der Palast des Sultans selbst. Vom Dach des Hotels schweift der Blick über Minarette und Moscheen, hinduistische Tempel und Kirchturmspitzen bis zum dahinter-liegenden Meer. Weiß getünchte Häuser, berühmt für ihre auf-wändig geschnitzten Türen reihen sich aneinander und säumen die engen, verwinkelten Straßen. Ein Spaziergang über den Markt, vorbei an Kunsthandwerkstätten, Moscheen, einer historischen Festung und Sultanspalästen bringt lebhafte visuelle und akustische Eindrücke mit sich.

Und die Luft ist voll vom Duft exotischer Aromen, welche die Meeresbrise herbeiträgt. Sansibar war einst der weltweit bedeu-tendste Anbauort für Gewürznelken und in den duftenden Gewürzgärten kann man die meisten bekannten tropischen Gewürze, wie Kardamom oder Vanille, wild wachsen sehen.

Buchtipp: »Leben im Sultanspalast. Memoiren aus dem 19. Jahrhundert« von Emily Ruete

L'île aux épices

En visite sur l'île de Zanzibar, le sultan d'Oman en tomba amoureux et décida de s'y installer sur-le-champ. Bien que cette anecdote remonte à plus d'un siècle, l'île n'a rien perdu de son charme envoûtant et son nom reste synonyme de fascination.

L'hôtel Emerson & Green, qui s'élève en plein cœur de Stone Town, la ville de pierre de Zanzibar, était la résidence de l'un des hommes les plus riches de l'empire swahili. En raison de ses liens étroits avec le sultan de l'époque, il fut autorisé à construire la maison la plus haute de la cité après le palais du sultan. La vue du toit de l'hôtel vous dévoile des minarets de mosquées, des temples hindous et des flèches d'églises et s'étend jusqu'à l'océan. Les rues étroites et tor-tueuses en contrebas sont bordées de maisons blanchies à la chaux, célèbres pour leurs portes d'entrée aux gravures complexes. Une visite au marché pittoresque, aux ateliers des artisans, aux mosquées, au fort historique et aux palais des sultans, et vous voilà transporté dans un univers plein de couleurs et de sons.

Des effluves exotiques transportés par la brise de mer embaument l'atmosphère : Zanzibar était jadis le principal producteur de clous de girofle et, dans ses jardins d'épices odorants, la plupart des épices tropicales connues, de la cardamome à la vanille, poussent à l'état naturel.

Livre à emporter : « Mémoires d'une princesse arabe » d'Emily Ruete

ANREISE	Kurze Fahrt vom Flughafen Sansibar
PREIS	150 US$ pro Doppelzimmer, inklusive Frühstück
ZIMMER	10 Doppelzimmer
KÜCHE	Das Dachterrassenrestaurant bietet eine überwältigende Aussicht und aufwändige arabische Speisen
GESCHICHTE	Ursprünglich erbaut im 19. Jahrhundert wurde es im Jahre 1994 zum Hotel umgestaltet und erstrahlt nun in seiner alten Pracht
X-FAKTOR	Opulente Innenausstattung und exotische Umgebung

ACCÈS	À quelques minutes de l'aéroport de Zanzibar en voiture
PRIX	150 $ US la chambre double, petit-déjeuner compris
CHAMBRES	10 chambres doubles
RESTAURATION	Le restaurant situé sur le toit de l'hôtel offre une vue exceptionnelle et propose des mets arabes exquis
HISTOIRE	Construit au XIXe siècle, le bâtiment a retrouvé sa splendeur passée en devenant hôtel en 1994
LES « PLUS »	Intérieur somptueux et environnement exotique

Barefoot luxury...
Chumbe Island Coral Park, Zanzibar

Chumbe Island Coral Park, Zanzibar

Barefoot luxury

Rising up on a small island between Zanzibar and Dar es Salaam is a lighthouse. Its flashing beam guides the dhows, boats that have crossed this sea for a thousand years. The tower also signals the location of one of the most spectacular coral gardens on earth. Beneath the water, corals in a kaleidoscope of colours teem with fish. Chumbe Island Coral Park is a private nature reserve, covered by an evergreen forest. This is an ecological sanctuary where the rare duiker antelope roam and giant coconut crabs climb to the top of trees in search of food. Few other buildings, or people, are here. Soaring thatched roofs amongst the foliage mark the existence of just seven bungalows. Water and energy are provided by nature, and they have solar-powered lights and hot water. All face the turquoise-blue ocean, and it takes just a few seconds to stroll to the beach and reef. Or you can just look at it, lying in your comfortable hammock. This is rather like camping out, but in comparative luxury, and sleeping, dreaming, under a palm thatched roof.
Book to pack: "Robinson Crusoe" by Daniel Defoe

Chumbe Island Coral Park
P.O. Box 3203
Zanzibar
Tanzania
Tel: + 255 (24) 223 10 40
Fax: + 255 (24) 223 10 40
E-mail: info@chumbeisland.com
Website: www.chumbeisland.com
Booking: www.great-escapes-hotels.com

DIRECTIONS	Fly to Zanzibar, take a boat from the beach at the Mbweni Ruins hotel
RATES	From US$150 per person full board, including transfers, all fees, taxes, services, snorkelling, forest walks
ROOMS	7 bungalows
FOOD	Zanzibarian, Arabic, Indian and African cuisine
HISTORY	The Government of Zanzibar declared it a closed forest in 1994, and the management was entrusted to the Chumbe Island Coral Park
X-FACTOR	Castaway in style

Der Luxus, barfuß zu laufen

Auf einer kleinen Insel zwischen Sansibar und Dar es Salaam steht ein Leuchtturm. Sein blinkender Lichtstrahl weist den Dhows die Richtung, Booten, die schon seit tausend Jahren durch dieses Meer segeln.

Der Leuchtturm weist auch den Weg zu einem der eindrucksvollsten Korallenriffe der Welt. In den Tiefen des Meeres kann man hier inmitten der bunten Farbenpracht der Korallen ganze Schwärme von Fischen bewundern.

Chumbe Island Coral Park ist ein privater Naturschutzpark, der von einem immergrünen Wald überzogen ist, ein ökologisches Heiligtum, in dem die seltene Duiker Antilope frei umherstreift und Riesenkokosnusskrabben bei ihrer Nahrungssuche in die Baumkronen hinaufklettern. Sonst gibt es hier wenig andere Gebäude oder Menschen. An den strohgedeckten Dächern die aus den Blättern ragen, lässt sich erkennen, dass es hier nicht mehr als sieben Bungalows gibt. Wasser und Strom liefert die Natur, die Bungalows haben solarbetriebenes Licht und heißes Wasser und sind alle auf das türkisblaue Meer hinaus ausgerichtet. Mit nur wenigen Schritten gelangt man an den Strand und das Riff. Oder man genießt einfach nur deren Anblick, während man in seiner bequemen Hängematte liegt.

Das ganze erinnert eher an Camping, aber mit vergleichsweise hohem Luxus; schlafen und träumen unterm Palmendach.

Buchtipp: »Robinson Crusoe« von Daniel Defoe

Les pieds nus dans le luxe

Sur une petite île entre Zanzibar et Dar es Salaam se dresse un phare. Son faisceau lumineux guide les boutres, des bateaux qui traversent l'océan depuis un millier d'années. Cette tour indique également la présence de l'un des jardins de corail les plus spectaculaires du monde. Sous l'eau, les coraux et leur kaléidoscope de couleurs foisonnent de poissons. Chumbe Island Coral Park est une réserve naturelle privée recouverte d'une forêt à feuillage persistant. Dans ce sanctuaire écologique, les céphalophes, antilopes rares, s'ébattent en toute liberté et les crabes géants de cocotier grimpent au sommet des arbres à la recherche de nourriture. Il n'y a guère d'autres constructions, et la solitude règne.

Des toits hauts et couverts de chaume dépassant du feuillage marquent la présence de sept bungalows seulement. L'eau est fournie par la nature et chauffée grâce à l'énergie solaire qui assure également l'éclairage. Tous les bungalows donnent sur l'océan bleu turquoise, et la plage et les récifs ne sont qu'à quelques secondes à pied. Bien sûr, vous pouvez aussi vous contenter de les observer de loin, confortablement installé dans votre hamac.

Vous aurez l'impression de camper, mais dans un camping de luxe, et vous dormirez et rêverez sous un toit recouvert de palmes.

Livre à emporter : « Robinson Crusoé » de Daniel Defoe

ANREISE	Fliegen Sie nach Sansibar, vom Strand des Mbweni Ruins Hotel aus nehmen Sie ein Boot
PREIS	Ab 150 US$ pro Person, inklusive Essen und Getränke, Transfers, Eintritt für den Park und Aktivitäten
ZIMMER	7 Bungalows
KÜCHE	Inseltypische Gerichte, arabische, indische und afrikanische Küche
GESCHICHTE	Im Jahre 1994 wurde der Wald von der Regierung Sansibars unter Naturschutz gestellt und Chumbe Island Coral Park die Verwaltung übertragen
X-FAKTOR	Romantische Einsamkeit

ACCÈS	Après un vol jusqu'à Zanzibar, le bateau se prend sur la plage de l'hôtel Mbweni Ruins.
PRIX	À partir de 150 $ US par personne en pension complète. Le prix comprend les transferts, les billets d'entrée dans la réserve, les taxes et les activités
CHAMBRES	7 bungalows
RESTAURATION	Cuisine arabe, indienne, africaine et typique de Zanzibar
HISTOIRE	La forêt de l'île a été décrétée forêt protégée par le gouvernement de Zanzibar en 1994, et sa gestion a été confiée au Chumbe Island Coral Park
LES « PLUS »	Isolement et style

Wilderness paradise...
Sausage Tree Camp, Lower Zambezi National Park

Sausage Tree Camp,
Lower Zambezi National Park

Wilderness paradise

There is such a thing as a sausage tree; meat eaters may be delighted to know this. Sadly, for fans of sausages, it is not a real source of these treats. It is linked just in name only, and so called because its seedpods look like huge salamis. On the banks of the Zambezi, under a large and shady specimen of this tree, a camp has been created. The large white tents of Sausage Tree Camp sit high along the riverbank. These are marquees for connoisseurs of canvas, and come with all the creature comforts. Spacious and cool, the tents are simple and stylish. Welcome breezes waft through. Mahogany and acacia trees join with the sausages to form a thick forest that surrounds the camp on three sides. The view is over the river and a field of reeds; channels dotted with water lilies and, at times, with heavier things like pods of hippos. In the distance blue tinged mountains seem to float on the horizon.

This remote and unspoiled park is Zambia's newest. Huge herds of buffalo, elephant, and hippo are found here, along with lion, leopard and cheetah. Elusive and prickly creatures such as porcupines and honey badgers are also seen. Over four hundred species of bird have been noted in the area; the cry of the widespread African fish eagle often cuts through the air. Perhaps it is a sign that the fishing is superb here – for tiger fish, bream and huge catfish.

Book to pack: "North of South: an African Journey" by Shiva Naipaul

Sausage Tree Camp	
Lower Zambezi National Park	
Zambia	
Tel: + 260 (1) 272 456	
Fax: + 260 (1) 272 456	
E-mail: info@sausagecamp.com	
Website: www.sausagetreecamp.com	
Booking: www.great-escapes-hotels.com	

DIRECTIONS	Access by light aircraft from Lusaka, Kariba, Mfuwe or Livingstone to Jeki airstrip, then a 45-minute game drive to camp. Road and boat transfer is also available from Lusaka or Kariba
RATES	US$295 per person per night fully inclusive. Open April 1 to November 15 only
ROOMS	6 tents
FOOD	Sometimes real sausages, always good
HISTORY	Opened in August 1996
X-FACTOR	River boating in a wilderness paradise

Paradiesische Wildnis

Es gibt tatsächlich einen sogenannten Würstchenbaum, Fleischesser werden dies mit Freude zur Kenntnis nehmen. Traurig für alle Wurstliebhaber ist, dass an diesen Bäumen nicht wirklich solche Leckereien wachsen. Nur der Name verweist auf sie. Der Baum wird deswegen so genannt, weil seine Samenschoten aussehen wie riesige Salamis. Am Ufer des Sambesi, unter einem großen und schattenspendenden Exemplar jener Art, hat man ein Camp errichtet. Entlang des Ufers liegen die weißen Zelte des Sausage Tree Camps – große Zelte für Kenner des feinen Segeltuches, die jeden erdenklichen Luxus bieten. Die geräumigen und kühlen Zelte sind einfach und stilvoll und ein angenehmer Lufthauch weht durch sie hindurch. Zusammen mit den Sausage Trees bilden Mahagoni- und Akazienbäume einen dichten Wald, der das Lager an drei Seiten umgibt. Der Ausblick geht auf den Fluss und ein Schilfrohrfeld hinaus; man blickt auf die Kanäle, die mit Wasserlilien und manchmal auch mit etwas schwereren Lebewesen, wie Nilpferdherden, übersät sind. Die in der Ferne gelegenen, bläulich gefärbten Berge scheinen am Horizont entlang zu treiben.

Dieser abgeschiedene und unberührte Park ist der jüngste in Zambia. Hier trifft man auf große Büffel-, Elefanten-, und Nilpferdherden, aber auch auf Löwen, Leoparden und Geparden.

Auch publikumsscheue und kratzbürstige Lebewesen, wie das Stachelschwein oder den Honigdachs kann man hier zu Gesicht bekommen. In der Gegend wird das Vorkommen von mehr als 400 verschiedenen Vogelarten verzeichnet, und oft durchschneidet der Schrei des weitverbreiteten afrikanischen Fischadlers die Luft. Dies ist womöglich ein Anzeichen dafür, wie hervorragend man hier Tigerfische, Brassen und Riesenkatzenwelse fischen kann.

Buchtipp: »North of South: an African Journey« von Shiva Naipaul

Paradis sauvage

Il existe bel et bien un arbre à saucisses. Voilà une nouvelle qui ravira les amateurs de charcuterie. Malheureusement pour eux, cet arbre ne produit pas réellement ces douceurs et n'a de saucisse que le nom, qu'il tire de ses cosses ressemblant à d'énormes salamis.

C'est sur les rives du Zambèze, à l'ombre d'un très grand spécimen d'arbre à saucisses, que le camp Sausage Tree Camp a été construit. Les grandes tentes blanches installées le long du fleuve sont équipées de tout le confort matériel et enchanteront les connaisseurs. Spacieuses, fraîches, elles sont simples et élégantes, et une brise bienvenue y circule en permanence. Les acajous, les acacias et les arbres à saucisses forment une épaisse forêt qui borde le camp sur trois côtés. Le côté ouvert donne sur le fleuve, sur un champ de roseaux et sur des canaux parsemés de nénuphars qui accueillent parfois des invités de poids, les hippopotames. Au loin, les montagnes teintées d'azur semblent flotter sur la ligne d'horizon.

Ce parc reculé et bien préservé est le plus récent du pays. D'immenses troupeaux de buffles, d'éléphants et d'hippopotames, des lions, des léopards et des guépards ou encore des créatures insaisissables et armées de piquants telles que le porc-épic et le ratel y cohabitent. Plus de quatre cents espèces d'oiseaux ont été répertoriées sur ce territoire, et le cri du pygargue vocifère, un aigle pêcheur très courant en Afrique, fend l'air à intervalles réguliers. C'est peut-être le signe que la pêche est de premier choix. Vous trouverez ici des poissons tigres, des brèmes et d'énormes poissons-chats.

Livre à emporter : « Au nord du Sud : Un voyage africain » de Shiva Naipaul

ANREISE	Mit dem Kleinflugzeug von Lusaka, Kariba, Mfuwe oder Livingstone aus zum Flugplatz Jeki, mit anschließender 45-minütiger Safarifahrt zum Camp. Von Lusaka oder Kariba aus ist auch ein Transfer mit dem Wagen oder per Boot möglich
PREIS	395 US$ pro Person und pro Nacht, alles inklusive. Nur zwischen 1. April und 15. November geöffnet
ZIMMER	6 Zelte
KÜCHE	Manchmal gibt es echte Würstchen, immer gut!
GESCHICHTE	Eröffnet im August 1996
X-FAKTOR	Flussschifffahrt in paradiesischer Wildnis

ACCÈS	En avionnette depuis Lusaka, Kariba, Mfuwe ou Livingstone jusqu'à la piste d'atterrissage de Jeki, puis transfert en voiture jusqu'au camp (45 min) pendant lequel vous pourrez observer la faune. Possibilité de transfert en voiture et en bateau depuis Lusaka ou Kariba
PRIX	395 $ US la nuit par personne, tout compris. Ouvert du 1er avril au 15 novembre uniquement
CHAMBRES	6 tentes
RESTAURATION	Cuisine de qualité. De vraies saucisses sont parfois au menu
HISTOIRE	Ouvert en août 1996
LES « PLUS »	Navigation sur le fleuve au cœur d'un paradis sauvage

Delta dawn...
Jao Camp, Okavango Delta

Jao Camp, Okavango Delta

Delta dawn

Most of the land of Botswana is a desert. Yet deep within this fierce aridity lies a wetland, one that obtains its water from rain that falls in central Africa; rain over a thousand kilometres away.

At full flood, the channels of the Okavango Delta are fringed with papyrus reeds, and lilies float on its tranquil lagoons. Moving through the waterways in a mokoro – a traditional canoe – is one of the best ways to see the wildlife that teems here. Propelled by boatmen, the canoes slide silently past scenes just waiting to be filmed. The lagoons are home to hippo and crocodile, and the pools of water act as a magnet for thousands of birds. In the midst of this harbour is an oasis, Jao Camp. Secluded under a thick canopy of ancient trees, the whole camp is raised on decks that lift it so that it appears to be floating above the lush palms below. Each of the stylish rooms has thatched roofs with canvas walls. From October to March, the waters of the Delta largely subside and vast plains come into view. This is the time when lions, cheetahs and leopards are more in evidence, on day and night drives.

Book to pack: "Henderson the Rain King" by Saul Bellow

Jao Camp		
Okavango Delta		
Botswana		
Tel: + 27 (11) 807 18 00		
Fax: + 27 (11) 807 21 00		
E-mail: enquiry@wilderness.co.za		
Website: www.wilderness-safaris.com		
Booking: www.great-escapes-hotels.com		

DIRECTIONS	Accessible by scheduled flights from Johannesburg to Maun or Kasane, followed by a 30-minute flight from Maun, or a 1.5-hour flight from Kasane and a short drive to the camp
RATES	US$300 to US$900, including all meals, activities, park fees and drinks
ROOMS	8 double room tents, 1 family tent
FOOD	Gourmet cuisine
HISTORY	Built in the Jao Reserve, the second reserve in Botswana not to hunt
X-FACTOR	Water and land combined

Water world...
Nxabega Okavango Safari Camp, Okavango Delta

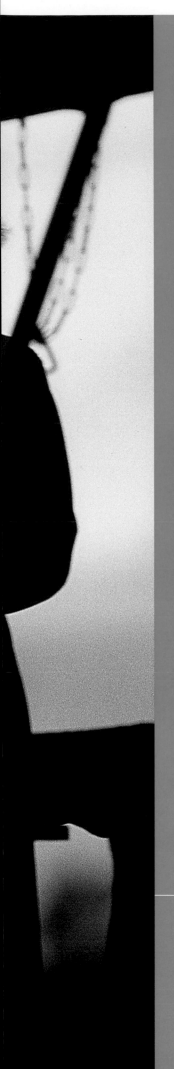

Nxabega Okavango Safari Camp, Okavango Delta

Water World

The money here is named after water, which seems a fitting choice in a country that is mostly dry. Its main unit is the pula, which means rain, and it is split into thebe – rain-drops. It is a gentle prompt that this is a land, and a continent, where water is precious.

Water is not scarce in this part. Botswana is dry, but not here, in the Delta. 'On safari' in this wilderness of clear water and tall grass, at dawn or at dusk, can be a truly buoyant event. A trip in a mokoro, just gliding in slow motion through the maze of channels, is a memory to treasure. Papyrus reeds edge the waterways; silver flashes of fish break the surface; all sorts of creatures move in and across the grass; the air is warm and still. It will come back to mind when you are on a clogged motorway.

In the language of the "river bushmen", Nxabega means "place of the giraffe". The tents are on high legs too, raised wooden platforms.

African ebony and strangler fig trees give shade to the camp; its style is one of subtle class, and from your veranda or the main lodge, the view is spectacular. There are few people here in this landscape, but it is full of wildlife. Birds are everywhere in and on the water in the reeds and the trees on the ground and in the air. This is one of the few places in Africa where you can see the animals from the waterways; and they can see you.

Book to pack: "Rain Fall" by Barry Eisler

Nxabega ("neh-sha-bay-ga") Okavango Safari Camp

Moremi Wildlife Reserve
Okavango Delta
Botswana
Tel: + 267 662 245
Fax: + 267 686 1972
E-mail: webenquiries@ccafrica.com
Website: www.ccafrica.com
Booking: www.great-escapes-hotels.com

DIRECTIONS	Accessible only by scheduled flights from Johannesburg to Maun or Kasane, followed by a 30-minute flight from Maun, or a 1.5-hour flight from Kasane and a short drive to the camp
RATES	US$380 to US$475 per person, including all meals, drinks, scheduled safari activities, and other extras
ROOMS	10 safari tents for up to 18 guests
FOOD	A fusion of local ingredients with African flavours
HISTORY	Opened in April 2000 under Conservation Corporation Africa (CC Africa)
X-FACTOR	The Delta itself, one of the most extraordinary wild places in Botswana

Wasserwelt

Die Bezeichnung für Geld leitet sich hier von der Bezeichnung für Wasser ab. Eine treffende Wortverwandtschaft, wenn man bedenkt, dass dies ein überwiegend trockenes Land ist. Die größere Einheit der hiesigen Währung heißt pula, was Regen bedeutet, und setzt sich aus den so genannten thebe, Regentropfen, zusammen – ein behutsamer Hinweis darauf, dass auf diesem Kontinent Wasser eine Kostbarkeit darstellt. In diesem Teil des Landes herrscht allerdings keine Wasserknappheit. Zwar ist Botswana sehr trocken, jedoch nicht hier im Delta. In der Morgen- oder Abenddämmerung kann man eine schwimmende Safaritour durch diese Wildnis aus klarem Wasser und hohem Gras machen. Eine solche Tour in einer Mokoro, bei der man langsam durch das Labyrinth von Kanälen gleitet, ist ein unvergessliches Erlebnis. Papyrus umsäumt die Wasserstraßen, silbern blitzen die Fische an der Wasseroberfläche, die verschiedensten Tiere bewegen sich im und über dem Gras, die Luft ist warm und ruhig. All diese Eindrücke werden plötzlich zu Ihnen zurückkommen, wenn Sie wieder einmal im Stau auf der Autobahn stehen.

In der Sprache der Flussbuschmänner bedeutet Nxabega »Ort der Giraffe«. Auch die Zelte haben hier lange Beine: Sie stehen auf hölzernen Plattformen. Afrikanisches Ebenholz und Würgefeigen spenden dem Camp, das in einem feinen, klassischen Stil gehalten ist, Schatten. Von der Veranda oder dem Hauptgebäude aus kann man eine spektakuläre Aussicht genießen. In dieser Gegend leben nur wenige Menschen, dafür umso mehr Tiere. Überall sind Vögel, in und auf dem Wasser, im Schilf und in den Bäumen, am Boden und in der Luft. Dieser Ort ist einer der wenigen in Afrika, von dem man die Tiere vom Wasser aus beobachten kann und sie uns.

Buchtipp: »Regenroman« von Karen Duve

Éclat aquatique

L'eau est à l'origine du nom de la monnaie botswanaise, ce qui est tout à fait approprié pour un pays où, dans l'ensemble, le climat est sec. L'unité monétaire de référence du pays est le *pula*, pluie, lui-même divisé en *thebe*, gouttes de pluie. Ceci montre à quel point l'eau est un bien précieux dans le pays et sur le continent. Contrairement à ce qui se passe dans le reste du pays, l'eau ne manque pas dans la région du delta. Partir en safari, à l'aube ou au crépuscule, dans cette vaste étendue sauvage couverte d'eau pure et de hautes herbes peut s'avérer une expérience extrêmement vivifiante. Vous chérirez longtemps le souvenir de votre excursion à bord d'un *mokoro* glissant au ralenti à travers un dédale de canaux : les papyrus bordant les voies navigables, l'éclair argenté des poissons rompant la surface de l'eau, les multiples créatures s'enfonçant dans l'herbe, l'air chaud et calme. Toutes ces images vous reviendront lorsque vous vous retrouverez coincé dans un embouteillage sur l'autoroute. Dans la langue des « bushmen du fleuve », Nxabega signifie « maison de la girafe ». Les tentes du camp sont elles aussi dressées sur de « hautes jambes », ces pilotis qui soutiennent des plates-formes en bois surélevées.

Installé à l'ombre des ébéniers africains et des figuiers des Banyans, le camp est d'une élégance subtile et la vue depuis votre véranda ou le hall principal est spectaculaire. La solitude du lieu n'est troublée que par l'abondance de la faune : les oiseaux sont partout, dans et sur l'eau, au milieu des roseaux et perchés dans les arbres, sur le sol ou dans les airs. Le delta est l'une des rares régions africaines où vous pouvez apercevoir les oiseaux depuis les voies navigables et où eux aussi peuvent vous observer...

Livres à emporter : « La ville du désert et de l'eau » de Jean-François Ménard
« Déluge » de Karen Duve

ANREISE	Nur per Linienflug von Johannesburg nach Maun oder Kasane mit anschließendem 30-minütigen Flug von Maun, oder 1,5-stündigen Flug von Kasane und kurzer Autofahrt zum Camp erreichbar
PREIS	Von 380 US$ bis 475 US$ pro Person, inklusive aller Mahlzeiten, Safari-Unternehmungen und andere Extras
ZIMMER	10 Safarizelte für maximal 18 Gäste
KÜCHE	Verschmelzung einheimischer Zutaten mit einer Auswahl afrikanischer Aromen
GESCHICHTE	Unter der Leitung von CC Africa im April 2000 eröffnet
X-FAKTOR	Das Delta selbst! Es ist einer der außergewöhnlichsten Orte in der Wildnis und mit großer Wahrscheinlichkeit Botswanas wertvollste natürliche Ressource

ACCÈS	Uniquement par vol régulier jusqu'à Maun ou Kasane, puis vol de 30 minutes à partir de Maun ou d'1H30 à partir de Kasane en avionnette et court trajet en voiture
PRIX	380 à 475 $ US par personne. Le prix comprend les repas, les boissons et les activités de safari planifiées
CHAMBRES	10 tentes accueillant 18 personnes maximum
RESTAURATION	Grand choix et possibilité de savourer des plats aux saveurs africaines
HISTOIRE	Ouvert en avril 2000 sous la direction de Conservation Corporation Africa (CC Africa)
LES « PLUS »	Le delta lui-même, l'un des sites les plus extraordinaires du Botswana et l'une de ses ressources naturelles plus précieux encore que les diamants

Where the buffalo roams...
Singita Boulders Lodge, Kruger National Park

Singita Boulders Lodge, Kruger National Park

Where the buffalo roams

In the heart of Africa, the search for prey is as old as time. As the sun starts to set and the heat of the day subsides, lions, leopards, cheetahs, hyenas and jackals begin to hunt. Whatever each of them outruns will be on their menu.

Of course your dinner will be served to you; unlike the animals, you are not required to hunt down your food.

At dusk, your personal game guard will escort you from your suite at the deluxe Boulders Lodge to the open-air boma, for pre-dinner drinks around a blazing fire. Seated here, you can gaze out over the vast plains inside the exclusive wildlife sanctuary of Singita.

For an animal watcher Singita is a dream come true. The park has a wealth of wildlife. The top five on the animal kingdom list, the elephant, lion, leopard, buffalo and rhinoceros are all here. From your private deck at this sumptuous lodge, you can watch hippos feeding nearby and cheetahs racing in the distance, and spot a giraffe moving gracefully past. Whether travelling by day in vehicles, on walking expeditions to get close to the smaller inhabitants of the bush, or on night safaris to view rare nocturnal creatures, there is much to observe.

Book to pack: "Disgrace" by J.M. Coetzee

Singita Boulders Lodge	
Sabi Sand Game Reserve	
Kruger National Park	
Mpumalanga Province	
South Africa	
Tel: + 27 (13) 735 54 56	
Fax: + 27 (13) 735 57 46	
E-mail: reservations@singita.co.za	
Website: www.singita.co.za	
Booking: www.great-escapes-hotels.com	

DIRECTIONS	A 75-minute flight northeast from Johannesburg to Skukuza, approximately 5 hours driving time from Johannesburg to Singita
RATES	From US$673 (from ZAR6,800) inclusive of all meals and drinks
ROOMS	9 double suites
FOOD	Traditional dishes and indigenous African venison specialities
HISTORY	Opened in December 1996
X-FACTOR	Panoramic wildlife views from a luxury vantage point

Im Königreich der Tiere

Das Jagen nach Beute ist im Herzen Afrikas so alt wie die Zeit selbst. Wenn die Sonne allmählich untergeht und die Hitze des Tages abklingt, begeben sich Löwen, Leoparden, Geparden, Hyänen und Schakale auf die Jagd. Was auch immer sie sich erhetzen, steht auf ihrem Speiseplan.

Im Gegensatz zu den Tieren müssen Sie nicht erst selbst auf die Jagd gehen. In der Abenddämmerung geleitet Sie Ihr persönlicher Wildwächter von Ihrer Suite in der luxuriösen Boulders Lodge zu der unter freiem Himmel gelegenen Boma, wo Sie, während Sie an einem lodernden Feuer sitzen, einen Aperitif einnehmen. Von hier kann man seinen Blick schweifen lassen über die weiten Ebenen, die innerhalb des Naturschutzparks von Singita liegen.

Für Tierbeobachter ist Singita ein wahr gewordener Traum. Der Park beheimatet eine Fülle von wild lebenden Tieren. Die fünf wohl imposantesten Mitglieder im Königreich der Tiere, der Elefant, der Löwe, der Leopard, der Büffel und das Nashorn – sie alle leben hier. Von Ihrer privaten Terrasse aus können Sie in dieser feudalen Unterkunft Nilpferde beim Fressen beobachten, Geparden zusehen, die in der Ferne jagen oder eine Giraffe entdecken, die anmutigen Schrittes vorüberzieht.

Ob auf Tagestouren mit dem Auto, bei Wanderexpeditionen, die einen näher an die kleineren Buschbewohner herankommen lassen, oder auf nächtlichen Safaris, bei denen man seltene Nachtwesen erspähen kann – es gibt viel zu beobachten.

Buchtipp: »Schande« von J.M Coetzee

Sur les traces du buffle

En Afrique, la chasse remonte à la nuit des temps.

Au crépuscule, lorsque la chaleur décroît, lions, léopards, guépards, hyènes et chacals commencent à traquer leur proie, et tout ce qui tombe sous leurs griffes figure à leur menu.

Quant à vous, ne vous inquiétez pas. À la différence des animaux, vous n'aurez pas à chasser pour manger à votre faim. Au crépuscule, vous quitterez votre suite du luxueux Boulders Lodge escorté par votre garde-chasse personnel et rejoindrez le boma à l'air libre pour un apéritif autour d'un grand feu. Vous pourrez alors contempler les vastes plaines de l'exceptionnelle réserve d'animaux sauvages de Singita. Avec sa faune abondante, le parc de Singita est un rêve devenu réalité pour les amateurs d'animaux. Les cinq espèces les plus emblématiques du règne animal, à savoir l'éléphant, le lion, le léopard, le buffle et le rhinocéros, sont toutes représentées. Depuis votre terrasse privée, vous verrez les hippopotames se nourrir à proximité, les guépards filer comme le vent dans le lointain et les girafes cheminer gracieusement aux abords de cet hôtel somptueux. Que vous partiez de jour, en voiture ou à pied, à la découverte des autres animaux de la brousse ou que vous observiez des créatures nocturnes rares lors d'un safari de nuit, vous aurez beaucoup à voir.

Livre à emporter : « Disgrâce » de J.M. Coetzee

ANREISE	75-minütiger Flug nordöstlich von Johannesburg nach Szukuza, mit dem Auto etwa 5-stündige Fahrt von Johannesburg nach Singita (500 km)	ACCÉS	75 minutes de vol, direction nord-est, de Johannesburg à Skukuza. En voiture, à environ 5 heures de Johannesburg (500 km)
PREIS	Ab 673 US$ (6.800 ZAR) inklusive aller Mahlzeiten und Getränke	PRIX	À partir de 673 $ US (6.800 R). Le prix comprend les repas et les boissons
ZIMMER	9 Suiten für je zwei Personen	CHAMBRES	9 suites pour deux personnes
KÜCHE	Traditionelle Gerichte und einheimische, afrikanische Wildspezialitäten	RESTAURATION	Plats traditionnels et spécialités indigènes de venaison africaine
GESCHICHTE	Eröffnet im Dezember 1996	HISTOIRE	Ouvert en décembre 1996
X-FAKTOR	Luxuriöser Aussichtspunkt mit Wildpark Panorama	LES « PLUS »	Point de vue luxueux permettant d'admirer le panorama de la faune et de la flore

Safari for the soul...
Garonga Lodge, Limpopo Province

Garonga Lodge, Limpopo Province

Safari for the soul

Everyone needs to take a safari for the soul, some 'time out' to find inspiration and to restore lost vigour.

The tent camp of Garonga, with its billowy ceilings of cream coloured canvas is just the place for such a mission. The floors and walls are sculpted from clay. In this place your senses too can be shaped and soothed. The camp is the perfect place to relax and reflect. To ease your stress, special treatments are at hand in a secluded "sala" in the bush. Taking a long soak in the deep bath that is nestled in the bush is one of the most memorable experiences. Being in the midst of such natural splendor is invigorating in itself. A night spent sleeping in a tree house out in the superb landscape that surrounds the camp is another way to relax. You can even cast off your clothes. To make this easy, a "kikoi" – a style of sarong – is given to each guest. It is suggested that it be worn during one's stay, even to dinner at night.

The camp looks out over a riverbed, one that an elephant herd is drawn to visit. Watching from the terrace or pool, you can be sure that elephants will come out from the bushes and feed just a few metres away from you.

Book to pack: "West with the Night" by Beryl Markham

Garonga Lodge	
P.O. Box 737	
Hoedspruit 1380	
Limpopo Province	
South Africa	
Tel: + 27 (11) 537 46 20	
Fax: + 27 (11) 447 09 93	
E-mail: reservations@garonga.com	
Website: www.garonga.com	
Booking: www.great-escapes-hotels.com	

DIRECTIONS	Daily scheduled flights from Johannesburg to Phalaborwa and Hoedspruit. Transfers are available from airport to the camp
RATES	US$116 (ZAR1,175) to US$602 (ZAR6,100) inclusive of all meals, drinks, game drives and bush walks
ROOMS	6 double rooms, 1 luxury suite
FOOD	To feed the soul
HISTORY	Built in 1997
X-FACTOR	Taking a bush bath under the stars

Seelensafari

Jeder sollte einmal auf Seelensafari gehen, einmal eine
Art Auszeit nehmen, um neue Inspirationen zu erlangen
und verloren gegangene Vitalität wieder aufzufrischen.
Das Zeltcamp von Garonga mit seinen gewölbten Decken
aus crèmefarbenem Segeltuch ist genau das Richtige für
solch ein Vorhaben. Boden und Wände sind aus Lehm
geformt. Hier können auch die Sinne neu geformt und
verwöhnt werden. Das Camp ist der ideale Ort zum
Entspannen und Nachdenken. Wer Stress abbauen möchte,
kann sich spezielle Entspannungsbehandlungen in einer
abgelegenen »Sala« im Busch gönnen. Ein langes erholsa-
mes Bad tief verborgen in der Wildnis ist wohl eine der ein-
prägsamsten Erinnerungen, die Sie mitnehmen werden.
Sich inmitten solcher Naturschönheit zu befinden, ist an
sich schon wohl tuend. Eine Nacht in einem Baumhaus in
dieser fantastischen Landschaft zu verbringen, ist eine
wunderbare Methode, um neue Kräfte zu schöpfen. Selbst
Ihre Kleider können Sie hier abstreifen. Damit dies leichter
fällt, bekommt jeder Gast einen »Kikoi« – eine Art Sarong.
Es ist vorgesehen, dass er während des gesamten Aufent-
haltes, selbst beim Abendessen getragen wird.
Das Camp öffnet sich zu einem Flussbett hin, das von
Elefantenherden aufgesucht wird. Wenn Sie auf der Terrasse
oder am Bassin stehen, können Sie so gut wie sicher sein,
dass Elefanten aus dem Busch kommen und nur einige
Meter von Ihnen entfernt auf Nahrungssuche gehen.

**Buchtipp: »Westwärts mit der Nacht. Mein Leben als Fliegerin
in Afrika« von Beryl Markham**

Un safari de l'âme

Tout le monde a besoin de reprendre des forces, de faire
une pause pour retrouver inspiration, énergie et vitalité.
Pour cela, rien de tel qu'un safari.
Le camp fixe de Garonga, avec ses tentes au plafond en toile
crème se gonflant et ondoyant sous le vent, est l'endroit le
mieux adapté à une telle entreprise. Tout comme les sols et
les murs sculptés dans l'argile, vos sens reprendront forme
et s'apaiseront. Le camp est le lieu idéal pour se détendre
et réfléchir : pour calmer votre stress, des soins spéciaux
vous sont proposés dans un « sala » retiré situé en pleine
brousse. Un long bain dans les vastes bassins à l'air libre est
une expérience inoubliable, et la nature alentour est en elle-
même revigorante. Vous pouvez également vous détendre
en passant une nuit dans une cabane perchée dans un arbre,
au milieu du superbe paysage qui entoure le camp. Vous
pouvez même oublier vos vêtements. En effet, chaque hôte
se voit remettre un « kikoi » (sarong), que nous vous suggé-
rons de porter pendant votre séjour, même au moment du
dîner.
Le camp donne sur le lit d'un fleuve près duquel vous apercevrez peut-être un troupeau d'éléphants. Si vous observez
le paysage depuis la terrasse ou la piscine, vous les verrez
sortir des buissons et se nourrir à seulement quelques
mètres de vous.

**Livre à emporter : « Vers l'ouest avec la nuit » de Beryl
Markham**

ANREISE	Tägliche Linienflüge von Johannesburg nach Phalaborwa und Hoedspruit. Transfer vom Flughafen zum Camp möglich	ACCÈS	Vols quotidiens en partance de Johannesburg jusqu'à Phalaborwa et Hoedspruit. Possibilité de transfert de l'aéroport jusqu'au camp
PREIS	Von 116 US$ (1.175 ZAR) bis 602 US$ (6.100 ZAR) inklusive aller Mahlzeiten, Getränke, Wildbeobachtungsfahrten und Buschwanderungen	PRIX	De 116 $ US (1 175 R) à 602 $ US (6 100 R). Le prix comprend tous les repas, les boissons, les safaris et les promenades en brousse
ZIMMER	6 Doppelzimmer und 1 Luxussuite	CHAMBRES	6 chambres doubles et 1 suite de luxe
KÜCHE	Zum Seele verwöhnen	RESTAURATION	Réconfortante et savoureuse
GESCHICHTE	Im Jahre 1997 erbaut	HISTOIRE	Construit en 1997
X-FAKTOR	Ein Bad im Busch unter Sternenhimmel	LES « PLUS »	Prendre un bain dans la brousse, sous les étoiles

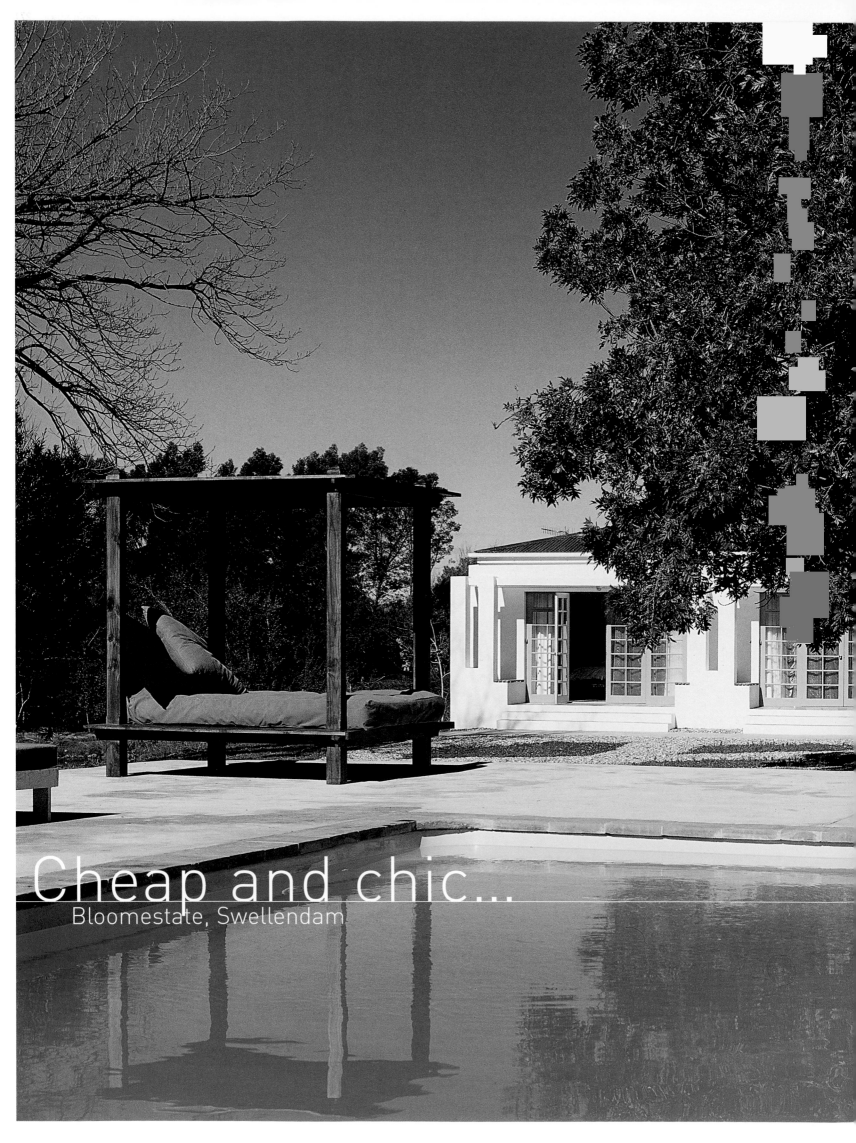

Cheap and chic...
Bloomestate, Swellendam

Bloomestate, Swellendam

Cheap and chic

A place where there are four seasons on one day? No, that is not the climate here; it's simply that each of the four guest suites has a seasonal theme. You could stay for a whole year and experience each one.

Whatever the weather is like where you are now, this chic guesthouse presents you with the opposite of it. You can choose the season inside. Winter is a good deal more appealing here than in most places.

The outside ambience is not as easy to select, but the climate is more often than not mild, whatever the time of year. Bloomestate is on the way to, and from, the Garden Route; a hideaway hotel set in a lush garden of its own. You can unwind here in this calming modern ambience. A spell lounging by the poolside just reading a book could be all you need to do. But if you do want to go out, Bloomestate borders one of the Cape's most attractive old towns. Swellendam is the third-oldest settlement in the country; its Cape Dutch and Victorian style buildings are a sign of its rich history. National parks and wineries are nearby; and this is the home of the graceful blue crane, the country's national bird.

It has been said that in nature, light creates colour, while artists use colour to create light. The landscape of rolling fields and stately mountains changes colour along with the seasons, and each interior here is creatively painted to reflect them.

Book to pack: "Cry, the Beloved Country: A Story of Comfort in Desolation" by Alan Paton

Bloomestate	
276 Voortrekstreet	
P.O. Box 672	
Swellendam 6740	
South Africa	
Tel: + 27 (28) 514 29 84	
Fax: + 27 (28) 514 38 22	
E-mail: info@ bloomestate.com	
Website: www.bloomestate.com	
Booking: www.great-escapes-hotels.com	

DIRECTIONS	200km/124 m from both Cape Town and George, from the N2 highway take the R60, at 4-stop turn right
RATES	From US$95 (ZAR950) per person, including a generous breakfast
ROOMS	4 suites
FOOD	Breakfast only: fresh fruit salad with fruits of the seasons, yoghurt, choice of cereals, freshly baked croissants and whole wheat bread, toast, homemade jams, eggs
HISTORY	First blossomed in 2002
X-FACTOR	Contemporary African chic

Cheap and chic

Wie? Ein Ort, an dem man an einem einzigen Tag vier Jahreszeiten erleben kann? Keine Angst, dies ist keine Beschreibung der klimatischen Bedingungen dieses Landes, sondern der Suiten: Jede von ihnen ist thematisch nach einer bestimmten Jahreszeit gestaltet worden. So können Sie problemlos ein ganzes Jahr hier verbringen und jede von ihnen kennen lernen.

Wie auch immer das Wetter an ihrem Aufenthaltsort, sein mag, diese elegante Pension kann Ihnen das genaue Gegenteil davon bieten. Sie selbst wählen die Jahreszeit aus. Der Winter ist hier übrigens sehr viel angenehmer als in den meisten anderen Ländern.

Das Außenklima lässt sich selbstverständlich nicht ganz so leicht bestimmen, doch unabhängig von der Jahreszeit ist es hier meist sehr mild. Bloomestate liegt an der »Garden Route«, ein kleines verstecktes Hotel inmitten eines sattgrünen Gartens. In diesem ruhigen, modernen Ambiente können Sie sich entspannen, indem Sie beispielsweise ganz einfach ein Weilchen am Pool liegen und in einem Buch schmökern. Ebenso können Sie aber auch etwas unternehmen, denn Bloomestate liegt am Rande einer der ältesten und schönsten Städte des Kaps. Swellendam ist die drittälteste Siedlung des Landes. Dass sie auf eine lange Geschichte zurückblicken kann, lässt sich an den Gebäuden im kapholländischen und viktorianischen Stil ablesen. Ganz in der Nähe befinden sich Nationalparks und Weinberge. Hier lebt auch der Landesvogel Südafrikas, der blaue Kranich.

In der Natur, sagt man, bringt Licht Farbe hervor, wohingegen Künstler Farbe benutzen, um Lichteffekte zu erzeugen. Die hiesige Landschaft mit ihren hügeligen Feldern und eindrucksvollen Bergen ändert mit den Jahreszeiten die Farbe. Die Innengestaltung der Suiten soll dies widerspiegeln.

Buchtipp: »Denn sie sollen getröstet werden« von Alan Paton

Chic et pas cher

Si vous pensez voir ici défiler les quatre saisons en une seule journée, vous vous trompez. En revanche, chacune des quatre suites du Bloomestate a pour thème une saison particulière. Vous pourriez séjourner à l'hôtel toute l'année et changer de chambre et de saison au gré de vos envies. Quel que soit le temps actuellement dans votre lieu de résidence, cette élégante pension de famille vous propose d'en changer. Vous constaterez aussi que l'hiver est ici plus agréable qu'ailleurs.

Impossible par contre de choisir le climat extérieur, ce qui n'est pas vraiment un problème puisque celui-ci est tempéré pendant pratiquement toute l'année. Bloomestate, qui se trouve sur le chemin de la Route des Jardins, est un hôtel retiré installé au cœur d'un jardin luxuriant. Son atmosphère paisible et son cadre moderne invitent à la détente. Un moment à paresser au bord de la piscine, un livre à la main, est peut-être juste ce qu'il vous faut. Mais si vous souhaitez sortir, Bloomestate jouxte l'une des vieilles villes les plus intéressantes du Cap. Troisième ville du pays en termes d'ancienneté, Swellendam présente en effet des bâtiments de style victorien et hollandais qui témoignent de sa riche histoire. Les parcs nationaux et les entreprises vinicoles ne sont qu'à un jet de pierre, et la région abrite l'oiseau national, l'élégante grue de paradis.

On dit que dans la nature, c'est la lumière qui crée la couleur et que les artistes utilisent la couleur pour rendre la lumière. Ici, le paysage formé par les terres aux formes gracieuses et les montagnes majestueuses se teinte de nouvelles nuances au fil des saisons, des nuances que reflètent avec originalité les couleurs utilisées à l'intérieur de chaque suite.

Livre à emporter : « Pleure, ô pays bien-aimé » d'Alan Paton

ANREISE	200 km von Kapstadt und George entfernt. Vom N2 Highway auf die R60, an der vierten Kreuzung rechts abbiegen
PREIS	Ab 95 US$ (950 ZAR) pro Person, inklusive großzügigem Frühstück
ZIMMER	4 Suiten
KÜCHE	Nur Frühstück: frische Obstsalate mit Früchten der Saison, Joghurt, einer Auswahl an Müslis, frisch gebakkenen Croissants und Vollkornweizenbrot, Toast, hausgemachten Marmeladen, Eiern
GESCHICHTE	Erblüht im Jahr 2002
X-FAKTOR	Zeitgemäßer afrikanischer Chic

ACCÈS	À 200 km du Cap et de George. Prendre la N2, puis la R60 et tourner à droite au quatrième stop
PRIX	À partir de 95 $ US (950 R) par personne, copieux petit-déjeuner compris
CHAMBRES	4 suites
RESTAURATION	Petit déjeuner uniquement : salade de fruits frais de la saison, yaourt, choix de céréales, pain complet et croissants tout juste sortis du four, pain grillé, confitures maison, œufs
HISTOIRE	Ouvert en 2002
LES « PLUS »	Style contemporain et chic typiquement africain

Soul searching...
Sossusvlei Wilderness Camp, Namib Naukluft Park

Sossusvlei Wilderness Camp, Namib Naukluft Park

Soul searching

"God created countries with water to enable mankind to live there, and deserts so that they may find their souls." A Namibian proverb.

Namibia has been called "the land that God made in anger." In a country made up of sweltering desert and mountains of sand and rock, man seems out of place. Yet the great sum of sand, the space and the vast silence draws us here.

The Namib Desert is the oldest in the world; at its heart are the Sossusvlei, some of the highest dunes on earth. Rich in contrast of colour and shape, the deep crescents are one of the most stunning sights in Africa. Great waves of them spread out in every direction, as far as the eye can see.

When the sun sets, the massive dunes change from pale apricot to bright orange to deep red. Above, against a clear dark sky, the Milky Way sweeps across in a dazzling light show.

At the entrance to this vast backdrop, is the Sossusvlei Wilderness Camp. Set close to the top of a hill, the little camp merges into the environment, built as it is of rock, timber and thatch. Its bungalows are a cool respite from the heat of the desert. Each has a commanding view out towards the plains and mountains. In the distance are the dunes.

The sheer physical beauty of the desert landscape is the main lure; seeing game much less so. But there are animals to be seen, more often ones that blend into the background, like the cape fox, the aardvark, springbok, and oryx. Eagles fly high above the ostrich – with its head in the sand and out.

Books to pack: "Wind, Sand and Stars" by Antoine de Saint Exupéry

"Desert and Wilderness" by Henryk Sienkiewicz

Sossusvlei Wilderness Camp

Namib Naukluft Park

Namibia

Tel: + 27 (11) 888 40 37

Fax: + 27 (11) 888 10 41

E-mail: enquiries@adventure.co.za

Website: www.africanadrenalin.co.za/ wildernesssafaris/index

Booking: www.great-escapes-hotels.com

DIRECTIONS	20 kms/12.5 miles south-east from Sesriem, and a one-hour flight from Windhoek International Airport
RATES	From US$200, including meals, activities and some drinks
ROOMS	8 double rooms, 1 honeymoon chalet
HISTORY	Opened in 1998
FOOD	Appetising and sand-free fare
X-FACTOR	Taking a balloon ride over the stunning canyon and dunes of this ancient desert

Seelensuche

»Gott hat Länder voll Wasser geschaffen, damit die Menschen dort leben können und Wüsten, damit sie dort ihre Seele erkennen...« Altes namibianisches Sprichwort.

Namibia nennt man »das Land, das Gott im Zorn erschuf«. Menschliches Leben scheint in einem Land, das aus flimmernd heißen Wüsten und Sand- und Felsgebirgen besteht, fehl am Platz zu sein. Dennoch sind es gerade die Massen von Sand, die Weiträumigkeit und die grenzenlose Stille, die uns hierher locken.

Die Namib Wüste ist die älteste der Welt, mitten in ihrem Inneren befinden sich die Sossusvlei, die zu den höchsten Dünen der Erde zählen. Mit ihren Farb- und Formkontrasten gehören diese unergründlichen Halbmonde zu den überwältigendsten Sehenswürdigkeiten Afrikas. So weit das Auge reicht, setzen sie sich wellenartig in alle Himmelsrichtungen fort. Bei Sonnenuntergang werden die gewaltigen Dünen zunächst in ein zartes apricotfarbenes, und kurz darauf in helloranges und schließlich blutrotes Licht getaucht. Und über all dies fegt die Milchstrasse wie eine glitzernde Lichtshow am dunklen, klaren Himmel hinweg.

Am Eingang zu dieser riesigen Kulisse befindet sich das Sossusvlei Wilderness Camp. Da es aus Fels, Holz und Dachstroh gebaut ist, verschmilzt das kleine, nahe dem Gipfel eines Hügels gelegene Lager mit der Umgebung. Seine Bungalows bieten eine kühle Ruhepause von der Hitze der Wüste. Von jedem Bungalow aus bietet sich ein eindrucksvoller Ausblick auf die Ebenen und Berge hinaus, und in der Ferne liegen die Dünen.

Was diesen Ort so verlockend macht, ist vor allem die bloße Schönheit der Wüstenlandschaft und weniger die Möglichkeit, auf Safari zu gehen. Dennoch gibt es durchaus Tiere zu beobachten, meist solche, die sich gegen ihren Hintergrund schwer ausmachen lassen, wie der Kamafuchs, das Erdferkel, der Springbock und die Säbelantilope. Adler fliegen über Strauße hinweg, die den Kopf im Sand stecken haben, oder auch nicht.

Buchtipps: »Wind, Sand und Sterne« von Antoine de Saint Exupéry »Desert and Wilderness« von Henryk Sienkiewicz

Introspection

« Dieu a créé des pays pleins d'eau pour que les hommes puissent y vivre et des déserts pour qu'ils puissent y découvrir leur âme. » Proverbe namibien.

On appelle la Namibie « la terre créée par un Dieu en colère ». Dans ce pays au climat torride fait de déserts et de montagnes de sable et de roche, l'homme ne semble pas à sa place. Pourtant, ce sont précisément les étendues de sable, l'espace et le profond silence qui nous attirent dans cette région.

Au cœur du désert de Namib, le plus ancien de la planète, se trouvent les dunes de Sossusvlei, qui sont parmi les plus hautes du monde. Ces grands croissants, qui se caractérisent par la richesse du contraste des couleurs et des formes, sont l'un des spectacles les plus impressionnants d'Afrique. Les énormes vagues de sable s'étendent dans toutes les directions, à perte de vue.

Au coucher du soleil, ces dunes immenses passent de l'abricot pâle à l'orange vif, puis au rouge profond. Par nuit claire, la Voie lactée balaie le ciel en un jeu de lumières éblouissant. Sossusvlei Wilderness Camp s'élève là où commence ce vaste désert. Installé à proximité du sommet d'une colline, ce camp de taille réduite, fait de roche, de bois et de chaume, se fond dans le paysage. Après la chaleur du désert, la fraîcheur des bungalows constitue un répit bienvenu. Chacun d'eux offre une vue panoramique sur les plaines et les montagnes, et sur les dunes au loin.

Le principal attrait du site est l'extraordinaire beauté du désert. En revanche, la faune y est rare. Il est toutefois possible d'apercevoir quelques animaux, surtout des espèces qui se confondent avec leur environnement, telles que le renard du Cap, l'oryctérope, le springbok ou l'oryx. Les aigles survolent les autruches, que vous verrez en mouvement ou immobiles, la tête enfouie dans le sable.

Livres à emporter : « Terre des Hommes » d'Antoine de Saint Exupéry « Le désert et la gloire » de Fathallah Sâyigh

ANREISE	20 km südöstlich von Sesriem, und einstündiger Flug von Windhuk International Airport
PREIS	Ab 200 US$ inklusive Mahlzeiten, Aktivitäten und teilweise Getränke
ZIMMER	8 Doppelzimmer, 1 Hochzeitszimmer
GESCHICHTE	Eröffnet im Jahr 1998
KÜCHE	Appetitliche und sandlose Speisen
X-FAKTOR	Eine Ballonfahrt über den beeindruckenden Canyon und die Dünen dieser alten Wüste

ACCÈS	À 20 Km au sud-est de Sesriem et à une heure en avion de Windhoek International Airport
PRIX	À partir de 200 $ US. Le prix comprend les repas, les activités et certaines boissons
CHAMBRES	8 chambres doubles et un chalet lune de miel
RESTAURATION	Appétissante et garantie sans sable !
HISTOIRE	Ouvert en 1998
LES « PLUS »	Excursion en ballon au-dessus du superbe canyon et des magnifiques dunes de ce désert ancestral

A dome of one's own...
Hotel Le Kambary, Bandiagara

Hotel Le Kambary, Bandiagara

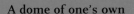

A dome of one's own

These white domes pop up in the desert like huge beehives. At first sight, they might look quite familiar. They will remind science fiction fans of a "Star Wars" space colony. But in fact it is a creative hotel on this planet, in the heart of one of Africa's largest but least known countries, Mali. Five hundred years ago one of the world's wealthiest nations, now it is among the poorest. Yet it is still rich in history and culture. In the 14th century, the Malian empire was one of the greatest on earth, endowed with two sources of great wealth – salt and gold. Both were equally valued, ounce for ounce. This is the homeland of Timbuktu, a legendary city once called 'the most distant place on earth'. It was the intellectual centre of the Arab world, and a thriving commercial city. Then it was the 'most glorious city' in medieval Africa. Little remains of its past glory now.

Mali is famous too for its mud architecture, from great temples to whole villages, and an intriguing people, the Dogon. Hotel Le Kambary is close to Dogon country. Aeons ago, to ward off conversion to Islam, they fled to the cliffs of Bandiagara, now dotted with ancient cliff dwellings and burial sites. The worship of their ancestors, as well as their architecture, farming ability and knowledge of the stars have long made them a magnet for visitors.

Books to pack: "The Fortunes of Wangrin" by Amadou Hampate Ba
"God's Bits of Wood" by Ousmane Sembene

Hotel Le Kambary
Bandiagara
Province de Mopti
Mali
Tel: + 223 420 388
Fax: + 223 420 388
Website: www.kambary.com
Booking: www.great-escapes-hotels.com

DIRECTIONS	A few minutes from Bandiagara, and aprox. 70 km/43 m from Mopti, Mali's Venice
RATES	From US$23 to US$33
ROOMS	14 rooms, 1 apartment
FOOD	The hotel restaurant Cheval-Blanc has African and European dishes on the menu
HISTORY	Designed by Italian architect Fabrizio Carola and opened in 1997. The architect's aim was to build without using wood, a scarce and expensive resource. Stone domes and arches are therefore among the main construction components
X-FACTOR	The hotel dining pods, the World Heritage site of the Dogon and the nearby Center for Traditional Medicine

Jedem seine Kuppel

Wie riesenhafte Bienenstöcke ragen diese weißen Kuppeln aus dem Wüstenboden. Auf den ersten Blick mögen sie ziemlich vertraut aussehen, zumindest für Science Fiction Fans, die sich unmittelbar an eine »Star Wars Weltraumsiedlung« erinnert fühlen.

In Wirklichkeit handelt es sich dabei um ein künstlerisches Hotel auf diesem unserem Planeten, im Herzen eines der größten und gleichzeitig unbekanntesten Länder Afrikas, Mali. War dieses Land vor rund fünfhundert Jahren eine der wohlhabendsten Nationen der Welt, so gehört es heute zu den ärmsten. Dennoch ist es immer noch reich an Geschichte und Kultur. Im 14. Jahrhundert war Mali eines der größten Imperien der Erde, gesegnet mit zwei Quellen großen Reichtums: Salz und Gold. Beides war von gleich hohem Wert, Unze für Unze. Auch liegt hier Timbuktu, die legendäre Stadt, die einst als der »abgelegenste Ort der Welt« bezeichnet wurde. Es war das intellektuelle Zentrum der arabischen Welt und eine blühende Handelsstadt. Dann wurde es bekannt, als die »prächtigste Stadt« im mittelalterlichen Afrika. Mag dieser Ruhm auch vergangen sein, so ist Mali heute noch berühmt für seine Schlammbauarchitektur, von großartigen Tempeln bis hin zu ganzen Dörfern, sowie für ein faszinierendes Volk, die Dogon. Das Hotel Le Kambary liegt nahe bei der Dogon-Region. Um einer Zwangsbekehrung zum Islam zu entgehen, flohen die Dogon vor langer Zeit in die Klippen von Bandiagara, welche nun mit uralten Klippensiedlungen und Grabstätten übersät sind. Ihre Ahnenverehrung, aber auch die für die Dogon typische Bauweise, ihr Talent beim Ackerbau und ihr Wissen über die Sterne haben die Besucher von jeher magisch angezogen.

Buchtipp: »Gottes Holzstücke« von Ousmane Sembene

Un dôme pour soi

Des dômes blancs qui émergent du désert telles des ruches géantes. Ce spectacle, qui vous sera peut-être familier, rappellera en tout cas aux fans de science-fiction une colonie spatiale de « La Guerre des Étoiles ».

Il s'agit en fait d'un hôtel original situé au cœur de l'un des pays les plus grands mais également les moins connus d'Afrique, le Mali, une nation parmi les plus riches du monde il y a cinq cent ans, et à l'heure actuelle l'une des plus pauvres. Le Mali conserve toutefois certaines richesses en matière d'histoire et de culture. Au XIVe siècle, l'empire malien était l'un des plus puissants du monde grâce à d'immenses revenus provenant du sel et de l'or, deux ressources alors considérées de valeur égale. Le Mali est aussi la patrie de Tombouctou, ville légendaire jadis qualifiée de « lieu le plus retiré du monde ». Centre intellectuel du monde arabe et cité commerciale florissante, elle était alors la « ville la plus merveilleuse » de l'Afrique médiévale. Aujourd'hui, ce glorieux passé n'est plus qu'un lointain souvenir.

Le Mali est également célèbre pour ses constructions en boue, qu'il s'agisse de grands temples ou de villages entiers, et en raison d'un peuple fascinant, les Dogons. L'hôtel Le Kambary est d'ailleurs proche du pays dogon. Il y a de cela bien des siècles, pour éviter d'être convertis à l'Islam, les Dogons s'enfuirent vers les falaises de Bandiagara où seules subsistent des habitations troglodytiques et des sépultures. Le culte des ancêtres, l'architecture ainsi que la science de l'agriculture et la connaissance des astres font de ce peuple un véritable pôle d'attraction, et ce depuis toujours.

Livre à emporter : « Les bouts de bois de Dieu » de Ousmane Sembene

ANREISE	Wenige Minuten von Bandiagara und 70 km von Mopti – dem Venedig von Mali – entfernt	ACCÈS	À quelques minutes de Bandiagara et à 70 km de Mopti, la Venise du Mali
PREIS	Von 23 US$ bis 33 US$	PRIX	De 23 à 33 $ US
ZIMMER	14 Zimmer, 1 Apartment	CHAMBRES	14 chambres, 1 appartement
KÜCHE	Die Karte des Hotel Restaurants Cheval-Blanc enthält sowohl afrikanische, als auch europäische Gerichte	RESTAURATION	La carte de l'hôtel restaurant Cheval-Blanc propose des mets africains et européens
GESCHICHTE	Entworfen von dem italienischen Architekten Fabrizio Carola; eröffnet im Jahr 1997. Ziel des Architekten war es, beim Bau auf Holz zu verzichten, da dies hier einen besonders seltenen und wertvollen Rohstoff darstellt	HISTOIRE	Hôtel ouvert en 1997 et conçu par l'architecte italien Fabrizio Carola. Son objectif était de ne pas utiliser le bois
X-FAKTOR	Das Weltkulturerbe der Dogon und das nahegelegene Zentrum für traditionelle Medizin	LES « PLUS »	Les « compartiments » du restaurant de l'hôtel, le site Dogon classé patrimoine de l'humanité et le Centre de médecine traditionnelle voisin

Asia

India • Sri Lanka • Myanmar • Thailand
Cambodia • Malaysia • Indonesia
The Philippines • Vietnam • China • Japan

Text by Christiane Reiter   *Edited by* Angelika Taschen

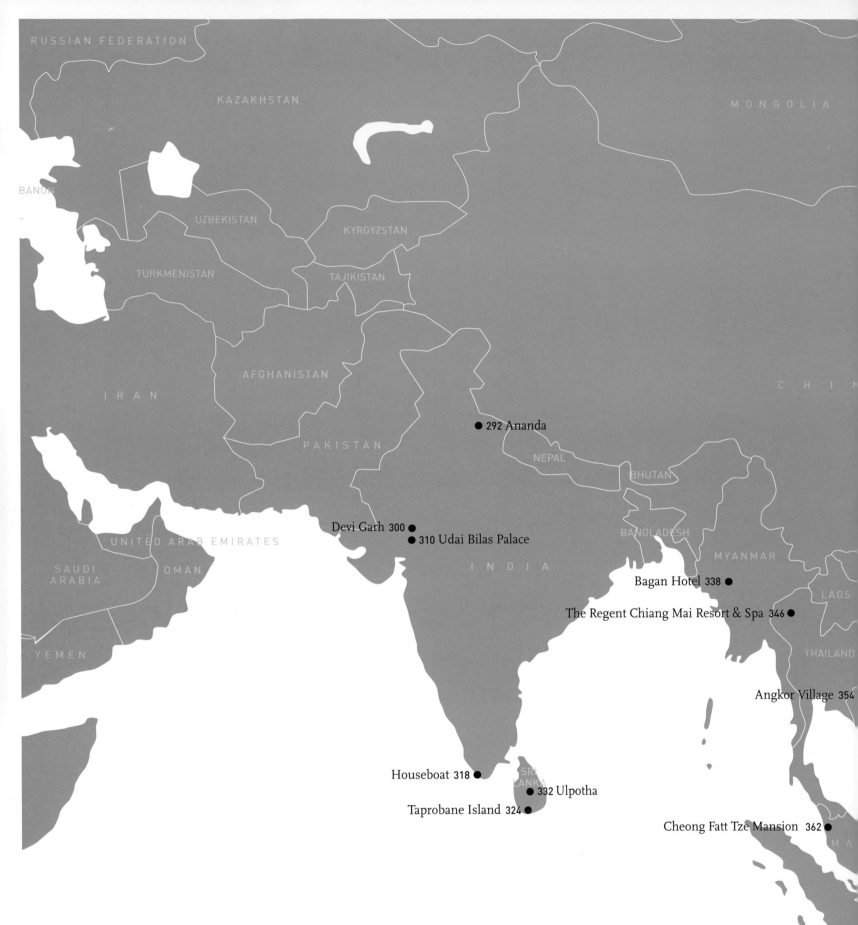

292 Ananda

Devi Garh 300
310 Udai Bilas Palace

Bagan Hotel 338

The Regent Chiang Mai Resort & Spa 346

Angkor Village 354

Houseboat 318

332 Ulpotha

Taprobane Island 324

Cheong Fatt Tze Mansion 362

"A journey of a 1,000 miles begins with the first step."
Chinese proverb

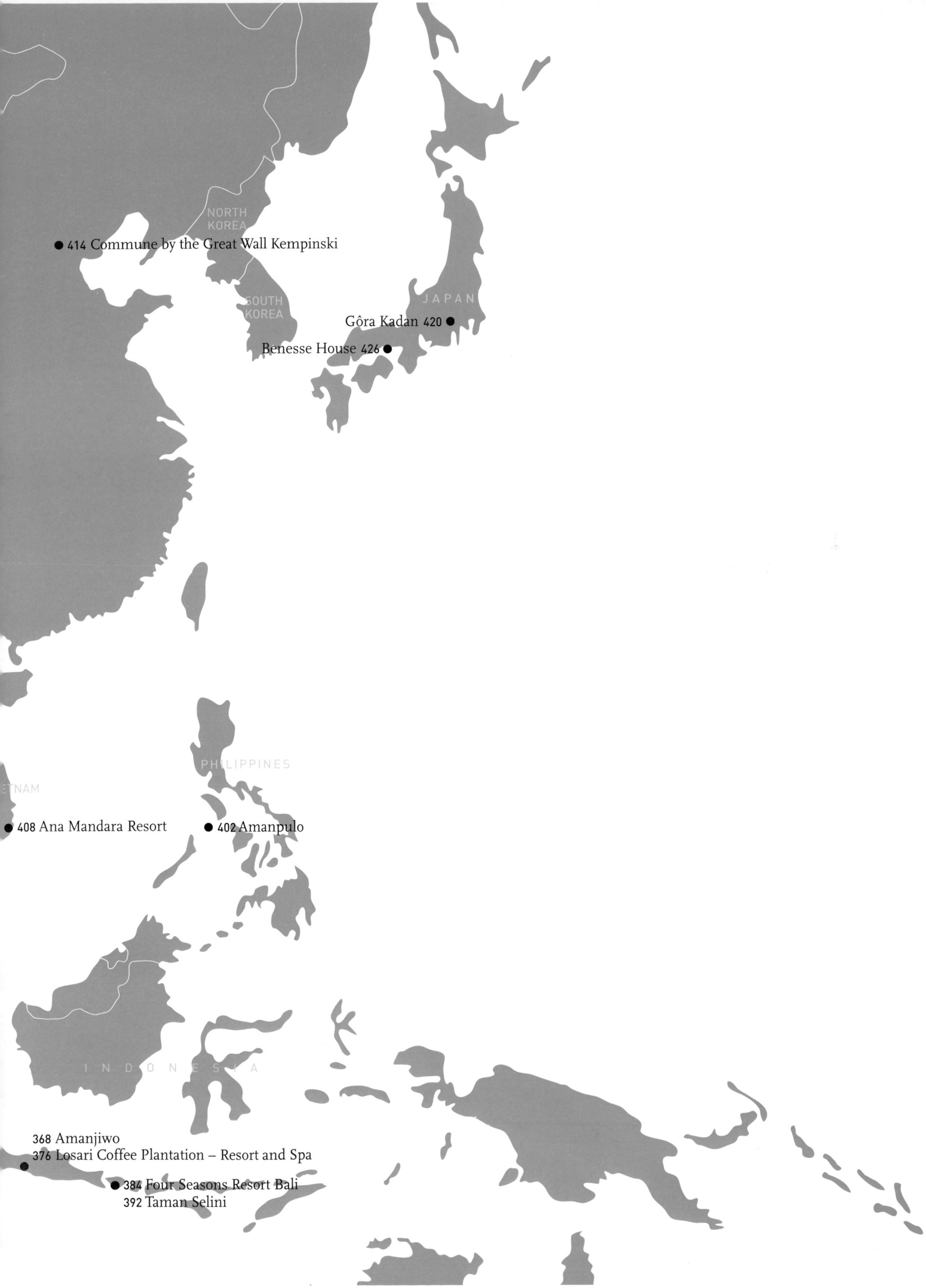
NORTH KOREA
414 Commune by the Great Wall Kempinski
SOUTH KOREA
JAPAN
Gôra Kadan 420
Benesse House 426
PHILIPPINES
TNAM
408 Ana Mandara Resort
402 Amanpulo
INDONESIA
368 Amanjiwo
376 Losari Coffee Plantation – Resort and Spa
384 Four Seasons Resort Bali
392 Taman Selini

Everything Flows...
Ananda – In the Himalayas, Uttaranchal

Ananda – Uttaranchal, In the Himalayas

Everything Flows

Vata, Pitta and Kapha can easily come out of balance in the stress of everyday life. What could make you happier than putting these physical energies back into balance with the help of Ayurveda therapy in one of India's most beautiful hotels? The Ananda, in the Himalayas, truly deserves the term "health temple" like no other. Situated against the cinematic backdrop of the Himalayas with a view across the valley of the Ganges, this white former maharaja's palace has a spa dedicated to Ayurveda for its guests. Okay, so the hard work of detoxification and purification is not always pleasurable, but afterwards one feels like one is wearing an eternal smile on one's face. One walks, as if on cotton wool, through the enchanting pavilions, the great ballroom or the winter garden and enjoys the peace in the rooms and suites. The Ananda Suite, for example, includes a private paradise garden, and the Vice-Regal Suite features a polished wooden floor, English antiques and a telescope to view the sparkling firmament over India. If, after days of meditation, you feel the need for an adrenalin kick then take a day trip on an elephant safari or a rafting tour of the Ganges.

Book to pack: "The Heart of God" by Rabindranath Tagore

Ananda – In the Himalayas

The Palace Estate

Narendra Nagar, District Tehri Garhwal

Uttaranchal – 249175, India

Tel. +91 (1378) 22 75 00

Fax +91 (1378) 22 75 50

Email: sales@anandaspa.com

Website: www.anandaspa.com

Booking: www.great-escapes-hotels.com

DIRECTIONS	Situated 260 km/161 miles north of Delhi (transfer from Delhi via aircraft in 40 min. or by train & car in 5 hr.).
RATES	Double rooms from US$300 per night, suites from US$550 per night (incl. breakfast and wellness offers).
ROOMS	70 luxury rooms, 3 Deluxe Suites, 1 Ananda Suite, 1 Vice-Regal Suite.
FOOD	5 restaurants with light "Ananda Spa Cuisine" and with fantastic views.
HISTORY	A former palace of the maharaja of Tehri Garhwal.
X-FACTOR	Everything is Ayurveda in one of the most beautiful spas in the world.

Alles im Fluss

Dass Vata, Pitta und Kapha aus dem Gleichgewicht geraten, kommt im Alltagsstress schnell einmal vor. Glücklich ist dann, wer diese Körperenergien mit Hilfe der Ayurvedatherapie und in einem der schönsten Hotels Indiens wieder ausbalancieren kann. Das Ananda – In the Himalayas verdient den Begriff »Wellness-Tempel« wie kaum ein anderes Haus. Vor der kinotauglichen Kulisse des Himalaja und mit Blick über das Tal des Ganges gelegen, lässt der weiße Palast die Zeiten der Maharadschas wieder aufleben und bittet seine Gäste in ein Spa, das sich dem Ayurveda verschrieben hat. Zugegeben: Entgiftung und Entschlackung sind nicht immer ganz angenehm – doch danach fühlt man sich, als trüge man auf ewig ein Lächeln im Gesicht. Wie auf Watte wandelt man durch die zauberhaften Pavillons, den großen Ballsaal oder den Wintergarten und genießt die Ruhe in den Zimmern und Suiten – zur Ananda Suite gehört beispielsweise ein eigener Paradiesgarten, und die Viceregal Suite bietet polierte Holzfußböden, britisch angehauchte Antiquitäten und ein Teleskop für den Blick in den glitzernden Sternenhimmel über Indien. Wer nach Tagen der Meditation wieder den Adrenalinkick sucht, plant einen Tagesausflug – eine Elefantensafari oder eine Raftingtour auf dem Ganges.

Buchtipp: »Das Herz Gottes« von Rabindranath Tagore

Le corps et l'âme en harmonie

Notre vie est un stress permanent, et que nous soyons de type vâta, pitta ou kapha, nous devons nous ressourcer. Heureux celui qui peut retrouver sa vitalité à l'aide de la médecine ayurvédique dans l'un des plus beaux hôtels de l'Inde.

Si l'un d'eux mérite la palme du bien-être, c'est bien l'Ananda Himalaya. Sur le décor grandiose des montagnes et avec vue sur la vallée du Gange, le palais blanc fait revivre l'époque des maharadjahs et offre à ses hôtes un centre de remise en forme voué à l'Ayurvéda.

Il faut bien sûr en passer par la désintoxication et la purification de l'organisme, ce qui n'a rien d'agréable, mais on se sent ensuite au septième ciel. Comme sur un nuage, on traverse les pavillons ravissants, la grande salle de bal ou le jardin d'hiver et on jouit du calme dans les chambres et les suites – la suite Ananda comprend par exemple un jardin particulier idyllique et la suite Viceregal offre des parquets polis, des antiquités « old England » et un télescope pour observer les étoiles au-dessus de l'Inde.

Si, après des jours passés à méditer, une envie d'action se fait sentir, il est possible de partir en excursion – en safari à dos d'éléphant ou en radeau sur le Gange.

Livre à emporter : « La demeure de la paix »
de Rabindranath Tagore

ANREISE	260 km nördlich von Delhi (Transfer von Delhi per Flugzeug in 40 min. oder per Zug & Auto in 5 h).
PREIS	Doppelzimmer ab 300 $ pro Nacht, Suite ab 550 $ pro Nacht (inklusive Frühstück und Wellnessangeboten).
ZIMMER	70 Luxuszimmer, 3 Deluxe-Suiten, 1 Ananda-Suite, 1 Viceregal-Suite.
KÜCHE	5 Restaurants, darunter »The Restaurant« mit leichter »Ananda Spa Cuisine« und »The Tree Top Deck« mit traumhaftem Blick.
GESCHICHTE	Ein ehemaliger Palast auf dem Gelände des Maharadscha von Tehri Garhwal.
X-FAKTOR	Alles Ayurveda – in einem der schönsten Spas der Welt.

ACCÈS	Situé à 260 km au nord de Delhi (de Delhi par avion en 40 min ou par train et voiture en 5 h).
PRIX	Chambre double à partir de 300 $, suite à partir de 550 $ (petit-déjeuner et accès au centre de remise en forme inclus. Prix de la suite transfert compris).
CHAMBRES	70 chambres, 3 suites, 1 suite Ananda, 1 suite Viceregal.
RESTAURATION	5 restaurants offrant une « Ananda Spa Cuisine » légère et un panorama sublime.
HISTOIRE	Situé dans l'enceinte du palais du maharadjah de Tehri Garhwal.
LE « PETIT PLUS »	Tout Ayurvéda – dans l'un des meilleurs centres de remise en forme du monde.

On Her Majesty's Secret Se

Devi Garh, Udaipur, Rajasthan

ice...

Devi Garh, Udaipur, Rajasthan

On Her Majesty's Secret Service

If a James Bond film director ever needed another setting in India – one where, on behalf of her majesty, 007 could hurl black-clad figures over walls and be seduced by long-legged women – then there would be no better place than Devi Garh. Both fascinating and awe-inspiring, the fort lords over the Aravalli Range near Udaipur; surrounded by mountains on three sides and a blue-grey velvet sky above. Its history really is something for the movies: Sajja Singh was given the building as thanks for his services and loyalty in the Battle of Haldighati (1576) when Maharana Pratap fought against the Mogul emperor Akbar. The palace presides over one of the three entrances to the valley of Udaipur and since being transformed into a luxury hotel is one of Rajasthan's most attractive addresses. Here, what you find beneath splendid archways and in the high halls, is more what you would expect of a loft residence in a big city: clear forms and colours, minimalist and functional design, marble and metal. Devi Garh reflects Asia's puristic side – which brings so much in terms of aesthetics and atmosphere, so much splendour and glamour, that it almost seems too beautiful to be real. A genuinely cinematic setting.

Book to pack: "The Sleeping Tiger" by Shashi Deshpande

Devi Garh
P. O. Box No. 144,
Udaipur – 313001
Rajasthan, India
Tel. +91 (2953) 28 92 11
Fax +91 (2953) 28 93 57
Email: devigarh@deviresorts.com and
reservations@deviresorts.com
Website: www.deviresorts.com
Booking: www.great-escapes-hotels.com

DIRECTIONS	Situated 26 km / 16 miles northeast of Udaipur (domestic flights from Delhi or Mumbai).
RATES	Tents starting at US$ 150 per night, suites starting at US$ 325 per night.
ROOMS	23 individually furnished suites. From October to March, 6 tents are also available.
FOOD	Innovative Asian cuisine based on the elaboration of traditional recipes. In addition, continental menus.
HISTORY	Built at the end of the sixteenth century. Following a 10-year period of renovation, it has been a luxury hotel since 2000.
X-FACTOR	One of the most beautiful Design Hotels in Asia.

Im Auftrag Ihrer Majestät

Sollte ein Regisseur von James Bond jemals wieder eine Kulisse in Indien suchen, vor der 007 im Auftrag Ihrer Majestät schwarz vermummte Gestalten über Mauern werfen und langbeinigen Frauen zum Opfer fallen kann – es gäbe keinen besseren Platz als Devi Garh. Faszinierend und Furcht einflößend zugleich thront das Fort in der Aravalli Range bei Udaipur; an drei Seiten von Bergen umgeben und über sich einen Himmel wie aus blaugrauem Samt. Seine Geschichte ist durchaus kinotauglich: Sajja Singh erhielt die Trutzburg als Dank für seine Verdienste und Loyalität in der Schlacht von Haldighati (1576), als Maharana Pratap gegen den Mogulkaiser Akbar kämpfte. Seitdem beherrscht der Palast einen der drei Eingänge ins Tal von Udaipur und gehört nach seiner Verwandlung in ein Luxushotel zu den attraktivsten Adressen Rajasthans. Was hier unter prachtvollen Torbögen und in hohen Hallen zu sehen ist, würde man sonst eher in einem Großstadtloft erwarten: klare Formen und Farben, minimalistisches und funktionales Design, Marmor und Metall. Devi Garh zeigt Asiens puristische Seite – und gewinnt genau dadurch so viel Ästhetik und Atmosphäre, so viel Glanz und Glamour, dass es beinahe unwirklich schön wirkt. Eine echte Kinokulisse eben.

Buchtipp: »Der schlafende Tiger« von Shashi Deshpande

Entre tradition et modernité

Si jamais un réalisateur voulait tourner un nouveau James Bond en Inde et cherchait un endroit où l'agent secret pourrait jeter des hommes emmitouflés de voiles noirs en bas des murailles et se laisser séduire par de ravissantes créatures – Devi Garh serait le cadre idéal.

A la fois fascinant et inquiétant, le fort trône au milieu des collines d'Aravali près d'Udaipur. Les montagnes l'enserrent sur trois côtés, un ciel de velours bleu gris le surplombe. Son histoire est de l'étoffe dont on fait les films à succès : Sajja Singh reçut la forteresse en récompense de ses bons et loyaux services à la bataille de Haldighati (1576), quand Maharana Pratap affrontait l'empereur mogol Akbar.

Depuis cette époque, le palais domine l'un des trois accès à la vallée d'Udaipur et, depuis sa transformation en hôtel de luxe, il est l'une des adresses les plus fameuses du Rajasthan – et des plus surprenantes : les formes et les couleurs nettes et claires, le design minimaliste et fonctionnel, le marbre et le métal que l'on peut voir ici sous les superbes arcades et dans les hautes salles, semblent échappés d'un loft de la métropole.

Devi Garh nous présente le côté puriste de l'Asie et acquiert ainsi tant de grâce harmonieuse et d'atmosphère, tant d'éclat et de glamour, qu'il semble d'une beauté quasi irréelle – un vrai décor de cinéma.

Livre à emporter : « La nuit retient ses fantômes » de Shashi Deshpande

ANREISE	26 km nordöstlich von Udaipur gelegen (Inlandsflüge ab Delhi oder Mumbai).	ACCÈS	Situé à 26 km au nord-est d'Udaipur (vols intérieurs à partir de Delhi ou Mumbai).
PREIS	Zelt ab 150 $ pro Nacht (zwei Personen), Suite ab 325 $ pro Nacht.	PRIX	Tente à partir de 150 $ la nuit (deux personnes), suite à partir de 325 $ la nuit.
ZIMMER	23 individuell ausgestattete Suiten. Von Oktober bis März stehen auch 6 Zelte zur Verfügung.	CHAMBRES	23 suites décorées de manière individuelle. 6 tentes disponibles d'octobre à mars.
KÜCHE	Innovative asiatische Küche, für die traditionelle Rezepte verfeinert wurden. Außerdem kontinentale Menüs.	RESTAURATION	Cuisine asiatique innovante avec plats traditionnels revisités. Menus continentaux.
GESCHICHTE	Ende des 16. Jahrhunderts erbaut, nach zehnjähriger Renovierung seit 2000 ein Luxushotel.	HISTOIRE	Construit à la fin du 16e siècle. Ouvert en 2000 après dix ans de restauration.
X-FAKTOR	Prachtvoller Palast und eines der schönsten Designhotels Asiens.	LE « PETIT PLUS »	A la fois palais sublime et l'un des plus beaux hôtels design d'Asie.

The Maharaja's Jewel...
Udai Bilas Palace, Dungarpur, Rajasthan

Udai Bilas Palace, Dungarpur, Rajasthan

The Maharaja's Jewel

Dungarpur has long been known as the "city of the hills" – but Udai Singhji never really acquired a taste for the rocky landscape when he wanted to build a new palace in the mid-nineteenth century. Nevertheless, he was fascinated by Lake Gaibsagar and so he decided to build his own island with the region's pale pareva stones. The palace's first residential wing turned out to be relatively modest; then Udai Singhji put his whole love for architectural details into the "single-column palace", Ek Thambia Mahal, which overflows with turrets, arches, balustrades and marble inlay work and to-day still forms the heart of the complex. Later, the original owner's descendants clearly wanted to do something which would contrast the concise traditional design: They furnished the rooms added in 1940 entirely in the Art Deco style and decorated the awe-inspiring banquet hall with hunting trophies from the nearby forest. Since 2001 the hotel has also had a pool where the raised trunks of two white marble elephants spurt fountains of water. The tracks of real animals can be followed on the banks of the lake and in the nature reserve, since Dungarpur is considered an El Dorado for ornithologists and safari fans: leopards, antelopes and even flying squirrels can be seen here. And for any of you who do not feel that the plain offers enough attractions: Dungarpur's Juna Mahal, for instance, is one of the most splendid and oldest palaces of the region – it dates back to the thirteenth century.

Book to pack: "Ten Princes or the Dasha-kumara-charita" by Grazia Dandin

Udai Bilas Palace Dungarpur – 314001 Rajasthan, India Tel. +91 (2964) 23 08 08 Fax +91 (2964) 23 10 08 Email: contact@udaibilaspalace.com Website: www.udaibilaspalace.com Booking: www.great-escapes-hotels.com	**DIRECTIONS** Situated at Lake Gaibsagar and at the edge of the nature reserve, 120 km/75 miles south of the airport at Udaipur. **RATES** Rooms starting at US$43, suites starting at US$71. **ROOMS** 10 rooms and 10 suites, all individually furnished in Art Deco style. **FOOD** Indian specialities; spiced more mildly than usual in consideration of western palates. **HISTORY** Built as a palace in the nineteenth century and extended in 1940. **X-FACTOR** A royal vacation just like on a private island.

Das Schmuckstück des Maharadschas

Seit jeher ist Dungarpur auch als »Stadt der Hügel« bekannt – doch mit dem felsigen Land konnte sich Udai Singhji nicht recht anfreunden, als er Mitte des 19. Jahrhunderts einen neuen Palast bauen wollte. Ihn faszinierte der Gaibsagar-See und hier schuf er aus dem hellen Pareva-Stein der Region seine eigene Insel. Der erste Wohnflügel fiel vergleichsweise bescheiden aus; Udai Singhji steckte seine ganze Liebe zu architektonischen Details in den »einsäuligen Palast« Ek Thambia Mahal, der von Türmchen, Bögen, Balustraden und Marmorintarsien nur so überquillt und noch heute das Herzstück des Komplexes ist. Dem geballten traditionellen Design wollten die Erben des einstigen Hausherrn offensichtlich einiges entgegensetzen: Sie richteten die 1940 angebauten Zimmer ganz im Art-déco-Stil ein und schmückten den Respekt einflößenden Bankettsaal mit Jagdtrophäen aus dem nahen Wald. Seit 2001 besitzt das Hotel auch einen Pool, in den zwei weiße Marmorelefanten aus erhobenen Rüsseln Wasserfontänen spritzen. Den Spuren echter Tiere kann man am Ufer des Sees und im Naturschutzgebiet folgen, denn Dungarpur gilt als Dorado für Ornithologen und Safarifans – hier werden regelmäßig Leoparden, Antilopen und sogar fliegende Eichhörnchen gesichtet. Und für alle, denen die Ebene noch nicht genug Attraktionen bietet, ist ebenfalls gesorgt: Mit dem Juna Mahal besitzt Dungarpur zum Beispiel einen der prachtvollsten und ältesten Paläste der Region – er stammt aus dem 13. Jahrhundert.

Buchtipp: »Krishnas Schatten« von Kiran Nagarkar

Le joyau du maharadjah

Depuis toujours Dungarpur est « la cité des collines », mais le maharawal Udai Singhji II ne la trouva pas à son goût quand il voulut construire un nouveau palais au milieu du 19e siècle. En revanche, il était fasciné par le lac Gaibsagar et fit d'abord élever juste au bord de celui-ci, en pierre bleu gris de Pareva locale, un pavillon modeste comparé à son autre palais : c'est que Udai Singhji II, grand amoureux de l'art et de l'architecture, consacra son énergie au « palais à une colonne » Ek Thambia Mahal qui offre une foule de tourelles, d'arcades, de balustrades et des frises en marbre sculpté, une merveille de l'architecture rajpoute, qui est resté le cœur du complexe.

Ses descendants ne partageaient manifestement pas sa prédilection pour le style traditionnel. Ils aménagèrent les chambres annexées en 1940 dans le plus pur style Art déco et décorèrent l'imposante salle de banquet avec des trophées de chasse – la jungle est toute proche. Depuis 2002, l'hôtel abrite aussi une piscine dans laquelle deux éléphants blancs en marbre font jaillir de l'eau de leur trompe fièrement dressée. On peut suivre les traces d'animaux sauvages sur les rives du lac et dans la réserve naturelle car Dungarpur est un véritable paradis pour les ornithologues et les amateurs de safaris. On y voit régulièrement des léopards, des antilopes et même des écureuils volants.

Et pour ceux à qui la plaine n'offre pas assez d'agréments – Dungarpur possède aussi le Juna Mahal, un des palais les plus splendides et les plus anciens de la région puisqu'il date du 13e siècle.

Livre à emporter : « Histoire des dix princes » de Grazia Dandin

ANREISE	Im Gaibsagar-See und am Rand eines Naturschutzgebietes gelegen, 120 km südlich des Flughafens von Udaipur.
PREIS	Zimmer ab 43 $, Suite ab 71 $.
ZIMMER	10 Zimmer und 10 Suiten, alle individuell im Art-déco-Stil eingerichtet.
KÜCHE	Indische Spezialitäten – mit Rücksicht auf westliche Gaumen sanfter gewürzt als üblich.
GESCHICHTE	Mitte des 19. Jahrhunderts als Palast errichtet und 1940 ausgebaut.
X-FAKTOR	Königlicher Urlaub wie auf einer privaten Insel.

ACCÈS	Situé sur les rives du lac Gaibsagar et au bord d'une réserve naturelle. A 120 km au sud de l'aéroport d'Udaipur.
PRIX	Chambre à partir de 43 $ la nuit, suite à partir de 71 $ la nuit.
CHAMBRES	10 chambres et 10 suites, toutes décorées individuellement dans le style Art déco.
RESTAURATION	Spécialités indiennes – moins épicées que ne le veut la coutume par égard pour les palais occidentaux.
HISTOIRE	Palais édifié au milieu du 19e siècle et agrandi en 1940.
LE « PETIT PLUS »	Des vacances royales.

The Journey is the Goal...
Houseboat, Kerala

Houseboat, Kerala

The Journey is the Goal

They look something like the scaly heads of reptiles, and when two of the boats swim towards one another and the helmsmen stir up the water with their long paddles, one thinks that a fight between two river dragons is about to break out. In comparison, life on board is very peaceful: Comfortably reclined in a deckchair, you let daily life on Kerala's shores pass by, doze in the shade of a sun roof made of palm leaves or sample the sharpness of the vegetable curry prepared by the onboard cook. "Kettuvallams" (rice boats) is the name for these long ships that traffic along Kerala's 1,500 kilometres of water – an extensive network of rivers, canals, lagoons and lakes, which comprises one of India's most enchanting landscapes. The boats are about 20 meters long and can be as wide as four meters. They have roofs made of bamboo poles, coconut fibres and palm leaves with numerous openings. They are furnished like small loggias with living spaces as well as a bathroom including a shower and toilet. They were formerly used to transport goods from one trading place to the next. Even today, postmen, campaigning politicians or missionaries use the kettuvallams to visit remote villages. But you need no special reason to board the ship as a tourist – on the boat, the journey is the goal.

Book to pack: "Nectar in a Sieve" by Kamala Markandaya

Houseboat, Kerala c/o Tourindia Post Box No. 163 Mahatma Gandhi Road Trivandrum – 695001, Kerala, India Tel. +91 (471) 233 04 37 and 233 15 07 Fax +91 (471) 233 14 07 Email: tourindia@vsnl.com Website: www.tourindiakerala.com Booking: www.great-escapes-hotels.com	**DIRECTIONS** Tours are available, for example, starting at the Green Magic Nature Resort. **RATES** Boats with cabins starting at US$185 per night (2 people, including full board), six-hour mini cruises starting at US$140 for up to 6 people. **ROOMS** Kettuvallams with one to three cabins (2 to 6 guests). **FOOD** Fresh fish and vegetable curries. **HISTORY** Backwater barges that are now houseboats for tourists. **X-FACTOR** A cruise with a difference that shows Kerala from a new perspective.

Der Weg ist das Ziel

Sie erinnern ein wenig an die schuppigen Köpfe von Reptilien; und wenn zwei der Boote aufeinanderzuschwimmen und die Steuermänner mit ihren langen Paddeln im Wasser herumrühren, erwartet man jeden Moment den Kampf zweier Flussdrachen. Dabei geht es an Bord so friedlich zu. Bequem im Deckchair zurückgelehnt lässt man den Alltag an Keralas Ufern an sich vorüberziehen, döst im Schatten eines Sonnendachs aus Palmwedeln oder testet die Schärfe des Gemüsecurrys, das der mitreisende Koch zubereitet hat. »Kettuvallams« (Reisboote) heißen die lang gezogenen Schiffe, die auf den 1500 Wasserkilometern von Kerala unterwegs sind – einem weit verzweigten Netz aus Flüssen, Kanälen, Lagunen und Seen, das eine der zauberhaftesten Landschaften Südindiens bildet. Um die zwanzig Meter lang und bis zu vier Meter breit sind die Boote, sie besitzen ein Dach aus Bambusstäben, Kokosfasern und Palmwedeln, das an mehreren Stellen geöffnet werden kann, und sind wie eine kleine Loggia mit Wohnräumen sowie einem Bad inklusive Dusche und Toilette ausgestattet. Früher transportierte man mit ihnen Waren von einem Handelsplatz zum nächsten, und noch heute sind Postboten, Politiker im Wahlkampf oder Missionare an Bord von Kettuvallams zu entlegenen Dörfern unterwegs. Wer sich als Tourist einschifft, braucht keine spezielle Aufgabe – auf dem Boot ist der Weg das Ziel.

Buchtipp: »Nektar in einem Sieb« von Kamala Markandaya

Au fil de l'eau

Les embarcations évoquent les têtes écailleuses de reptiles gigantesques, et lorsqu'elles s'avancent l'une vers l'autre, que les hommes fouillent l'eau de leurs longues perches, on s'attend à tout instant à voir s'affronter deux dragons aquatiques. Et dire que la vie est si paisible à bord. Confortablement installé dans une chaise longue sur le pont, on regarde défiler les rives du Kerala, on somnole sous un toit en feuilles de palmier ou on savoure un curry de légumes bien épicé préparé par le cuisinier du bord.

Les longues embarcations naviguent sur les 1500 kilomètres de cours d'eau du Kerala – un réseau dense de rivières, de canaux, de lagunes et de lacs qui forme l'un des paysages les plus enchanteurs du sud de l'Inde. Longs d'une vingtaine de mètres et jusqu'à quatre mètres de large, les « kettuvalam », ou bateaux à riz, ont un toit en bambou, en fibre de coco et en branches de palmier qui peut être ouvert à plusieurs endroits. Ils sont dotés, comme un petite loggia, de pièces à vivre, d'une salle de bains avec douche et de W.-C. Autrefois, les kettuvallam transportaient les marchandises d'une centre de commerce à l'autre et aujourd'hui encore les facteurs, les politiciens en campagne et les missionnaires les empruntent pour se rendre dans les villages isolés. Le touriste qui s'embarque ici le fait sans objectif précis – ici, le chemin est le but.

Livre à emporter : « Le riz et la mousson » de Kamala Markandaya

ANREISE	Angeboten werden Touren zum Beispiel ab dem Green Magic Nature Resort.
PREIS	Boot mit einer Kabine ab 185 $ pro Nacht (2 Personen, inklusive Vollpension). Sechsstündige Mini-Kreuzfahrt ab 140 $ für bis zu 6 Personen.
ZIMMER	Kettuvallams mit ein bis drei Kabinen (2 bis 6 Gäste).
KÜCHE	Frischer Fisch und Gemüsecurrys.
GESCHICHTE	Aus den ursprünglichen Transportbooten in den Backwaters von Südindien wurden Hausboote für Touristen.
X-FAKTOR	Die etwas andere Kreuzfahrt zeigt Kerala aus neuen Perspektiven.

ACCÈS	Choix de promenades, par exemple à partir du Green Magic Nature Resort.
PRIX	Bateau à une cabine à partir de 185 $ la nuit (2 personnes, repas compris), mini-croisière de six heures à partir de 140 $ pour jusqu'à 6 personnes.
CHAMBRES	Kettuvallam de 1 à 3 cabines (2 à 6 personnes).
RESTAURATION	Poisson frais et curry de légumes.
HISTOIRE	Les bateaux de transport circulant dans les back waters, ont été transformés en embarcations aménagées pour les touristes.
LE « PETIT PLUS »	Une croisière pour découvrir l'autre visage du Kerala.

A Storybook Island...
Taprobane Island, Galle

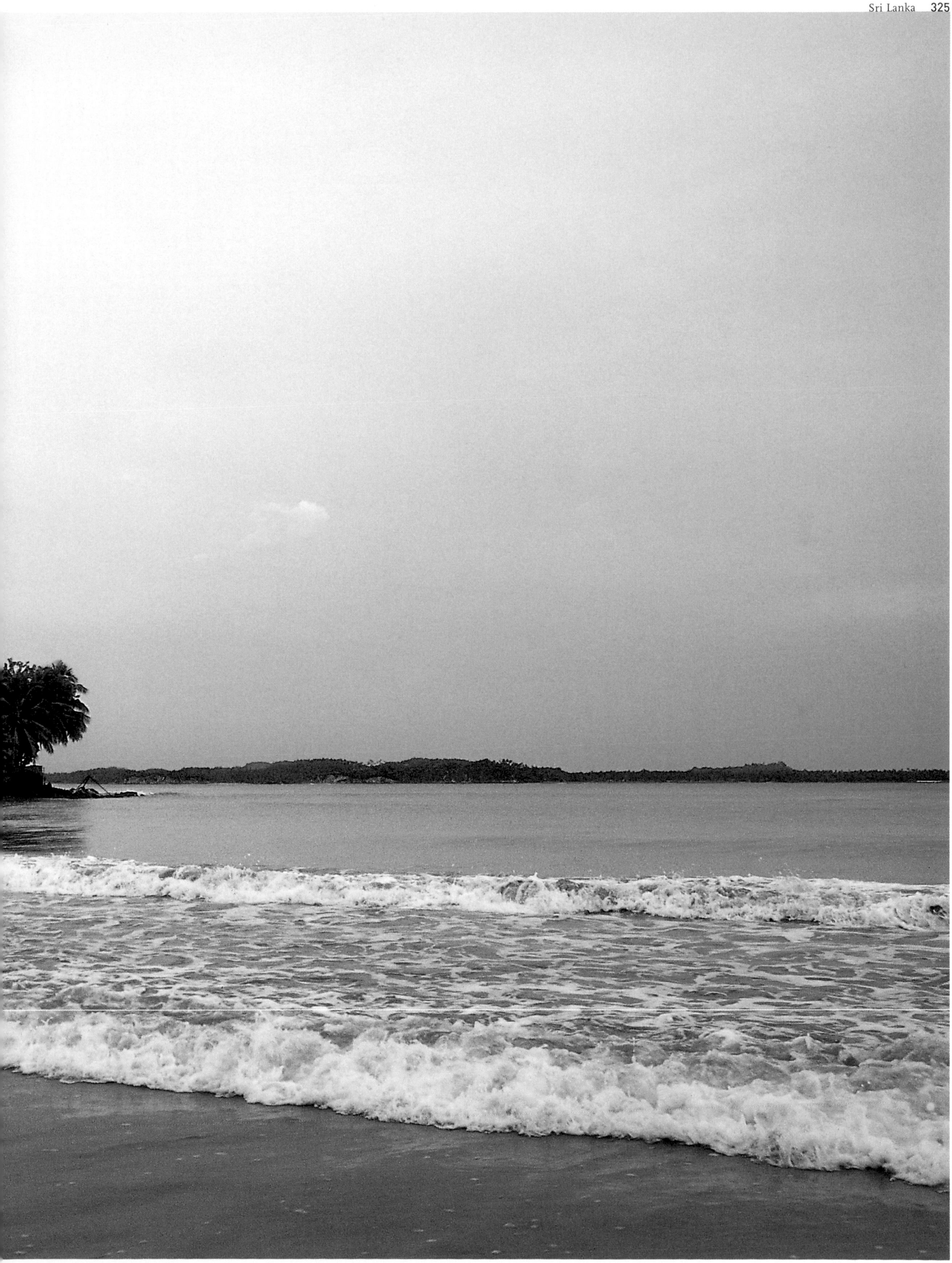

Taprobane Island, Galle

A Storybook Island

It is one of those photos that makes you close your eyes and pray that when you open them again you will be at the place in the picture. Warm salty air, waves rolling gently over the sand, an island packed with palm trees and on which there is only one house. Taprobane is a dream island *par excellence,* a dream that you might think could never come true. But unfulfilled dreams did not feature in the life of Count de Mauny. In 1922 this eccentric Brit and descendent of a general in Napoleon's army had a villa built on the island at Weligama Bay. It was intended to be not so much an enclosed house as a pavilion that was open to its surroundings as much as possible. And it really worked: spacious and sparingly furnished rooms are arranged around a hexagonal hall with projecting terraces that allow a 360-degree view. In the ensuing decades, a very artistic clientele enjoyed these premises. None other than Arthur C. Clarke said that this is where he was freed from the "tyranny of the keyboard" and learned to wear a sarong. Paul Bowles even went so far as to buy the island and wrote "The Spider's House" here and Peggy Guggenheim lay in the sun for days just at this spot. Today, the villa provides space for a maximum of 10 visitors and a new pool to experience their very own private Sri Lanka, which is appropriate since "Taprobane" was the Greek name for ancient Ceylon.

Book to pack: "The Spider's House" by Paul Bowles

Taprobane Island
18 Upper Dickson Road
Galle, Sri Lanka
Tel. + 94 (74) 38 02 75
Fax + 94 (9) 226 24
Email: taproban@sri.lanka.net
www.taprobaneisland.com
Booking: www.great-escapes-hotels.com

DIRECTIONS	Situated on Sri Lanka's southern coast by Weligama (3 hours or a 1-hour flight from Colombo, transfer available upon request), passage by foot, elephant or palanquin.
RATES	Upon request.
ROOMS	4 en-suite rooms, 1 suite (each with its own bath). Looked after by a service team (6 people).
FOOD	Curries from Sri Lanka; seafood and continental dishes.
HISTORY	Built in 1922 by Count de Mauny; a destination for many artists right up to the 1990s.
X-FACTOR	Own your own island just for once – even if only for a vacation.

Eine Bilderbuchinsel

Es ist eines jener Fotos, bei deren Anblick man die Augen schließt und betet, genau am Ort dieser Aufnahme zu stehen, wenn man sie wieder öffnet. Warme Salzluft, Wellen, die leise über den Sand rauschen, eine Insel, die von Palmen überquillt und auf der nur ein einziges Haus steht. Taprobane Island ist ein Sehnsuchtsziel par excellence, ein Traum, von dem man eigentlich annimmt, er könne nie Wirklichkeit werden. Doch unerfüllte Träume kamen im Leben des Count de Mauny nicht vor. 1922 ließ der exzentrische Brite und Nachfahre eines Generals in Napoleons Heer auf der Insel in der Weligama Bay eine Villa bauen, die weniger ein abgeschlossenes Haus werden sollte als vielmehr ein Pavillon, der sich der Umgebung so weit wie möglich öffnet. Rund um eine sechseckige Halle liegen Räume, die diesen Namen wirklich verdienen – großzügig und sparsam möbliert –, sowie ausladende Terrassen mit einem 360-Grad-Panorama. Das genoss in den folgenden Jahrzehnten eine künstlerische Klientel – Arthur C. Clarke wurde hier nach eigenen Aussagen von der »Tyrannei der Tastatur« befreit und lernte, einen Sarong zu tragen; Paul Bowles kaufte die Insel sogar und schrieb auf ihr »Das Haus der Spinne«; Peggy Guggenheim lag hier tagelang in der Sonne. Heute bietet die Villa maximal zehn Personen Platz, die im Haus und am neuen Pool ihr ganz privates Sri Lanka erleben – und das im wahrsten Sinne des Wortes: »Taprobane« ist der griechische Name für das alte Ceylon.

Buchtipp: »Das Haus der Spinne« von Paul Bowles

Une île enchantée

C'est le genre de photo que l'on regarde avant de fermer les yeux et de prier le ciel de se trouver exactement là en les rouvrant. Air chaud et salé, des vagues qui bruissent doucement sur le sable, une île plantée de palmiers à profusion et sur laquelle ne se dresse qu'une seule maison. S'il est un lieu auquel l'âme aspire, un rêve dont on croit qu'il ne deviendra jamais réalité, c'est bien Taprobane Island.

Il ne serait jamais venu à l'idée du comte de Mauny, descendant d'un général de l'armée napoléonienne, que ses désirs ne pussent être exaucés. En 1922, l'excentrique Anglais fit édifier sur l'île une villa dans la baie de Weligama. Il recherchait moins une maison fermée sur elle-même qu'un pavillon s'ouvrant le plus possible à la nature environnante. Tout autour d'une salle hexagonale se déploient des pièces aux proportions généreuses et sobrement meublées et de vastes terrasses qui offrent une vue circulaire sur l'île et la mer. Au fil du temps, de nombreux artistes ont su profiter de ce panorama fascinant – l'auteur de science-fiction Arthur C. Clarke a été libéré ici, selon ses dires, de «la tyrannie du clavier» et a appris à porter un sarong ; Paul Bowles, quant à lui, à même acheté l'île et a rédigé dans ces lieux « La maison de l'araignée » ; Peggy Guggenheim passait ici des journées entières au soleil.

Aujourd'hui, la villa offre le gîte et le couvert à dix personnes qui veulent découvrir Sri Lanka en toute liberté dans la maison et au bord de la nouvelle piscine et prendre le temps de vivre dans cette île qui a su préserver le nom sonore que les Grecs avaient donné à Ceylan : Taprobane.

Livre à emporter : « La maison de l'araignée » de Paul Bowles

ANREISE	An der Südküste Sri Lankas vor Weligama gelegen (3 Fahrt- oder 1 Flugstunde von Colombo entfernt, Transfer auf Wunsch), Passage zu Fuß, per Elefant oder Sänfte.	ACCÈS	Sur la côte sud du Sri Lanka, devant Weligama (à 3 h de voiture ou 1 h d'avion de Colombo), passage à pied, à dos d'éléphant ou en chaise à porteurs.
PREIS	Auf Anfrage.	PRIX	Sur demande.
ZIMMER	4 Ensuite-Zimmer, 1 Suite (jeweils mit eigenem Bad). Betreut von einem Serviceteam (6 Personen).	CHAMBRES	4 en-suite chambres et 1 suite (avec salle de bains annexe). Une équipe de 6 personnes veille au bien-être des hôtes.
KÜCHE	Currys aus Sri Lanka, Meeresfrüchte und kontinentale Gerichte.	RESTAURATION	Curries sri lankais, fruits de mer et plats continentaux.
GESCHICHTE	1922 vom Count de Mauny gebaut, bis in die neunziger Jahre Ziel vieler Künstler.	HISTOIRE	Edifié en 1922 par le comte de Mauny. But de voyage de nombreux artistes jusqu'aux années 90.
X-FAKTOR	Einmal Inselbesitzer sein – und sei es nur für einen Urlaub.	LE « PETIT PLUS »	Posséder une île, rien qu'une fois, et ne serait-ce que pour y passer ses vacances.

Nature Pure...
Ulpotha, Galgiriyawa Mountains

Ulpotha, Galgiriyawa Mountains

Nature Pure

Ulpotha has never been short of legends: This small village in the deepest Sri Lankan jungle is supposedly the holy place, described in ancient myths, where Shiva's son had a shrine built to which Prince Saliya and Asokamala fled to live out their love which was not tolerated by the royal palace. Even today, secrets and spirituality still play an important role in Ulpotha – as a source of inspiration for one of the most unusual eco-tourist projects in Asia. Two private, non-profit organizations have rebuilt Ulpotha as a traditional farming village with organic farm and reforestation project. With the help of old irrigation systems, traditional working methods and a large helping of idealism, the aim is to bring back the original Ceylon. Ulpotha is only open to visitors from November to March and in June/July – where a mixture of eco-lodge, vacation camp and introductory courses in spiritual exercises await them. Yoga courses, massages and Ayurveda are regular rituals filling the days, which pass quietly and gently between the jungle, sea and campfire site. Every visitor to Ulpotha will enjoy nature in its purest form – and experience that as a luxury.

Book to pack: "Running in the Family" by Michael Ondaatje

Ulpotha	
c/o Neal's Yard Agency	
BCM Neal's Yard	
London WC1N 3XX, Great Britain	
Tel./Fax +44 (870) 444 27 02	
and +44 (7000) 78 37 04	
Email: info@ulpotha.com	
www.ulpotha.com	
Booking: www.great-escapes-hotels.com	

DIRECTIONS	Situated at the foot of the Galgiriyawa Mountains, 30 km/18 miles north of Kurunegala, 140 km/87 miles from Colombo Airport.
RATES	14-day packages starting at US$ 1570 per person in double rooms (including all meals, yoga, massage, Ayurveda and excursions)
ROOMS	A maximum of 19 guests live in 7 simple cottages (double rooms).
FOOD	Strictly vegetarian, with products from its own organic farm. Cooking is done over an open fire.
HISTORY	The legendary Ulpotha turns ambitious eco-tourist project.
X-FACTOR	Insights into Sri Lanka's soul.

Natur pur

An Legenden hat es Ulpotha noch nie gemangelt: Das kleine Dorf im tiefsten Dschungel von Sri Lanka soll der heilige Ort sein, der in jahrtausendealten Mythen beschrieben ist. Wo Shivas Sohn einen Schrein errichten ließ und wohin Prinz Saliya und Asokamala flohen, um ihre vom Königspalast nicht geduldete Liebe zu leben. Auch heute noch spielen Geheimnisse und Spiritualität eine wichtige Rolle in Ulpotha – als Inspirationsquelle für eines der außergewöhnlichsten Ökotourismus-Projekte Asiens. Zwei private und gemeinnützige Organisationen haben Ulpotha als traditionelles Bauerndorf wieder aufgebaut, als Biofarm und Aufforstungsbetrieb. Mit Hilfe alter Bewässerungssysteme, überlieferten Arbeitsmethoden und einer großen Portion Idealismus soll hier das ursprüngliche Ceylon wieder aufleben. Nur von November bis März sowie im Juni und Juli ist Ulpotha für Besucher geöffnet – sie erwartet dann eine Mischung aus Eco-Lodge, Feriencamp und Einführungskurs in spirituelle Übungen. Yogakurse, Massagen und Ayurveda sind feste Bestandteile der Tage, die zwischen Urwald, See und Feuerstelle ruhig und sanft dahinfließen. Wer nach Ulpotha kommt, soll die Natur in ihrer reinsten Form erleben – und das als Luxus empfinden.

Buchtipp: »Es liegt in der Familie« von Michael Ondaatje

Pour les amoureux de la nature

Ulpotha est un lieu saint entouré de légendes. Selon les mythes ancestraux, c'est là en effet, dans ce petit village enfoui dans la jungle du Sri Lanka, que le fils de Shiva aurait fait bâtir un mausolée et que le prince Saliya se serait réfugié avec la belle Asokamala pour fuir les foudres de son père qui désapprouvait cet amour. Mais les mystères et la spiritualité jouent aujourd'hui encore un rôle important à Ulpotha – et ils ont inspiré l'un des projets de tourisme écologique les plus exceptionnels d'Asie. Deux organisations privées d'utilité publique ont reconstruit Ulpotha en village traditionnel, lui ajoutant une ferme bio et une entreprise de reboisement. Le but est de faire revivre le Ceylan d'origine tout en s'aidant de systèmes d'irrigation, de méthodes de travail classiques et d'une bonne dose d'idéalisme. Ouvert aux visiteurs de novembre à mars et durant les mois de juin et de juillet, Ulpotha est un mélange de lodge écologique, de camp de vacances et de cours d'initiation aux exercices spirituels. Le yoga, les massages et l'Ayurvéda rythment les journées qui s'écoulent paisiblement avec pour toile de fond la végétation luxuriante, les eaux du lac et les feux de camp. Celui qui vient à Ulpotha découvrira la nature sous sa forme originelle et la percevra comme un luxe.

Livre à emporter : «Un air de famille» de Michael Ondaatje

ANREISE	Am Fuß der Galgiriyawa Mountains gelegen, 30 km nördlich von Kurunegala, 140 km vom Flughafen Colombo entfernt.	ACCÈS	Au pied du Galgiriyawa, à 30 km au nord de Kurunegala et à 140 km de l'aéroport de Colombo.
PREIS	14 Tage ab 1570 $ pro Person im Doppelzimmer (inklusive Vollpension, Yoga, Massage, Ayurveda und Ausflüge).	PRIX	Formule de 14 jours à partir de 1570 $ par personne en chambre double (comprenant pension complète, yoga, massages, Ayurvéda et excursions)
ZIMMER	Maximal 19 Gäste wohnen in 7 einfachen Cottages (Doppelzimmer).	CHAMBRES	19 hôtes au maximum résident dans 7 cottages simples (chambre double).
KÜCHE	Ausschließlich vegetarisch und mit Produkten aus eigenem Bio-Anbau. Gekocht wird über dem offenen Feuer.	RESTAURATION	Exclusivement végétarienne avec des produits bios cultivés sur place. Cuisine au feu de bois.
GESCHICHTE	Aus dem sagenhaften Ort Ulpotha wurde in den neunziger Jahren ein ambitioniertes Ökotourismus-Projekt.	HISTOIRE	Le lieu légendaire d'Ulpotha est devenu dans les années 90 un projet de tourisme écologique ambitieux.
X-FAKTOR	Einblicke in Sri Lankas Seele.	LE « PETIT PLUS »	Incursion dans l'âme du Sri Lanka.

Enchanted Gardens...
Bagan Hotel, Bagan

Bagan Hotel, Bagan

Enchanted Gardens

The first king of Bagan's greatest fears were not war, sickness or even the disfavour of his people: Thammoddarit was afraid of tigers, flying squirrels, boars, birds and gourd plants. It was the last one that mainly kept him awake nights, because night after night they grew like in a time-lapse photograph, slowly covering the country, enabling the feared animals to live a life of paradise – until a brave man named Pyusawhti drew his bow and fatally wounded all five "dangers." As a reward, he was allowed to marry Thammoddarit's daughter and years later become king himself. On that very day, he had pagodas built on all five spots where he had once conquered the animal and plant world – a good foundation! Today Bagan is one of the greatest archaeological sites in Asia. Over an area of about 35 square kilometres, one can visit 5000 temple ruins and almost 70 restored holy relics. One of the best places to start is the Bagan Hotel, which is situated at the foot of the Gawdawpalin Temple and directly on the shores of the Ayeyarwady, just a few steps away from Old Bagan's archaeological museum. The buildings of red-brown stone are linked by small paths and situated in the midst of enchanted gardens. If you take a little time for exploration, you will be surprised by a statue of Buddha behind just about every corner and in almost every room, and after a few days you will feel like picking up a shovel and brush and taking part in the excavations in and around Bagan. But pulling up supposed weeds is hardly worth it – a king no longer reigns over the city with a daughter of marriageable age.

Book to pack: "Freedom From Fear and Other Writings" by Aung San Suu Kyi

Bagan Hotel		
Bagan, Old Bagan, Myanmar		
Tel. +95 (2) 671 45		
Fax +95 (2) 673 11		
Email: olbagho1@bagan.nel.mm		
Website: www.myanmars.net/baganhotel		
Booking: www.great-escapes-hotels.com		
	DIRECTIONS	Situated in Old Bagan and directly on the banks of the Ayeyarwady, 16 km/10 miles west of Nyaung U Airport.
	RATES	Superior Room US$ 80 per night (2 people, with breakfast), Deluxe Room US$ 90 per night, Junior Suite US$ 120 per night, Bagan Suite US$ 150 per night, Riverview Suite US$ 180 per night.
	ROOMS	50 Superior Rooms, 36 Deluxe Rooms, 12 Junior Suites, 4 Bagan Suites, 4 Riverview Suites.
	FOOD	Good traditional specialties from Myanmar as well as Western dishes.
	HISTORY	Built on historical ground and at the foot of the pagodas.
	X-FACTOR	Living like in a giant open-air museum.

Die Spur der Steine

Die größte Angst des ersten Königs von Bagan war nicht Krieg, nicht Krankheit und auch nicht die Ungnade seines Volkes: Thammoddarit fürchtete sich vor Tigern, Flughörnchen, Ebern, Vögeln und Kürbispflanzen. Vor allem letztere raubten ihm den Schlaf, da sie Nacht für Nacht wie im Zeitraffer das Land überwucherten und den gefürchteten Tieren ein paradiesisches Leben ermöglichten – bis ein tapferer Mann namens Pyusawhti seinen magischen Bogen spannte und alle fünf »Gefahren« tödlich traf. Zum Dank durfte er die Tochter Thammoddarits heiraten und Jahre später selbst den Thron besteigen. An diesem Tag ließ er an allen fünf Stellen Pagoden errichten, an denen er einst über die Tier- und Pflanzenwelt gesiegt hatte – ein guter Grundstock! Heute ist Bagan eine der größten archäologischen Stätten Asiens – auf rund 35 Quadratkilometern kann man 5000 Ruinen und knapp 70 restaurierte Heiligtümer besichtigen. Einer der besten Ausgangspunkte ist das Bagan Hotel, das zu Füßen des Gawdawpalin Tempels und direkt am Ufer des Ayeyarwaddy steht, nur wenige Schritte vom Archäologischen Museum Old Bagans entfernt. Die Gebäude aus rotbraunem Stein liegen inmitten verwunschener Gärten und sind durch schmale Pfade miteinander verbunden – wer sich Zeit für Entdeckungen nimmt, wird hinter beinahe jeder Ecke und in fast jedem Zimmer von einer Statue des Buddha überrascht und bekommt nach ein paar Tagen Lust, bei den Ausgrabungen in und um Bagan selbst Schaufel und Pinsel in die Hand zu nehmen. Das Zupfen vermeintlichen Unkrauts lohnt sich allerdings kaum – über die Stadt herrscht kein König mit heiratsfähiger Tochter mehr.

Buchtipp: »Der Weg zur Freiheit« von Aung San Suu Kyi

Les jardins enchantés

Le premier roi du Bagan ne redoutait ni la guerre, ni la maladie pas plus qu'il n'avait peur de tomber en disgrâce auprès de son peuple. En revanche Thammoddarit craignait plus que tout au monde le tigre, les écureuils volants, les verrats, les oiseaux et les courges. Ces dernières en particulier l'empêchaient de dormir car, nuit après nuit, elles pullulaient à une telle rapidité que tout le pays en était envahi et qu'elles offraient un abri aux animaux indésirables. Un jour toutefois arriva un jeune homme courageux, qui s'appelait Pyusawhti. Bandant son arc magique, il transperça les cinq « dangers ». Pour le remercier, Thammoddarit lui accorda la main de sa fille et, plusieurs années plus tard, Pyusawhti monta sur le trône. Ce jour-là, il fit ériger des pagodes aux cinq endroits où il avait jadis vaincu le monde animal et végétal. Bagan est l'un des sites archéologiques les plus vastes d'Asie, il s'étend sur trente-cinq kilomètres carrés et compte cinq milles temples en ruines ainsi que soixante-dix sanctuaires restaurés. Celui qui désire visiter le site prendra comme point d'attache le Bagan Hotel, situé au pied du temple Gawdawpalin, sur les rives de l'Irrawaddy et à quelques pas seulement du musée archéologique Old Bagan. Les constructions en pierre brun-rouge sont nichées au milieu de jardins enchanteurs et reliées entre elles par d'étroits sentiers. Le visiteur désireux de partir à la découverte sera surpris de trouver une statue de Bouddha à chaque détour du chemin et dans presque toutes les chambres. Au bout de quelques jours, l'envie lui viendra de participer aux fouilles effectuées à Bagan et dans les alentours. Il se gardera toutefois d'arracher les plantes envahissantes car il n'y a plus de roi ayant une fille en âge de se marier.

Livre à emporter : « Nationalisme et littérature en Birmanie : Quelques aspects de la vie intellectuelle sous le colonialisme » d'Aung San Suu Kyi

ANREISE	In Old Bagan und direkt am Ufer des Ayeyarwady gelegen, 16 km westlich des Flughafens Nyaung U.
PREIS	Superior Room 80 $ pro Nacht (2 Personen, mit Frühstück), Deluxe Room 90 $ pro Nacht, Junior-Suite 120 $ pro Nacht, Bagan-Suite 150 $ pro Nacht, Riverview-Suite 180 $ pro Nacht.
ZIMMER	50 Superior Rooms, 36 Deluxe Rooms, 12 Junior-Suiten, 4 Bagan-Suiten, 4 Riverview-Suiten.
KÜCHE	Gute traditionelle Spezialitäten aus Myanmar, außerdem westliche Gerichte.
GESCHICHTE	Auf historischem Boden zu Füßen der Pagoden gebaut.
X-FAKTOR	Wohnen wie in einem riesigen Freiluftmuseum.

ACCÈS	Situé à Old Bagan, sur les rives de l'Irrawaddy, à 16 km à l'ouest de l'aéroport de Nyaung U.
PRIX	Superior Room 80 $ la nuit (2 personnes, petit-déjeuner compris), Deluxe Room 90 $ la nuit, Junior Suite 120 $ la nuit, Bagan Suite 150 $ la nuit, Riverview Suite 180 $ la nuit.
CHAMBRES	50 Superior Rooms, 36 Deluxe Rooms, 12 Junior Suites, 4 Bagan Suites, 4 Riverview Suites.
RESTAURATION	Spécialités traditionnelles de Myanmar, ainsi que plats occidentaux.
HISTOIRE	Construit sur un site historique au pied des pagodes.
LE « PETIT PLUS »	On se croirait dans un immense musée en plein air.

The Wellspring of Light...

The Regent Chiang Mai Resort & Spa, Chiang Mai

The Regent Chiang Mai Resort & Spa, Chiang Mai

The Wellspring of Light

Every morning the gods let gold dust rain on Chiang Mai. When shortly before dawn the torches flare up, the papyrus lanterns gently swing back and forth and the lanterns emit a fragile glow; the hotel gardens look like a glittering golden carpet. One is almost cross with the sky for turning blue and yet more blue, but by daylight the view across the houses is also close to pure magic. With pointed roofs, small stairwells, gazebos and many little turrets, the pavilions recall the typical "Lanna" architecture, the style of the "land of a million rice fields". The setting here is also, naturally, pre-programmed with its green-tinted rice terraces and gently curved hills – a brief glance is enough to touch the soul. The spa will also do you the world of good; thanks to its seven exclusive spa suites, the Chiang Mai Resort is famous for being one of the best in Thailand. This also applies to the restaurants, whose delicacies one can learn to prepare in the hotel's own cooking school. And should, by your endeavours, a touch too much salt land in the soup or the meat burn in the wok then do not worry, the evening brings consolation. Because the moment darkness falls over the hotel, the divine rain falls for a second time and everything turns gold.

Book to pack: "The King and I" by Margaret Landon

The Regent Chiang Mai Resort & Spa	
Mae Rim-Samoeng Old Road	
Mae Rim, Chiang Mai 50180, Thailand	
Tel. +66 (53) 29 81 81	
Fax +66 (53) 29 81 89	
Website: www.regenthotels.com	
Booking: www.great-escapes-hotels.com	

DIRECTIONS	Situated in the heart of the valley of Mae Rim, 20 minutes north of Chiang Mai (airport transfer upon request).
RATES	Suites starting at US$ 340 per night.
ROOMS	64 pavilion suites, 16 residence suites (these with personal "Mae Baan" or butler).
FOOD	Two restaurants with the finest Thai cooking and the "Elephant Bar" for drinks. The hotel has its own cooking school.
HISTORY	Opened in April 1995 and constructed in traditional Thai "Lanna" style.
X-FACTOR	Majestic – Relax like King of Siam himself.

Die Quelle des Lichts

Jeden Morgen lassen die Götter Goldstaub auf Chiang Mai regnen – wenn kurz vor der Dämmerung die Fackeln aufflackern, die Papyruslaternen sanft hin- und herschaukeln und die Windlichter einen zerbrechlichen Schein aussenden, sehen die Hotelgärten aus wie ein goldglitzernder Teppich. Man ist dem Himmel fast ein wenig böse, dass er blau und blauer wird; doch die Aussicht über die Häuser kommt auch bei Tageslicht reiner Magie ziemlich nahe. Mit spitz zulaufenden Dächern, kleinen Treppen, Erkern und ungezählten Türmchen erinnern die Pavillons an die typische »Lanna«-Architektur, den Stil des »Landes der Millionen Reisfelder«. Da ist natürlich auch die Kulisse vorprogrammiert: Grün schattierte Reisterrassen und sanft geschwungene Hügel – schon ein einziger Blick darauf streichelt die Seele. Ihr wird auch im Spa alles erdenklich Gute getan. Dank seiner sieben exklusiven Spa-Suiten ist das Chiang Mai Resort als eine der besten Wellness-Adressen Thailands berühmt. Das gilt auch für die Restaurants, deren Köstlichkeiten man in der hoteleigenen Cooking School nachkochen kann. Und sollte eine Prise Salz zu viel in der Suppe landen oder das Fleisch im Wok verkohlen, bringt der Abend Trost. Denn sobald sich die Dunkelheit über das Hotel legt, fällt ein zweites Mal der göttliche Regen – alles wird golden.

Buchtipp: »Der König und ich« von Margaret Landon

Aux sources de la lumière

Tous les matins, les dieux répandent une poudre d'or sur Chiang Mai. Lorsque juste avant l'aube les flambeaux se raniment une dernière fois, lorsque les lanternes en papyrus se balancent doucement et les chandelles jettent leur lueur tremblotante, les jardins des hôtels ressemblent à des tapis scintillants. On pourrait presque en vouloir au ciel de s'éclaircir inexorablement. Mais on se console bien vite car à la lumière du jour, la vue sur les toits des maisons est elle aussi magique. Avec leurs toits pointus, leurs petits escaliers, leurs encorbellements et leurs tours innombrables, les pavillons évoquent l'architecture « Lanna », le style caractéristique du pays aux mille rizières. Les collines aux formes arrondies et les rizières en terrasse déclinant leurs nuances de vert forment un décor qui ne peut que réjouir l'âme. Et celle-ci est particulièrement choyée dans ce centre de beauté et de remise en forme. Disposant de sept suites exclusives, le Chiang Mai Resort est l'une des meilleures adresses de Thaïlande. Cela vaut aussi pour ses restaurants dont vous pourrez apprendre les préparations exquises à la Cooking School de l'hôtel. Et si par mégarde vous avez salé un peu trop le potage ou laissé brûler la viande dans le wok, la tombée du jour vous fera oublier vos déboires, car dès que l'obscurité enveloppe l'hôtel, les dieux répandent leur poudre d'or une seconde fois.

Livre à emporter : « Le Roi et moi » de Margaret Landon

ANREISE	Mitten im Tal von Mae Rim gelegen, 20 Fahrtminuten nördlich von Chiang Mai (Flughafentransfer auf Wunsch).
PREIS	Suite ab 340 $ pro Nacht.
ZIMMER	64 Pavilion-Suiten, 16 Residence-Suiten (mit persönlichem »Mae Baan«/Butler).
KÜCHE	2 Restaurants mit feinster thailändischer Küche, »Elephant Bar« für Drinks. Hoteleigene Kochschule.
GESCHICHTE	Eröffnet im April 1995 und im altthailändischen »Lanna«-Stil erbaut.
X-FAKTOR	Majestätisch – entspannen wie der König von Siam persönlich.

ACCÈS	Dans la vallée de Mae Rim, au nord de Chiang Mai, à 20 min de voiture (transfert par avion sur demande).
PRIX	Suite à partir de 340 $ la nuit.
CHAMBRES	64 suites pavillon, 16 suites résidence (avec « Mae Baan »/majordôme individuel).
RESTAURATION	2 restaurants proposant une cuisine thaïlandaise raffinée, « Elephant Bar » pour les drinks. Ecole gastronomique appartenant à l'hôtel.
HISTOIRE	Ouvert en avril 1995 et construit dans le style traditionnel thaïlandais « Lanna ».
LE « PETIT PLUS »	Majestueux – se détendre comme le roi de Siam en personne.

Adventure in Wonderland...
Angkor Village, Siem Reap

Eine blaue Pause

Auch in Asien gibt es Karrieren, die vom Tellerwäscher zum Millionär führen: Als Cheong Fatt Tze 1856 mit 16 Jahren seine Heimatstadt verließ, tat er es ohne eine Münze in der Tasche – und nur wenige Jahrzehnte später war er einer der reichsten Männer der Welt, stand Eisenbahnunternehmen sowie Banken vor und wurde in wirtschaftspolitischen Kreisen nur noch »Chinas letzter Mandarin und erster Kapitalist« oder »Rockefeller des Ostens« genannt. Zwischen seinen Reisen durch ganz Asien kam er immer wieder nach Malaysia, in sein Haus in Penang, das schon damals zu den schönsten Gebäuden der Stadt zählte. Nach einer Rundumrenovierung 1990 wurde es von der Unesco preisgekrönt und verlieh dem Kinofilm »Indochine« mit Catherine Deneuve Farbe – heute ist es ein Hotel, das Mythos und Magie Chinas mit Glanz und Glorie des Britischen Empire verbindet. Die Cheong Fatt Tze Mansion, die dank ihrer Fassade in leuchtendem Indigo auch als Blue Mansion bekannt ist, hat sich den Stil des späten 19. Jahrhunderts bewahrt. Die 16 individuell eingerichteten Zimmer schmücken filigrane chinesische Holzschnitzereien, schottische Lampen, Vorhänge aus handgewebtem Gaze und Seide, mundgeblasenes Glas und feines Porzellan. Wer in einem der fünf Innenhöfe sitzt, durch den Garten schlendert oder versucht, die 220 kleinen Fenster zu zählen, wird in die Geschichte der Blue Mansion zurückversetzt und an die große Karriere des Cheong Fatt Tze erinnert.

Buchtipp: »Sternenhimmel über Malaysia« von Marion Nikola

La maison bleue

En Asie, un cireur de chaussures peut aussi devenir millionnaire. Un jour de 1856, Cheong Fatt Tze, âgé de seize ans, quitta sa ville natale sans un sou en poche. Quelques dizaines d'années plus tard, il était l'un des hommes les plus riches du monde. Propriétaire de banques et de chemins de fer, on le surnommait dans les milieux économiques et politiques « le dernier mandarin de Chine et le premier capitaliste » ou encore « le Rockefeller de l'Orient ». Entre ses nombreux voyages à travers l'Asie, il revenait toujours en Malaisie dans sa maison de Penang, jadis des plus beaux bâtiments de la ville. Après une rénovation complète en 1990, elle fut primée par l'Unesco et on peut l'admirer dans le film « Indochine » avec Catherine Deneuve. Aujourd'hui cette maison est un hôtel qui marie les mythes et la magie de la Chine avec la splendeur et la gloire de l'Empire britannique. La Cheong Fatt Tze Mansion qui, en raison de sa façade bleu indigo, est aussi connue sous le nom de Blue Mansion a conservé le style de la fin du 19e siècle. Les 16 chambres, aménagées de façon individuelle, sont décorées avec de filigranes sculptures en bois chinoises, des lampes écossaises, des rideaux en gaze et en soie, tissés à la main, du verre soufflé à l'ancienne et de la porcelaine fine. Le visiteur qui s'assoit dans l'une des cinq cours intérieures, se promène dans le jardin ou essaie de compter les multiples petites fenêtres (220 en tout !), se retrouve transporté dans le passé de la Blue Mansion et pense bien sûr à la grande carrière de Cheong Fatt Tze.

Livre à emporter : « Malaisie, cœur de l'Asie du Sud-Est » de Gavin Young

ANREISE	Im historischen Zentrum von Penang gelegen, 30 bis 45 Fahrtminuten vom Flughafen Penang entfernt.
PREIS	Doppelzimmer von 61 bis 184 $ pro Nacht (inklusive Frühstück).
ZIMMER	16 individuell eingerichtete Doppelzimmer im Stil des späten 19. Jahrhunderts.
KÜCHE	Frühstück in einem Innenhof, außerdem Afternoon-Tea und Drinks (Bar mit Weinkeller).
GESCHICHTE	Aus dem ehemaligen Haus von Cheong Fatt Tze wurde eines der schönsten chinesisch inspirierten Courtyard-Houses.
X-FAKTOR	Ein Höhepunkt der Handwerkskunst.

ACCÈS	Situé dans le centre historique de Penang, à 30–45 min en voiture de l'aéroport de Penang.
PRIX	Chambre double de 61 à 184 $ la nuit (petit-déjeuner compris).
CHAMBRES	16 chambres doubles aménagées individuellement dans le style de la fin du 19e siècle.
RESTAURATION	Petit-déjeuner dans une cour intérieure. Thé de cinq heures et boissons (bar doté d'une cave à vins).
HISTOIRE	L'ancienne maison de Cheong Fatt Tze est devenue l'une des plus belles courtyard-houses d'inspiration chinoise.
LE « PETIT PLUS »	L'artisanat d'art à son apogée.

A Building for Buddha...
Amanjiwo, Java

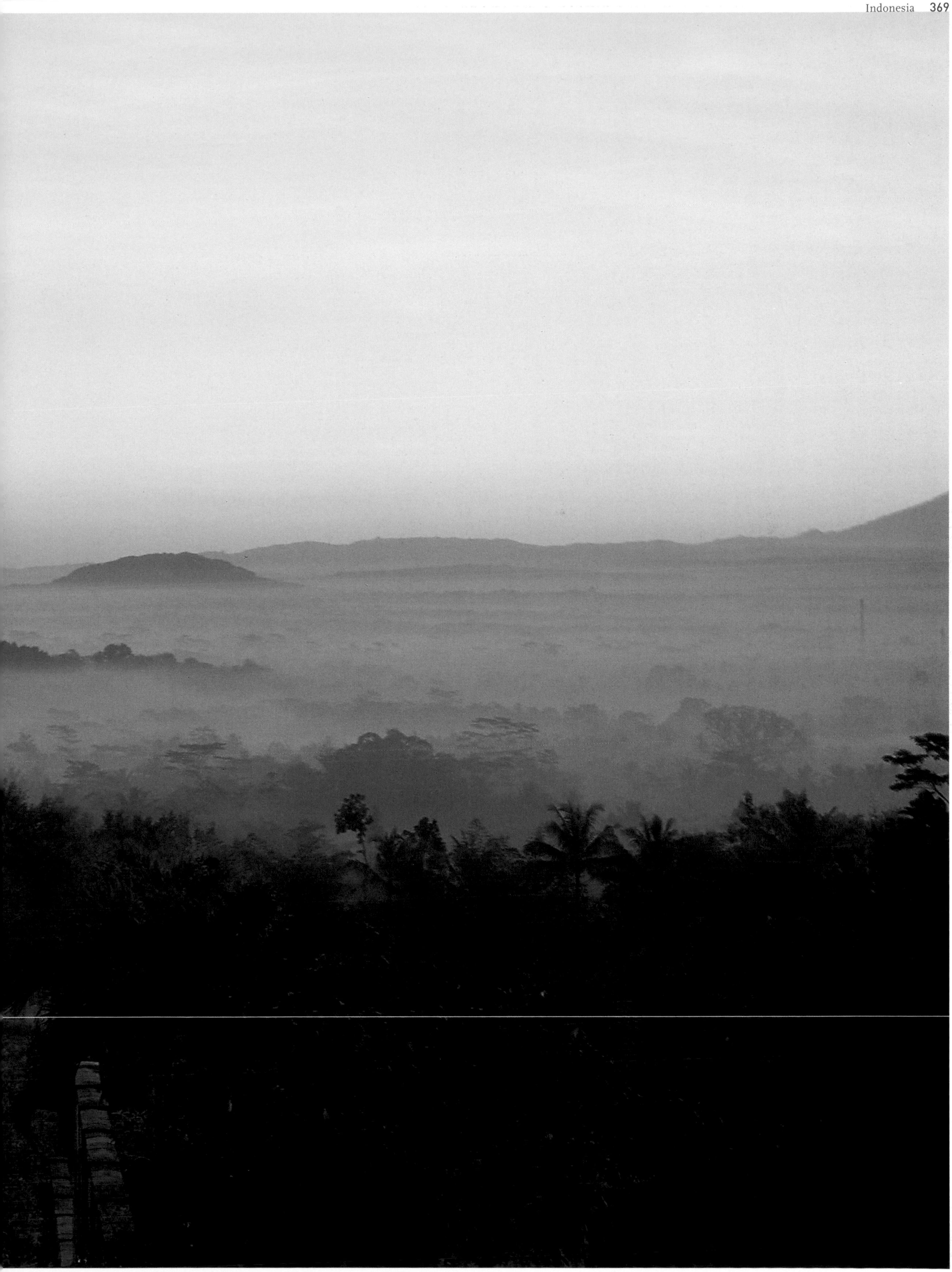

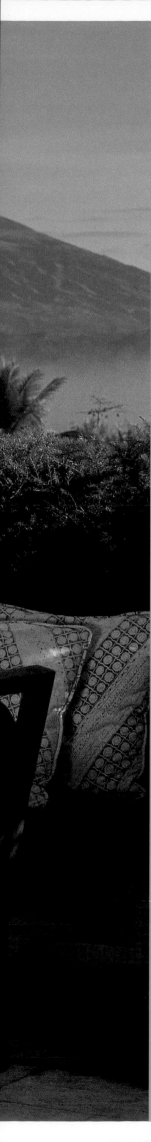

Amanjiwo, Java

A Building for Buddha

Ten thousand craftsmen slaved away for almost an entire century, dragging stone after stone, shaping and piling them on top of one another – and when the Temple of Borobudur was complete, Merapi Volcano erupted and buried the lot under lava and ashes. But the legend of Borobudur lived on, and excavations began at the start of the nineteenth century. Thirty years ago, Unesco supported the complete restoration of the temple and today Borobudur is again the largest and perhaps most beautiful temple complex in southeast Asia. The architecture of Amanjiwo was influenced by its splendour – it reflects ideas and details of the complex, radiates the same solemnity and peace, and when one looks across the rice fields, one looks directly at Borobudur itself. Opened only a few years ago, Amanjiwo simply seems to have merged with the nature of Central Java. The light "paras yogya" limestone stems from the region and assumes the colour of the tree trunks. The green, brown and cream tones of the forest and earth can also be found on pillow cases and bedspreads, and the pale wash of blue sky over the island gives the pool its own unique shimmer. If you stay in one of the suites with the cool terrazzo floor and high ceilings, you experience the classic, elegant style of Java with light accents on dark wood, rattan furniture and traditional glass painting. The "normal" windows present a view of your choice, either the hills, the farmland or Borobudur – inspiration in its purest form.

Book to pack: "Child of All Nations" by Pramoedya Ananta Toer

Amanjiwo	
Borobudur, Java, Indonesia	
Tel. +62 (293) 78 83 33	
Fax +62 (293) 78 83 55	
Email: reservations@amanresorts.com	
Website: www.amanresorts.com	
Booking: www.great-escapes-hotels.com	

DIRECTIONS	Situated in Central Java, 1.5 hr. northwest of Yogyakarta Airport and 2 hr. southwest of Solo Airport.
RATES	Suites starting at US$ 700 per night, pool suites starting at US$ 1000 per night, Dalem Jiwo Suites starting at US$ 2800 per night.
ROOMS	36 suites, including 5 pool suites, 10 deluxe pool suites and 1 Dalem Jiwo Suite.
FOOD	Indonesian specialities.
HISTORY	Opened in 1997 and designed to mirror the holiness of the Borobudur Temple.
X-FACTOR	Buddha was never so close.

Ein Bauwerk für den Buddha

Fast ein ganzes Jahrhundert hatten sich insgesamt 10 000 Handwerker abgemüht, hatten Steine herangeschleppt, in Form gebracht und aufeinandergetürmt – und als der Tempel von Borobudur vollendet war, brach der Vulkan Merapi aus und begrub ihn unter Lava und Asche. Doch die Legende von Borobudur lebte fort, zu Beginn des 19. Jahrhunderts begannen die Ausgrabungen, vor dreißig Jahren unterstützte die UNESCO eine umfassende Sanierung und heute präsentiert sich Borobudur wieder als größter und vielleicht schönster Tempelkomplex Südostasiens. Von seinem Glanz ließ sich die Architektur von Amanjiwo beeinflussen – sie spiegelt Ideen und Details der Anlage wieder, strahlt dieselbe Erhabenheit und Ruhe aus, und wenn man über die Reisfelder blickt, blickt man direkt auf Borobudur selbst. Erst vor wenigen Jahren eröffnet, scheint Amanjiwo schon wie selbstverständlich mit der Natur Zentraljavas verwachsen zu sein. Der helle Kalkstein »paras yogya« stammt aus der Region und nimmt die Farbe der Baumstämme auf; die Grün-, Braun- und Cremetöne von Wald und Erde entdeckt man auch auf Kissenbezügen und Tagesdecken, und der verwaschen blaue Himmel über der Insel verleiht den Pools ihren ganz eigenen Schimmer. Wer in einer der Suiten mit kühlem Terrazzoboden und hohen Decken wohnt, erlebt den klassisch-eleganten Stil Javas; mit hellen Akzenten auf dunklem Holz, Rattanmöbeln und traditionellen Glasmalereien. Die »normalen« Fenster zeigen im übrigen ganz nach Wunsch auf die Hügel, das Farmland oder Borobudur – Inspiration in ihrer reinsten Form.

Buchtipp: »Kind aller Völker« von Pramoedya Ananta Toer

Une construction pour Bouddha

Pendant près d'un siècle, les dix milles artisans s'étaient tués à la tâche, ils avaient apporté péniblement les pierres sur le site, les avaient taillées, puis les avaient amoncelées – et lorsque le temple de Borobudur fut achevé, le volcan Merapi se réveilla et l'ensevelit sous la lave et les cendres. Pourtant la légende continua de vivre, au 19e siècle des fouilles furent entreprises et, il y a trente ans, l'UNESCO mit des fonds à disposition en vue d'une restauration complète. Aujourd'hui, Borobudur est le complexe le plus grand, et peut-être le plus beau, de toute l'Asie du Sud-Est. Son éclat a inspiré l'architecture d'Amanjiwo, qui reflète les idées et les détails du temple, dégage la même sérénité et lorsque le regard glisse au-dessus des rizières, il tombe directement sur Borobudur. Ouvert seulement depuis quelques années, Amanjiwo semble s'être intégré tout naturellement au paysage du centre de Java. La pierre calcaire de couleur claire, appelée ici « paras yogya », provient des environs et absorbe la couleur des troncs d'arbre ; les tons de vert, de marron et de crème de la forêt réapparaissent sur les coussins et les nappes, et le bleu délavé du ciel confère aux piscines une brillance qui n'existe nulle part ailleurs. Le client qui séjourne dans l'une des suites au sol en terre cuite et au plafond élevé peut voir dans toute sa splendeur le style classique et élégant de Java avec ses accents clairs sur les bois sombres, ses meubles en osier et ses peintures sur verre traditionnelles. Suivant les préférences de l'hôte, les fenêtres « normales » de sa chambre donnent sur les collines, les fermes ou Borobudur – l'inspiration sous sa forme la plus pure.

Livre à emporter : « Le Monde des hommes » de Pramoedya Ananta Toer

ANREISE	In Zentraljava gelegen, 1,5h nordwestlich vom Flughafen Yogyakarta und 2h südwestlich vom Flughafen Solo.
PREIS	Suite ab 700 $ pro Nacht, Pool-Suite ab 1000 $ pro Nacht, Dalem-Jiwo-Suite ab 2800 $ pro Nacht.
ZIMMER	36 Suiten, darunter 5 Pool-Suiten und 10 Deluxe-Pool-Suiten und 1 Dalem-Jiwo-Suite.
KÜCHE	Indonesische Spezialitäten.
GESCHICHTE	1997 eröffnet und wie ein Spiegelbild des Heiligtums Borobudur gestaltet.
X-FAKTOR	Noch nie war Buddha so nah.

ACCÈS	Situé dans le centre de Java à 1 h ½ au nord-ouest de l'aéroport de Yogyakarta et à 2 h au sud-ouest de l'aéroport de Solo.
PRIX	Suite à partir de 700 $ la nuit, suite avec piscine à partir de 1000 $ la nuit, suite Dalem Jiwo à partir de 2800 $ la nuit.
CHAMBRES	36 suites, dont 5 suites avec piscine, 10 suites de luxe avec piscine et 1 suite Dalem Jiwo.
RESTAURATION	Spécialités indonésiennes.
HISTOIRE	Ouvert en 1997 et décoré comme un miroir du lieu saint de Borobudur.
LE « PETIT PLUS »	Bouddha n'a jamais été aussi proche.

Enchanted on Bali...

Four Seasons Resort Bali, Sayan

Four Seasons Resort Bali, Sayan

Enchanted on Bali

Ubud, the most famous artist's city on Bali, is beautiful without doubt– but also quite loud as well: with gamelan musicians on every corner, tinny pop music issuing from souvenir shop speakers and the roar of motorbikes in the streets. It is hard to believe that there's a whole different world only a few kilometres away. But in the mountains near Sayan one hears only bird calls and the murmur of the Ayung. Here the air is simultaneously so dense and clear that you can see every single leaf of the plants on the rice terraces, and the jungle glows in an endless array of almost supernatural green tones. The Four Seasons Bali at Sayan has been situated in the midst of this scenery for only a few years, but it is as if it had always belonged here. The modern and reduced design is not at all the kind that makes one shiver and where one prefers not to touch anything for fear of making fingerprints – old Balinese furniture, warm teakwood and light natural stone make the rooms into real living spaces. The spa offers traditional massages and flower petal baths; the restaurants feature both eastern and western menus as well as a breathtaking view of the river and the mountains shielding Ubud. Far, far away.

Book to pack: "A Tale from Bali" by Vicki Baum

Four Seasons Resort Bali
Gianyar, Ubud
Bali, Indonesien 80571
Tel. +62 (361) 97 75 77
Fax +62 (361) 97 75 88
Website: www.fourseasons.com
Booking: www.great-escapes-hotels.com

DIRECTIONS	35 km / 22 miles north of Denpasar Airport, on the outskirts of the village of Sayan (transfer upon request).
RATES	Suites starting at US$ 450 per night, villas starting at US$ 575 per night.
ROOMS	18 suites, 42 villas.
FOOD	Eastern and western cuisine as well as light, altnernative dishes on the "Ayung Terrace", "The Riverside Café". Drinks in the "Jati Bar".
HISTORY	Opened in March 1998 to reflect the mystic landscape in the mountains near Sayan.
X-FACTOR	From nowhere else does Bali seem so beautiful.

Verzaubert auf Bali

Ubud, die berühmteste Künstlerstadt auf Bali, ist zweifellos schön – aber auch schön laut: mit Gamelanmusikern an den Ecken, blechernem Pop aus den Lautsprechern der Souvenirshops und knatternden Motorrädern auf den Straßen. Kann nur wenige Kilometer entfernt eine andere Welt beginnen? Sie kann. In den Bergen bei Sayan sind nur die Lockrufe der Vögel und das Rauschen des Ayung zu hören, hier ist die Luft so dicht und klar zugleich, dass jedes einzelne Blatt der Pflänzchen auf den Reisterrassen erkennbar wird, und der Dschungel leuchtet in unendlich vielen und fast übernatürlichen Grüntönen. Inmitten dieser Kulisse steht das Four Seasons Bali at Sayan – seit wenigen Jahren erst und doch so, als hätte es schon immer hierher gehört. Das moderne und reduzierte Design ist keines von der Sorte, bei der man leicht fröstelt und aus Sorge vor Fingerabdrücken lieber nichts anfasst – alte balinesische Möbel, warmes Teakholz und heller Naturstein machen die Räume zu wirklichen Wohnräumen. Im Spa werden traditionelle Massagen und Blütenbäder angeboten, in den Restaurants östliche wie westliche Menüs und ein zauberhafter Blick auf den Fluss und die Berge, hinter denen Ubud liegt. Weit, weit weg.

Buchtipp: »Liebe und Tod auf Bali« von Vicki Baum

Les deux visages de Bali

Ubud, la ville artistique la plus célèbre de Bali, est sans nul doute une belle ville – mais aussi bien bruyante avec les joueurs de gamelan aux coins des rues, la musique pop diffusée par les haut-parleurs des magasins de souvenirs et les mobylettes qui pétaradent toute la journée. On a peine à croire qu'à quelques kilomètres d'ici, existe un autre univers. Dans les montagnes de Sayan, on n'entend en effet que le chant des oiseaux et le murmure de la rivière. Ici l'air est si limpide que l'on peut distinguer chaque feuille sur les rizières en terrasses. La jungle décline ses tons de vert presque à l'infini et sa luminosité semble presque surnaturelle. Dans ce décor est situé le Four Seasons Bali at Sayan – de construction récente même si on a l'impression qu'il a toujours été là. Sa décoration moderne et minimaliste n'est pas de celles qui donnent le frisson ni de celles où l'on préfère ne rien toucher par crainte de laisser des traces de doigts – ici les vieux meubles balinais, le bois de teck et les pierres naturelles de couleur claire rendent les pièces vraiment accueillantes. Le centre de remise en forme propose des massages traditionnels et des bains de pétales de fleurs, les restaurants des menus orientaux et occidentaux ainsi qu'une vue splendide sur la rivière et les montagnes.

Livre à emporter : « Sang et volupté à Bali » de Vicki Baum

ANREISE	35 km nördlich vom Flughafen Denpasar gelegen, am Rand des Dorfes Sayan (Transfer auf Wunsch).
PREIS	Suite ab 450 $ pro Nacht, Villa ab 575 $ pro Nacht.
ZIMMER	18 Suiten, 42 Villen.
KÜCHE	Östliche und westliche Küche sowie leichte alternative Gerichte im »Ayung Terrace«, »The Riverside Café«. Drinks in der »Jati Bar«.
GESCHICHTE	Im März 1998 und als Spiegelbild der mystischen Landschaft in den Bergen bei Sayan eröffnet.
X-FAKTOR	Nirgendwo sonst ist der Blick auf Bali so schön.

ACCÈS	Situé à 35 km au nord de l'aéroport de Denpasar, en bordure du village de Sayan (transfert sur demande).
PRIX	Suite à partir de 450 $ la nuit, villa à partir de 575 $ la nuit.
CHAMBRES	18 suites, 42 villas.
RESTAURATION	Cuisine orientale et occidentale ainsi que repas légers au « Ayung Terrace » et au « The Riverside Café ». Drinks au « Jati Bar ».
HISTOIRE	Ouvert en mars 1998. Reflet du paysage mystique dans les montagnes de Sayan.
LE « PETIT PLUS »	La vue sur Bali n'est nulle part ailleurs aussi belle.

A Room with a View...
Taman Selini, Bali

Taman Selini, Bali

A Room with a View

They can only be seen early in the morning and only by those who watch the ocean with great patience: the dolphins shoot up like tense, slightly chubby arches and spray water as they dive back in. Their favourite spots are off of Bali's northwest coast; there, where fewer ships sail than in the south, where the dark beaches are more secluded and the face of the island creases into gentle wrinkles. The volcanic mountain chain also forms a backdrop for the bungalows of Taman Belini in Pemuteran. The fishing village is not only an address for the small resort; it is also a home to the locals. The buildings were primarily built by local craftsmen using Balinese materials. Many village residents took part in English classes and cooking courses and now tend to the guests of Taman Selini, and inviting foreign visitors to family celebrations or religious ceremonies is nothing unusual. The bungalows attain an unusual balance: You feel both like a guest and at home. You enjoy tea on the terrace with a view of the ocean. You take walks through the garden and touch the enchanting flowers of the bougainvilleas, frangipanis and jacarandas, just to check whether they are real or actually coloured plastic. And voluntarily get up early every morning – just because of the dolphins.

Book to pack: "The Islands" by Albert Alberts

Taman Selini	
Beach Bungalows	
Desa Pemuteran, Gerogkak,	
Singaraja, Bali, Indonesia	
Tel. +62 (362) 947 46	
Fax +62 (362) 934 49	
Booking: www.great-escapes-hotels.com	

DIRECTIONS	Situated in Pemuteran on the northwest coast of Bali, 10 km / 6 miles west of Singaraja (4 hours to the airport, the transport is organized).
RATES	Bungalows starting at US$ 70 per night (2 people).
ROOMS	11 bungalows.
FOOD	Simple Balinese dishes. Occasional Greek specialties as well.
HISTORY	Built by a Balinese-Greek couple.
X-FACTOR	Far away but still feels like home.

Zimmer mit Aussicht

Sie zeigen sich nur früh am Morgen und nur denen, die
mit viel Geduld aufs Meer hinausschauen: die Delfine, die
wie gespannte, ein wenig dickliche Bogen aus dem Wasser
schnellen und spritzend wieder untertauchen. Ihre Lieb-
lingsplätze liegen vor der Nordwestküste Balis, dort, wo
weniger Schiffe fahren als im Süden, die dunklen Strände
einsamer sind und das Gesicht der Insel zarte Falten zeigt.
Die vulkanische Bergkette bildet auch die Kulisse für die
Bungalows von Taman Belini in Pemuteran. Das Fischerdorf
ist für die kleine Anlage nicht nur eine Adresse – es ist eine
Heimat. So wurden die Häuser hauptsächlich aus balinesi-
schen Materialien und von hiesigen Handwerkern erbaut,
viele Dorfbewohner nahmen an Englisch- und Kochkursen
teil und kümmern sich jetzt um die Gäste von Taman Selini.
Und dass die gerade noch fremden Besucher zu Familien-
festen oder religiösen Zeremonien eingeladen werden, ist
keine Seltenheit. Die Bungalows schaffen einen seltenen
Spagat: Man fühlt sich in ihnen zu Gast und zu Hause
zugleich. Genießt den Tee auf der Terrasse mit Blick aufs
Meer, testet beim Spaziergang durch den Garten, ob die
zauberhaften Blüten der Bougainvilleen, Frangipanis und
Jakarandas wirklich echt oder nicht doch aus farbigem
Plastik sind. Und steht jeden Morgen freiwillig früh auf –
einzig um der Delfine willen.

Buchtipp: »Die Inseln« von Albert Alberts

Une chambre avec vue

Les dauphins ne se montrent qu'à ceux qui se lèvent tôt et
ont de la patience. Ils surgissent alors des flots comme des
arcs tendus, un peu rondelets, pour y replonger dans un
grand jet d'écume. Leurs endroits préférés sont situés
devant la côte nord-ouest de Bali : là où la circulation est
moins dense que dans le Sud, là où les plages sombres sont
plus isolées et où le visage de l'île montre des rides délicates.
La chaîne de massifs volcaniques sert aussi de décor aux
bungalows de Taman Selini à Pemuteran.
Le village de pêcheurs n'est pas seulement une adresse
mais une patrie, les maisons ont essentiellement été construites à l'aide de matériaux balinais et par des artisans de la
région ; de nombreux villageois ont pris des cours d'anglais
et des cours de cuisine et s'occupent maintenant des hôtes
de Taman Selini – il n'est pas rare que les visiteurs encore
inconnus soient invités à participer aux fêtes de famille et
aux cérémonies religieuses.
Les bungalows réussissent à concilier deux aspects para-
doxaux puisque l'on s'y sent chez soi et aussi en visite chez
des amis. On se détend en buvant le thé sur la terrasse avec
vue sur la mer, on hume en se promenant dans le jardin les
fleurs éblouissantes des bougainvillées, des frangipaniers et
des jacarandas – les unes ont une odeur, les autres pas. Et on
se lève de bonne heure le matin uniquement pour pouvoir
observer les dauphins.

Livre à emporter : « The Islands » de Albert Alberts

ANREISE	In Pemuteran an der Nordwestküste Balis gelegen, 10 km westlich von Singaraja (4 Fahrtstunden zum Flughafen, Transfer wird organisiert).
PREIS	Bungalow ab 70 $ pro Nacht (2 Personen).
ZIMMER	11 Bungalows.
KÜCHE	Einfache balinesische Gerichte. Gelegentlich auch griechische Spezialitäten.
GESCHICHTE	Von einem balinesisch-griechischen Ehepaar erbaut.
X-FAKTOR	Weit weg und trotzdem zu Hause sein.

ACCÈS	Situé à Pemuteran sur la côte nord-ouest de Bali, à 10 km à l'ouest de Singaraja (4 h de voiture jusqu'à l'aéroport, transfert organisé).
PRIX	Bungalow à partir de 70 $ la nuit (2 personnes)
CHAMBRES	11 bungalows.
RESTAURATION	Cuisine balinaise simple. A l'occasion spécialités grecques.
HISTOIRE	Construit par un couple gréco-balinais.
LE « PETIT PLUS »	Se sentir chez soi au bout du monde.

Between Sky and Sea...
Amanpulo, Pamalican Island

Amanpulo, Pamalican Island

Between Sky and Sea

Don't let yourself be misled by the word Amanpulo which means "peaceful island". A visit to this island will definitely not be peaceful in the boring sense of the word. Because a fantastic reef encircles Amanpulo, making the small private island 300 kilometres south of Manila one of the best things that could happen to water sports fans. Underwater, divers feel like they are in a gigantic 3-D picture filled with maritime motifs; skippers see how many beaches they can visit while island hopping for the day and counting the whales, dolphins or sea cows between the waves, and romantics sail through the sunset right into the moonlight. One could almost worry that the dry land has nothing to offer in contrast to the sea – but this is far from the case. The 40 *casitas* of Amanpulo are small dream houses, built in a traditional Philippine way and furnished with favourite spots like hammocks and observation terraces. If you live at the ocean, a private woodland path leads to the beach; if you go up in the hills, you enjoy even more peace, a view that is at most slightly obstructed by the greenery of the neighbouring islands and with a bit of luck a *casita* from whose veranda you can watch both sunrise and sunset. Whichever house you reside in, almost half of the living space is taken up by a splendid marble bath – even where it is dry, everything here has to do with water.

Book to pack: "Infanta" by Bodo Kirchoff

Amanpulo

Pamalican Island, Philippines

Tel. +63 (2) 759 40 40

Fax +63 (2) 759 40 44

Email: reservations@amanresorts.com

Website: www.amanresorts.com

Booking: www.great-escapes-hotels.com

DIRECTIONS	The private island of Pamalican is situated 300 km/ 186 miles south of Manila; the transfer via aircraft is organized (US$ 300 per person).
RATES	Treetop Casita US$ 625 per night, Hillside Casita US$ 750 per night, Beach Casita US$ 800 per night, villa for 6 to 8 people starting at US$ 2425 per night.
ROOMS	4 treetop casitas, 7 hillside casitas, 29 beach casitas, 2 villas.
FOOD	Fantastic seafood, as well as Asian dishes and barbeque on the beach.
HISTORY	Opened in 1993.
X-FACTOR	Beach, sun, sailboats – paradise complete.

Zwischen Himmel und Meer

Amanpulo heißt übersetzt »friedliche Insel« – doch lassen Sie sich nicht täuschen: friedlich im Sinne von langweilig wird es hier ganz bestimmt nicht. Denn rund um Amanpulo zieht sich ein fantastisches Riff und macht die kleine Privatinsel 300 Kilometer südlich von Manila zum Besten, was Wassersportlern passieren kann. Taucher fühlen sich in der Unterwasserwelt wie in einem gigantischen 3-D-Bild voller maritimer Motive, Skipper testen aus, wie viele Strände sie innerhalb eines Island-Hopping-Days anlaufen können und zählen zwischen den Wellen Wale, Delfine oder Seekühe, und Romantiker segeln durch den Sonnenuntergang geradewegs ins Mondlicht. Man hat fast ein wenig Sorge, das Festland könne den Geheimnissen des Meeres nichts entgegensetzen – doch dies ist unbegründet. Die 40 *Casitas* von Amanpulo sind kleine Traumhäuser; gebaut nach traditioneller philippinischer Art und mit Lieblingsplätzen wie Hängematten oder Aussichtsterrassen ausgestattet. Wer am Ozean wohnt, erreicht den Strand über einen privaten Buschpfad; wer hinauf in die Hügel zieht, genießt noch mehr Ruhe, höchstens von etwas Grün verstellte Sicht auf die Nachbarinseln und mit etwas Glück eine *Casita*, von deren Veranda aus sowohl Sonnenaufgang als auch Sonnenuntergang zu sehen sind. Und egal, für welches Haus man sich entscheidet: Beinahe die Hälfte der Wohnfläche nimmt ein prächtiges Marmorbad ein – selbst auf dem Trockenen dreht sich hier eben alles ums Wasser.

Buchtipp: »Infanta« von Bodo Kirchoff

Entre le ciel et la mer

Amanpulo signifie « l'île paisible », mais, soyez sans inquiétude, vous ne vous y ennuierez certainement pas. En effet, Amanpulo est entourée d'une sublime barrière de corail qui fait de la petite île privée située à 300 kilomètres au sud de Manille un véritable paradis pour les amateurs de sports aquatiques. Les plongeurs ont l'impression de se trouver dans un film présentant les merveilles sous-marines, les skippers cherchent combien de plages ils peuvent accoster en un Island-Hopping-Day et comptent les baleines, les dauphins et les lamantins qui surgissent au creux des vagues ; quant aux romantiques, il naviguent pendant que le soleil se couche pour jouir ensuite du clair de lune. On craindrait presque que l'île ne puisse être à la hauteur de la mer qui l'entoure et de ses mystères – mais ce n'est pas le cas. Les 40 *casitas* d'Amanpulo ne sont pas des demeures de rêve, mais des maisons philippines traditionnelles équipées de hamacs ou de terrasses d'où l'on peut contempler le paysage par exemple. Celui qui habite près de l'océan, accède à la plage par un sentier privé ; celui qui s'installe sur les collines, jouit encore plus du calme, bénéficie d'une vue sur les îles voisines que lui cache tout au plus la végétation et, s'il a de la chance, il peut admirer le lever et le coucher de soleil de sa véranda. Mais qu'importe l'endroit choisi : une superbe salle de bains en marbre occupe près de la moitié de l'habitation – même sur la terre ferme, tout tourne autour de l'eau.

Livre à emporter : « Infanta » de Bodo Kirchhoff

ANREISE	Die Privatinsel Pamalican liegt 300 km südlich von Manila, der Transfer per Flugzeug wird organisiert (300 $ pro Person).
PREIS	Treetop Casita 625 $ pro Nacht, Hillside Casita 750 $ pro Nacht, Beach Casita 800 $ pro Nacht, Villa für 6 bis 8 Personen ab 2425 $ pro Nacht.
ZIMMER	4 Treetop Casitas, 7 Hillside Casitas, 29 Beach Casitas, 2 Villen.
KÜCHE	Fantastische Meeresfrüchte, außerdem asiatische Gerichte und Barbecue am Strand.
GESCHICHTE	1993 eröffnet.
X-FAKTOR	Strand, Sonne, Segelboote – fertig ist das Paradies.

ACCÈS	L'île privée de Pamalican est située à 300 km au sud de Manille, le transfert par avion est organisé (300 $ par personne).
PRIX	Treetop Casita 625 $ la nuit, Hillside Casita 750 $ la nuit, Beach Casita 800 $ la nuit, villa pour 6 à 8 personnes à partir de 2425 $ la nuit.
CHAMBRES	4 Treetop Casitas, 7 Hillside Casitas, 29 Beach Casitas, 2 villas.
RESTAURATION	Fruits de mer fantastiques, cuisine asiatique et barbecue sur la plage.
HISTOIRE	Ouvert en 1993.
LE « PETIT PLUS »	Le soleil, la plage et les voiliers, qui dit mieux ?

Naturally Beautiful...
Ana Mandara Resort, Nha Trang

Ana Mandara Resort, Nha Trang

Naturally Beautiful

On the beach at Nha Trang, Vietnam shows its polished side. The white sand extends along the ocean for seven kilometres, palm-lined and so soft that you think you are lying in cotton wool. During the day you gaze at pure aquamarine, in the evening at a gently tinted play of colours with which the sun fades into the ocean. If you turn your gaze inland, you see nature in all of the green tones of a painter's palette merging with the houses, as well as people with a friendly, shy smile in their eyes – and the Ana Mandara Resort. In the style of a typical Vietnamese village, the hotel is situated in the midst of a tropical garden, is furnished with local wood, rattan and light-coloured fabrics, has shady boardwalks on which the sand crunches, open verandas and one of the most respected spas in the country. Beneath coconut palms and with the quiet murmur of the sea and waterfalls in the background, one relaxes here with massages in the open-air sala, under the Vichy shower or in the Japanese-inspired bath. Within just a few hours the tensions of a whole year dissolve into pleasure – the newly won energy can later be used for an excursion to one of the small islands off of Nha Trang, a diving trip or a drive to the nearby Bao Dai Villa. This is where Bao Dai, Vietnam's last emperor, spent his summers – with a dazzling view of the city, the sparkling water and a view to the horizon where, even then, the sun was already setting in such a cinematic way.

Book to pack: "The Moon Bamboo" by Thich Nhat Hanh

Ana Mandara Resort

Beachside Tran Phu Boulevard

Nha Trang, Vietnam

Tel. +84 (58) 82 98 29

Fax +84 (58) 82 96 29

Email: resvana@dng.vnn.vn

Website: www.sixsenses.com/ana-mandara

Booking: www.great-escapes-hotels.com

DIRECTIONS	Situated 450 km/280 miles northeast of Ho Chi Minh City and 2 km/1.2 miles from Nha Trang (15 minute drive to the airport).
RATES	Garden View Rooms starting at US$ 216, Sea View Rooms starting at US$ 246, Deluxe Rooms starting at US$ 278 per night, Ana Mandara Suites starting at US$ 407 (all per night and including breakfast).
ROOMS	32 Garden View Rooms, 8 Sea View Rooms, 24 Deluxe Rooms and 4 Ana Mandara Suites.
FOOD	Vietnamese dishes and ambitious East-meets-West menus.
HISTORY	Opened in September 1997.
X-FACTOR	Relax in one of Vietnam's best spas.

Von Natur aus schön

Am Strand von Nha Trang zeigt sich Vietnam von seiner Hochglanzseite. Über sieben Kilometer zieht sich der weiße Sand am Ozean entlang, palmengesäumt und so weich, dass man meint, in Watte zu liegen. Tagsüber fällt der Blick auf reines Aquamarin, abends auf ein weichgezeichnetes Farbspiel, mit dem die Sonne im Meer verglüht. Wer in Richtung Land schaut, sieht die Natur in sämtlichen Grüntönen des Malkastens auf Tuchfühlung mit den Häusern gehen, Menschen mit einem freundlich-schüchternen Lächeln in den Augen – und das Ana Mandara Resort. Im Stil eines typisch vietnamesischen Dorfes liegt das Hotel inmitten eines tropischen Gartens, ist mit einheimischen Hölzern, Rattan und hellen Stoffen ausgestattet, besitzt schattige *boardwalks*, auf denen der Sand knirscht, offene Veranden und eines der angesehensten Spas des Landes. Unter Kokospalmen und mit dem leisen Rauschen von Meer und Wasserfällen im Hintergrund entspannt man hier bei Massagen in der Open-air-Sala, unter der Vichy-Dusche oder im japanisch angehauchten Bad. Innerhalb weniger Stunden lösen sich die Verspannungen eines ganzen Jahres in Genuss auf – die neu gewonnene Energie wird später für den Ausflug auf eine der kleinen Inseln vor Nha Trang genutzt, einen Tauchgang oder die Fahrt zur nahen Bao Dai Villa. Dort verbrachte Vietnams letzter König Bao Dai seine Sommerfrische – mit Traumblick auf die Stadt, das glitzernde Wasser und einem Horizont, an dem die Sonne schon damals so kinotauglich unterging.

Buchtipp: »Der Mondbambus« von Thich Nhat Hanh

Une beauté naturelle

La plage de Nha Trang est l'une des plus belles du Viêt-nam. Bordée de palmiers, elle s'étire sur sept kilomètres le long de l'océan, et le sable est si blanc et si doux que l'on a l'impression de marcher sur de la ouate. Le jour les vagues ont une teinte aigue-marine, le soir une symphonie de couleurs floues s'élève pendant que le soleil embrase la mer. Celui qui regarde en direction des terres voit la végétation dans une superbe palette de verts se marier aux habitations, des gens timides et souriants et l'Ana Mandara Resort.
Edifié dans le style d'un village traditionnel vietnamien, l'hôtel est situé dans un vaste jardin tropical. L'intérieur fait la part belle aux bois régionaux, au rotin et aux étoffes claires. Il possède des caillebotis ombragés sur lesquels le sable crisse, des vérandas ouvertes et un des centres de remise en forme les plus renommés du pays. Sous les cocotiers et avec en fond sonore le doux grondement de la mer et des cascades, on se détend ici en se faisant masser en plein air, sous la douche Vichy ou dans la salle de bains aux accents nippons.
En l'espace de quelques heures, les tensions accumulées pendant toute l'année cèdent la place au plaisir. Ce regain d'énergie sera utile plus tard durant l'excursion sur une des petites îles qui se trouvent devant Nha Trang, pour aller faire de la plongée ou se rendre en voiture jusqu'à la villa de Bao Dai. C'est là en effet, que le dernier empereur du Viêt-nam se réfugiait durant les grandes chaleurs. Il avait d'ici une vue superbe sur la ville, sur l'eau scintillante et sur les couchers de soleil que le cinéma n'avait pas encore découvert.

Livre à emporter : « La plénitude de l'instant » de Thich Nhat Hanh

ANREISE	450 km nordöstlich von Ho Chi Minh City gelegen und 2 km von Nha Trang entfernt (15-minütige Fahrt zum Flughafen).
PREIS	Gardenview Room ab 216 $, Seaview Room ab 246 $, Deluxe Room ab 278 $, Ana Mandara-Suite ab 407 $ (alle pro Nacht und inklusive Frühstück).
ZIMMER	32 Gardenview Rooms, 8 Seaview Rooms, 24 Deluxe Rooms und 4 Ana-Mandara-Suiten.
KÜCHE	Vietnamesische Gerichte und ambitionierte East-meets-West-Menüs.
GESCHICHTE	Im September 1997 eröffnet.
X-FAKTOR	Eines der besten Spas in Vietnam.

ACCÈS	A 450 km au nord-est de Ho Chi Minh City et à 2 km de Nha Trang (15 min en voiture jusqu'à l'aéroport).
PRIX	Gardenview Room à partir de 216 $, Seaview Room à partir de 246 $, Deluxe Room à partir de 278 $, Ana Mandara Suite à partir de 407 $ (prix par nuit petit-déjeuner compris).
CHAMBRES	32 Gardenview Rooms, 8 Seaview Rooms, 24 Deluxe Rooms et 4 Ana Mandara Suites.
RESTAURATION	Cuisine vietnamienne et menus East-meets-West.
HISTOIRE	Ouvert depuis septembre 1997.
LE « PETIT PLUS »	Un des plus beaux centres de remise en forme du Viêt-nam.

Ein leuchtendes Beispiel

Selten sieht ein Berg so sanft aus. Der Fuji liegt mit seinen weichen Flanken da, als wäre er nicht aus Fels gemacht, sondern bloß ein Haufen grünbrauner Sand, den eine Riesenhand zu Boden rieseln ließ und mit Schneekristallen bestreut hat. Doch Japans heiliger Gipfel ist durchaus eine Herausforderung. Nur im Juli und August erlaubt er Wanderern, sich ihm zu nähern – wer hier einen Sonnenaufgang erleben möchte, muss warme Kleidung, Kondition und ein Faible für überfüllte Matratzenlager mitbringen. Da ist es eine Überlegung wert, auf das morgendliche Farbspiel zu verzichten und dafür hundertfach entspannter zu logieren – im Gôra Kadan etwa. Das märchenhafte Haus steht im Nationalpark von Hakone, um sich herum nur Bäume, deren Konturen so scharf gezeichnet sind, als wären es bunte Scherenschnitte und Musterbeispiele an Klarheit und Symmetrie. Einst verbrachte die kaiserliche Familie hier ihre Sommerwochenenden – seit 1952 ist das Gôra Kadan ein Hotel mit typischen Tatami-Matten, Zypressenbädern und einer Lichtdramaturgie, die den besten Theaterbühnen der Erde Konkurrenz machen könnte. Hier eine schimmernde Laterne, dort fünf Lampen, die goldglänzende Kegel auf den Steinweg werfen, und über dem Pool ein kassettenartiges Glasdach, das aus Sonnenstrahlen einen Regenbogen zaubert. Es ist ein Konzentrat des stillen Japan – noch im Energiefeld des Fuji gelegen, aber weit weg vom Trubel rund um den Puderzuckergipfel.

Buchtipp: »Naokos Lächeln« von Haruki Murakami

Calme et lumière

Rares sont les montagnes qui ont l'air aussi peu menaçantes. Le Fuji-yama aux doux versants ne donne pas l'impression d'être fait de pierres et de roches, mais d'être un tas de sable vert-brun qu'une main de géant aurait fait ruisseler sur le sol et poudré de cristaux de neige. Pourtant l'ascension de la montagne sacrée du Japon n'en représente pas moins un défi. Ce n'est que durant les mois de juillet et d'août qu'il permet aux promeneurs de l'approcher – celui qui veut assister ici au lever du soleil, doit apporter des vêtements chauds, jouir d'une bonne condition physique et avoir un faible pour les campement surpeuplés. A tout prendre, mieux vaut peut-être renoncer à ce flamboiement des couleurs matinal et prendre ses aises au Gôra Kadan par exemple. Ressemblant à une maison de conte de fées, l'hôtel est situé dans le parc national de Harkone. Exemple de clarté et de symétrie, il est entouré d'arbres aux contours si nets qu'on les croirait découpés au ciseau. Jadis la famille impériale y venait durant l'été passer les fins de semaine. Depuis 1952, le Gôra Kadan est un hôtel traditionnel avec tatamis, cuves de cyprès et une dramaturgie de la lumière qui pourrait entrer en compétition avec les meilleures scènes de théâtre du monde entier. Ici la lueur tremblotante d'une lanterne, là les boules d'or que dessinent cinq lampes sur le chemin de pierre, et, au-dessus de la piscine, un toit de verre en cassettes qui métamorphose les rayons du soleil en arc en ciel. L'hôtel reflète toute la sérénité du Japon et s'il se trouve encore dans le champ d'énergie du Fuji-yama, il est à mille lieux de toute cette agitation qui règne autour de lui.

**Livre à emporter : « Au sud de la frontière, à l'ouest du soleil »
de Haruki Murakami**

ANREISE	90 km südwestlich von Tokio (Stadtzentrum) gelegen, 170 km vom Flughafen Tokio-Narita entfernt.	ACCÈS	Situé à 90 km au sud-ouest de Tokyo (centre) et à 170 km de l'aéroport de Tokyo-Narita.
PREIS	Standardzimmer ab 450 $ pro Nacht, Suite ab 630 $ pro Nacht.	PRIX	Chambre standard à partir de 450 $ la nuit, suite à partir de 630 $ la nuit.
ZIMMER	38 Zimmer, darunter 12 Suiten.	CHAMBRES	38 chambres, dont 12 suites.
KÜCHE	Traditionelle Kaiseki-Küche; fast zu schön zum Aufessen.	RESTAURATION	Cuisine kaiseki traditionnelle ; si belle qu'on hésite à la consommer.
GESCHICHTE	Einst der kaiserliche Sommersitz, 1952 als Hotel eröffnet und 1989 renoviert.	HISTOIRE	Résidence d'été impériale, l'hôtel a ouvert ses portes en 1952 et a été rénové en 1989.
X-FAKTOR	Die Ruhe selbst – inmitten einer traumhaften Natur.	LE « PETIT PLUS »	Le calme dans une nature enchanteresse.

South America

Brazil • Uruguay • Argentina
Chile • Bolivia
Peru • Ecuador • Colombia

Photos by Tuca Reinés   *Text by* Christiane Reiter   *Edited by* Angelika Taschen

"Nothing is certain, but all things are possible."
Peruvian saying

"If you look after your land, the trees and all of nature will shed their light.
It is then that we know we can benefit greatly from the earth."
Inca saying

"He who has once drunk the waters of the Amazon will always return."
Brazilian saying

● 552 Hotel San Pedro de Majagua

VENEZUELA

GUYANA

COLOMBIA

SURINAME FRENCH GUIANA

ECUADOR

● 544 Kapawi Ecolodge & Reserve

PERU

BRAZIL

● 536 Hotel Monasterio

● 436 Txai Resort

● 446 Pousada Etnia

BOLIVIA

Vila Naiá – Paralelo 17° 462 ● 454 Ponta do Camarão

● 528 Hotel de Sal

CHILE

PARAGUAY

● 476 Yacutinga Lodge

● 484 Pirá Lodge

URUGUAY

ARGENTINA

● 470 La Posada del Faro

● 492 La Escondida
500 Estancia Santa Rita

Hotel Antumalal 518 ●

explora en Patagonia 510 ●

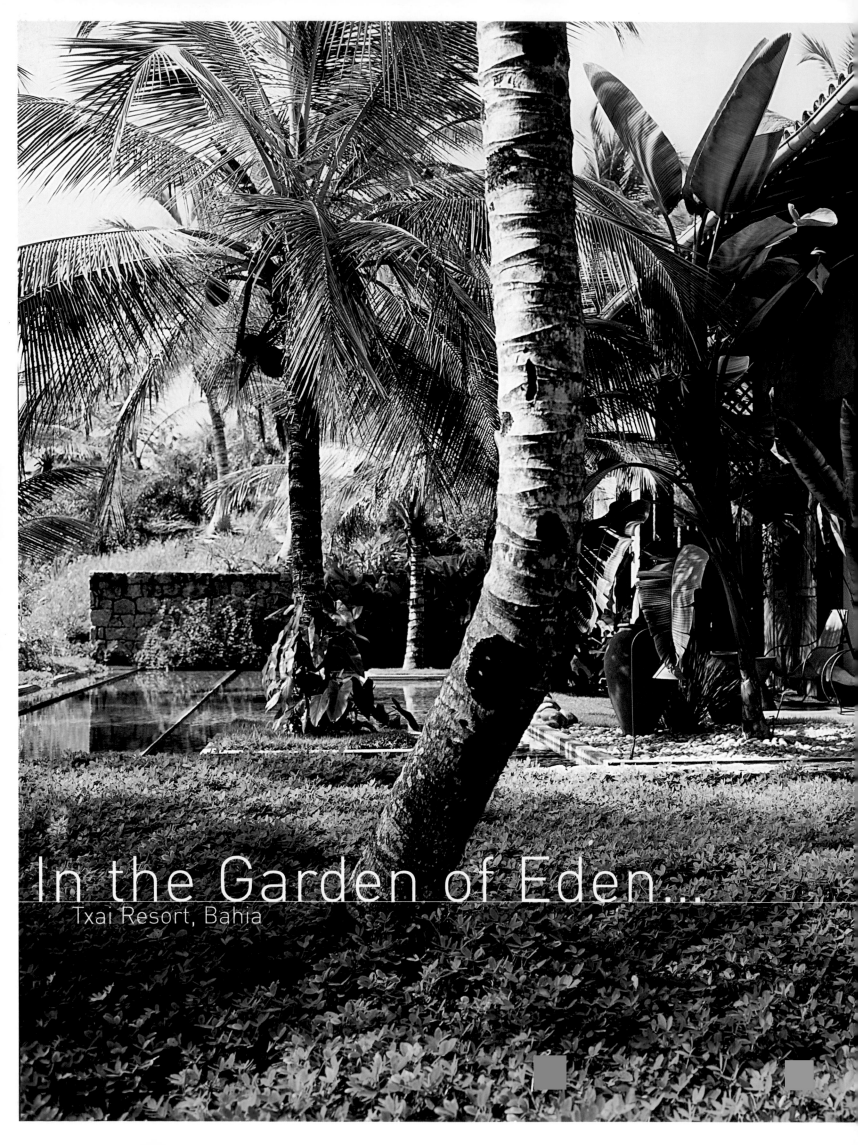

In the Garden of Eden...
Txai Resort, Bahia

Txai Resort, Bahia

In the Garden of Eden

Itacaré is in the south of Bahia, on the Cocoa Coast. In the mid-19th century, the "black gold" made it famous, and it became the foremost port of export in the region. Brazil's great writer Jorge Amado immortalised that cocoa boom in his novel "Gabriela, Clove and Cinnamon" – Amado was born in the region himself, on a cocoa plantation near Ilhéus. But ever since 1989 a fungal blight has annually been wiping out almost the entire crop all along the entire coast, and with it the regional economy – which has made tourism all the more important. One of the most appealing destinations is the Txai Resort, set amid a 100-hectare coconut grove which looks like a soft green pillow from the air. In the language of the Kaxinawa Indians, "Txai" means "companion", and in the spirit of this philosophy every guest is received as a family friend. The bungalows, built up on stilts, have all the distinctive atmosphere of private homes, and are furnished in the snug, rustic style of Bahia – no superfluous frills, dark wood, light fabrics, and colourwashed walls. The moment you wake you're looking at a picture-book natural setting, through the gossamer haze of the mosquito net. You can idle the day away on a recliner or at the beach, and succumb to the rhythms of Brazilian music in the evening. The resort supports re-afforestation projects and offers natural history excursions into the surrounding area. There's also a spa for relaxing massages, and yoga classes, and a restaurant where you can feed your eyes on the fabulous view as you dine on phenomenal fish.

Book to pack: "Gabriela, Clove and Cinnamon" by Jorge Amado

Txai Resort	
Rodovia Ilhéus Itacaré, km 48	
Itacaré	
Bahia, Brazil	
CEP 45530000	
Tel. (55) 736346936	
Fax (55) 736346956	
E-mail: txairesort@txai.com.br	
Website: www.txai.com.br	
Booking: www.great-escapes-hotels.com	

DIRECTIONS	15 km/10 miles south of Itacaré, 50 minutes by road from Ilhéus airport (transfer can be arranged on request)
RATES	Suite from US$ 275 for 2 persons, bungalow from US$ 310. Full board included (excluding drinks)
ROOMS	16 bungalows, 10 suites (for 2)
FOOD	Restaurant serving Bahian dishes such as "moqueca" (seafood and fish)
HISTORY	Opened in 2001
X-FACTOR	It's like spending your vacation with good friends

Our little realm...
Pousada Etnia, Bahia

Pousada Etnia, Bahia

Our little realm

There are times when your ticket quite clearly reads "Porto Seguro, Brazil" – and all the same you land in the oriental world of the Arabian Nights, or on the shores of the Mediterranean. In fact you're on vacation at the Pousada Etnia, a charming retreat tucked away in a dreamy Trancoso park. It entirely lives up to its name, and the bungalows and apartments are conceived in homage to a variety of places and cultures. The "Trancoso" is the apartment closest in feel to the Brazilian setting. It is simply furnished with rattan armchairs, native wood, and light-hued fabrics, and its understated grace sets off the exuberance of the outside world on the doorstep all the more. Dark furniture reminiscent of colonial times, animal prints, and African-inspired art are the hallmark of the "Tribal" apartment, with its discreet safari mood. In the "Cottage" you can enjoy the bright and breezy style of tropical islands such as the Seychelles, with just a hint of the English south. If other European moods are what you crave, relax in the "Mediterráneo" on the blue-and-white cushions and marvel at the model sailing ships. Finally, all the magic of the Orient is yours in the "Maroccos" bungalow with its typical pointed doors, the golden gleam of brass, and hand-woven carpets. The proprietors of Etnia aim to transcend borders and create a cosmopolitan kaleidoscope where the best of various cultures is juxtaposed and possesses a new fascination in the encounter. The hotel shop sells antiques and art to match the styles – and throws in a boundless enthusiasm for the Pousada philosophy for free.

Book to pack: "Brazil" by John Updike

Pousada Etnia
Rua Principal
Trancoso – Porto Seguro
Bahia, Brazil
CEP 458 18 000
Tel. (55) 73 6681137
Fax (55) 73 6681549
E-mail: etniabrasil@etniabrasil.com.br
Website: www.etniabrasil.com.br
Booking: www.great-escapes-hotels.com

DIRECTIONS	Situated 40 km/25 miles south of Porto Seguro international airport. Transfer by ferry (Porto Seguro-Arrial d'Ajuda) and road or by road only
RATES	Apartments from US$ 118 for 2 persons, bungalow from US$ 153 for 2 persons. Breakfast included
ROOMS	1 Bungalow "Maroccos" and 4 apartments
FOOD	Light cuisine in the poolside restaurant. The bar is famed for its drinks
HISTORY	Opened in December 2002
X-FACTOR	A meeting place for the world's cultures

Unsere kleine Welt

Manchmal steht auf dem Flugschein ganz deutlich »Porto Seguro, Brasilien« – und man landet doch in tausendundeiner Nacht des Orients oder an den Gestaden des Mittelmeers ... Dann nämlich, wenn man seinen Urlaub in der Pousada Etnia verbringt, einer charmanten Anlage mitten in einem verwunschenen Park von Trancoso. Sie macht ihrem Namen alle Ehre und hat die Bungalows und Apartments als Hommage an unterschiedliche Destinationen und Kulturen entworfen. Der brasilianischen Umgebung am nächsten ist das Apartment »Trancoso«, das schlicht mit Rattansesseln, einheimischem Holz und hellen Stoffen eingerichtet ist und dank seiner Zurückhaltung die üppige Natur vor der Tür nur noch besser zur Geltung bringt. Dunkle und an Kolonialzeiten erinnernde Möbel, Animalprints und afrikanische inspirierte Kunst zeichnen die Wohnung »Tribal« aus und sorgen für dezentes Safari-Feeling; das luftige Flair tropischer Inseln wie der Seychellen, gemischt mit einem Hauch Südengland, herrscht im »Cottage«. Wer sich nach weiteren europäischen Einflüssen sehnt, zieht in die Unterkunft »Mediterrâneo« und entspannt dort auf blau-weiß-gestreifen Kissen oder bewundert Segelschiff-Modelle. Die Magie des Orients schließlich besitzt das Haus »Maroccos« – mit den typischen, spitz zulaufenden Türen, goldglänzendem Messing und handgewebten Teppichen. Es geht den Besitzern von Etnia darum, Grenzen aufzuheben und ein kosmopolitisches Kaleidoskop zu schaffen, in dem das Beste aus verschiedenen Kulturkreisen unvermittelt aufeinander trifft und gerade deshalb so faszinierend ist. Im hoteleigenen Shop werden passende Antiquitäten und Kunst verkauft – die Begeisterung für die Philosophie der Pousada gibt es gratis mit dazu.

Buchtipp: »Brasilien« von John Updike

Citoyens du monde

On peut très bien lire « Porto Seguro, Brésil » sur le billet d'avion et se retrouver dans une ambiance de Mille et Une Nuits ou sur les rivages de la Méditerranée... C'est ce qui arrive si l'on passe ses vacances a la Pousada Etnia, un hôtel charmant situé dans un parc ravissant à Trancoso. Son nom est tout un programme et, de fait, les bungalows et les appartements ont été conçus et décorés en hommage à divers pays et cultures. L'appartement « Trancoso » se rapproche le plus de l'environnement brésilien avec ses fauteuils de rotin, ses essences locales et ses étoffes claires – sa sobriété met en valeur la végétation exubérante qui s'épanouit au pied de la porte. L'appartement « Tribal », quant à lui, est doté de meubles sombres évoquant l'ère coloniale, d'impressions animalières et d'œuvres inspirées de l'art africain. Le « Cottage » marie l'atmosphère des îles heureuses et des accents cosy du sud anglais. Celui qui désire d'autres influences européennes s'installe dans l'appartement « Mediterrâneo », se détend sur des coussins rayés bleu et blanc ou admire des maquettes de voiliers. Et enfin la maison « Maroccos » avec ses portes en ogive, ses laitons étincelants et ses tapis tissés à la main offre toute la magie de l'Orient. Les propriétaires d'Etnia veulent abolir les frontières et créer une mosaïque cosmopolite réunissant le meilleur de ce que les diverses cultures ont à offrir, et cette rencontre est fascinante. La boutique de l'hôtel vend les antiquités et les œuvres d'art correspondants – l'enthousiasme pour la philosophie qui règne en ces lieux est gracieusement offert en sus.

Livre à emporter : « Brésil » de John Updike

ANREISE	40 Kilometer südlich des Internationalen Flughafens Porto Seguro gelegen. Transfer per Fähre (Porto Seguro-Arrial d'Ajuda) und Auto oder nur per Auto
PREISE	Apartment ab US$ 118 für 2 Personen, Bungalow ab US$ 153 für 2 Personen. Mit Frühstück
ZIMMER	1 Bungalow »Maroccos« und 4 Apartments
KÜCHE	Leichte Küche am Pool-Restaurant. Die Bar ist für ihre Drinks berühmt
GESCHICHTE	Im Dezember 2002 eröffnet
X-FAKTOR	Ein Treffpunkt der Kulturen

ACCÈS	Situé à 40 kilomètres au sud de l'aéroport international de Porto Seguro. Transfert par ferry (Porto Seguro-Arrial d'Ajuda) et voiture ou seulement par voiture
PRIX	Appartement à partir de US$ 118 pour deux personnes, bungalow à partir de US$ 153 pour 2 personnes. Petit-déjeuner inclus
CHAMBRES	1 bungalow « Maroccos » et 4 appartements
RESTAURATION	Cuisine légère au restaurant de la piscine. Le bar est renommé pour ses cocktails
HISTOIRE	Ouvert en décembre 2002
LE « PETIT PLUS »	Le rendez-vous des cultures

The discovery of solitude...
Ponta do Camarão, Bahia

Ponta do Camarão, Bahia

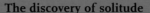

The discovery of solitude

If you make the journey to Caraíva, you can leave the trunk behind and travel light. "Flip-flops, tennis shoes, shorts, T-shirts, swimming gear, a sun hat, suntan lotion, and money" – that is all the Caraíva website recommends visitors bring with them. Caraíva is tucked away on the south coast of Bahia, cut off by the ocean on the one side and the river on the other. There are no surfaced roads, no cars, no electricity. And nonetheless the village offers sheer luxury: the discovery of solitude, closeness to nature, and the exclusive bungalows of Ponta do Camarão amid the greenery, with a view so gloriously close to kitsch it rivals any picture postcard. The turquoise of the water is taken up in the colour the walls are painted, and the sunlight is echoed in the yellow door frames and orange valances. A maximum of four guests at a time are spoilt rotten by Fernanda and Flavio. Revel in being the master, for a time, of this bright and spacious house. At the thermal pool you can enjoy massages with natural oils or relax in a mineral bath. And every day you can order the choicest of fare – Flavio's fish is sheer poetry, and the home-baked bread is to die for. On a day that begins in this paradise, everything's bound to be perfect. Take a walk by Satu Lagoon, for instance, and drink cool coconut milk straight from the coconut at the plantation. If you like boats, explore a whole new world of rain forest and mangroves on the Rio Caraíva, or if fishing is your preference you can go in search of supper. No one here bothers with travel agents – all you need do is have a word with your amiable hosts, or one of the fishermen on the beach, and ask for their tips. But do be sure to plan your evenings. Keep the hours of darkness free for gazing out from your Ponta do Camarão bungalow – the night sky over Caraíva is truly awash with stars.

Book to pack: "By the River Piedra I sat down and wept" by Paulo Coelho

Ponta do Camarão between Praia do Espelho and Caraíva Bahia Brazil Tel. (55) 73 99796269 E-mail: flanana@uol.com.br No website. Caraíva can be found in the Internet at: www.caraiva.com.br Booking: www.great-escapes-hotels.com	**DIRECTIONS** Situated 115 km/72 miles south of Porto Seguro airport. The two-hour road transfer is organised. The final stretch, by river, is done by canoe **RATES** Bungalow US$ 400 for 2 people. Includes airport transfer and full board **ROOMS** 2 Bungalows for 2 people (each offering 100 square metres/1,076 square feet of accommodation) **FOOD** Brazilian cuisine with a hint of the oriental. Proprietor Flavio likes to cook fish and to prepare the food according to his guests' personal wishes **HISTORY** Opened in October 2002 **X-FACTOR** Definitely an insider tip

Die Entdeckung der Einsamkeit

Wer nach Caraíva reist, kann den Schrankkoffer getrost zu Hause lassen. »Flip Flops, Tennisschuhe, Shorts, T-Shirts, Badesachen, Sonnenhut, Sonnencreme und Geld« – das ist alles, was die ortseigene Website künftigen Gästen an Gepäck empfiehlt. Caraíva versteckt sich an der Südküste von Bahia, isoliert vom Ozean auf der einen und dem Fluss auf der anderen Seite, ohne asphaltierte Straßen, ohne Autos, ohne Strom. Und dennoch bietet das Dorf Luxus: die Entdeckung der Einsamkeit, die Nähe zur Natur und die exklusiven Bungalows von Ponta do Camarão – im Grünen gelegen und mit einer Aussicht so kitschig-schön wie eine Fototapete. Das Türkisblau des Wassers spiegelt sich in der Wandfarbe wieder und das Sonnenlicht in den gelben Tür-rahmen und Einfassungen sowie den orangefarbenen Volants. Maximal vier Personen genießen hier das Verwöhn-programm von Fernanda und Flavio: Sie sind Herren auf Zeit über ein helles Haus mit fast 100 m², können sich im Thermalbad mit natürlichen Ölen massieren lassen oder im Salzbad entspannen und sich jeden Tag ihr Leibgericht wünschen – Flavios Fisch ist ein Gedicht, und ins selbst gebackene Brot möchte man sich am liebsten hineinlegen. An Tagen, die in diesem Paradies beginnen, kann eigentlich nichts mehr schief gehen. Man spaziert z. B. an der Lagune von Satu entlang und trinkt bei der kleinen Plantage kühle Kokosmilch frisch aus der Nuss. Bootsfreunde schippern auf dem Rio Caraíva durch Regenwald und Mangroven in eine andere Welt, und Angler machen sich geduldig auf die Suche nach ihrem Abendessen. Reiseagenturen braucht hier niemand – es reicht vollkommen aus, die liebenswerten Gastgeber oder einen der Fischer am Strand anzusprechen und um die besten Tipps zu bitten. Nur den Abend sollte man fest planen und vor den Bungalows von Ponta do Camarão einfach in die Nacht schauen – der Himmel über Caraíva ist ein Sternenmeer.

Buchtipp: »Am Ufer des Rio Piedra saß ich und weinte« von Paulo Coelho

La découverte de la solitude

Celui qui se rend à Caraíva, n'a pas besoin d'emmener de grosses valises. « Tongs, tennis, t-shirts, shorts, maillots de bain, chapeau, crème solaire et de l'argent », voilà ce qu'on peut lire sur le site web de Caraíva. Caraíva est niché sur la côte sud de Bahia, isolé du reste du monde par l'Océan d'un côté et par le fleuve de l'autre, sans route goudronnée, sans voitures ni électricité. Et pourtant le village offre un luxe qui n'a pas de prix : la découverte de la solitude, la proximité de la nature et les bungalows de Ponta do Camarão absolument uniques dans leur genre – avec la végétation luxuriante qui les entoure et leur vue digne d'une carte postale. Le bleu turquoise de l'eau se reflète sur les murs et la lumière du soleil, dans les encadrements jaunes de portes et de fenêtre ainsi que dans les étoffes orangées. Quatre personnes au maximum peuvent se laisser choyer ici par Fernanda et Flavio. Résidant dans une demeure claire de près de 100 mètres carrés, les clients peuvent se faire masser avec des huiles naturelles ou se détendre dans un bain de sel marin. Ils peuvent aussi commander tous les jours leur plat favori, le poisson préparé par Flavio est un poème et son pain mai-son, un vrai régal. Les jours passés dans ce paradis sont des moments de rêve. On peut se promener par exemple le long du lagon de Satu et boire un lait de coco bien frais dans la petite plantation. Les amoureux du bateau descendront le Rio Caraíva à travers la forêt tropicale et les mangroves, les pêcheurs attendront avec patience que leur repas du soir frétille au bout de la ligne. Il suffit de demander à l'hôte plein de gentillesse quels sont ses meilleurs tuyaux. Mais n'entreprenez rien le soir, contentez-vous de regarder l'obscurité devant les bungalows de Ponta do Camarão – le ciel étoilé au-dessus de Caraíva est une splendeur.

Livre à emporter : « Sur le bord de la rivière Piedra » de Paulo Coelho

ANREISE	115 Kilometer südlich des Flughafens von Porto Seguro gelegen. Zweistündiger Transfer per Auto wird organisiert. Das letzte Stück über den Fluss legt man im Kanu zurück	ACCÈS	Situé à 115 kilomètres au sud de l'aéroport de Porto Seguro. Le transfert en voiture (deux heures) est organisé. La dernière partie sur le fleuve se fait en canoë
PREISE	Bungalow US$ 400 für 2 Personen. Mit Flughafentransfer und Vollpension	PRIX	Bungalow US$ 400 pour 2 personnes. Transfert depuis l'aéroport et pension complète compris
ZIMMER	2 Bungalows für je 2 Personen (je 100 Quadratmeter Wohnfläche)	CHAMBRES	2 bungalows pour 2 Personen (de 100 mètres carrés chacun)
KÜCHE	Brasilianische Küche mit leicht orientalischem Touch. Besitzer Flavio kocht viel Fisch und ganz nach persön-lichem Geschmack der Gäste	CUISINE	Cuisine brésilienne avec une légère note orientale. Le propriétaire Flavio cuisine beaucoup de plats à base de poisson et tient compte des goûts de ses clients
GESCHICHTE	Im Oktober 2002 eröffnet	HISTOIRE	Ouvert depuis octobre 2002
X-FAKTOR	Ein Geheimtipp	LE « PETIT PLUS »	Une adresse à garder pour soi

A hidden paradise...
Vila Naiá – Paralelo 17°, Bahia

Vila Naiá – Paralelo 17°, Bahia

A hidden paradise

This paradise isn't one with an address. There's no zip code, no streeet name, no house number. No guidebook or map will help you find it – to get to Vila Naiá, you need the sixth sense for orientation that a pilot, rally driver, or helmsman has. It's a small resort, opened only in September 2004, on the Atlantic coast near Corumbau, on the edge of the Monte Pascoal National Park and a fishing reservation where only the indigenous population are allowed out to sea. Bahia, otherwise so temperamental, seems worlds away. All you can hear is the breeze in the palm fronds and the wavelets lapping on the beach. The air you breathe has a mild salty tang, and the sun is warm on your skin. For ten years, architect Renato Marques and owner Renata Mellão worked at the Vila Naiá concept, till the buildings were as plain and true to the local spirit as the natural world all around – not too much the ecological resort, and not too understated on the luxuries for guests who like their creature comforts. The four apartments and four houses are simple of line, panelled in dark wood within, and not over-furnished. The only strong colours added to the natural hues are the chairs, hammocks and throws. The kitchen is a no-frills affair as well. At Vila Naiá, Maria Alice Solimene prepares typical Brazilian specialities and plans her menu to fit the fishermen's catch that morning and according to what the garden provides. Those with even more purist tastes can eat at Rafael Rosa, where the manager and second maitre is probably the only chef in the country to be serving "raw living food".

Book to pack: "Captains of the Sands" by Jorge Amado

Vila Naiá – Paralelo 17°	DIRECTIONS	Situated 60 km/38 miles south of Porto Seguro airport. Transfer by light aircraft (20 minutes, US$ 323), Landrover (approx. 4 hours, US$ 145) or Landrover and boat (2 hours 45 minutes, US$ 340)
Corumbau		
Bahia		
Brazil	RATES	Apartment US$ 260 per night for 2 persons, house US$ 388 per night for 2. Full board included
Tel. (55) 73 5731006		
Fax (55) 73 5731006	ROOMS	4 apartments for 2 persons, 4 houses for 3 persons
E-mail: info@vilanaia.com.br	FOOD	Brazilian cuisine and "raw living food"
Website: www.vilanaia.com.br	HISTORY	Ten years in the making, it opened in 2004
Booking: www.great-escapes-hotels.com	X-FACTOR	Right in the heart of nature

Das versteckte Paradies

Das Paradies hat keine genaue Adresse – keine Straße, keine Hausnummer, keine Postleitzahl. Bei seiner Entdeckung nützt kein Reiseführer und keine Landkarte – wer zur Vila Naiá möchte, muss dem Orientierungssinn des Piloten, Fahrers oder Bootsmannes vertrauen. Das kleine, erst im September 2004 eröffnete Resort liegt an der Atlantikküste bei Corumbau; am Rand des Nationalparks Monte Pascoal und eines Fischreservats, in dem nur die Einheimischen hinaus aufs Meer fahren dürfen. Hier scheint das sonst so temperamentvolle Bahia Welten entfernt zu sein; man hört den Wind in den Palmen und die Wellen an den Strand rauschen, atmet salzig-sanfte Luft und spürt die Sonne auf der Haut. Zehn Jahre lang haben Architekt Renato Marques und Besitzerin Renata Mellão am Konzept der Vila Naiá getüftelt, bis die Häuser genau so schlicht und ursprünglich wie die umliegende Natur waren, nicht zu sehr in Richtung »Öko-Resort« abdrifteten und nicht zu wenig Luxus für anspruchsvolle Gäste bieten. Die vier Apartments und vier Häuser wurden innen mit dunklem Holz verkleidet und zeigen einfache Linien und sparsame Möblierung – einige bunte Stühle, Hängematten und Decken sind die einzigen Akzente inmitten der Naturtöne. Ohne Schnörkel kommt auch die Küche aus: In der Vila Naiá kocht Maria Alice Solimene typisch brasilianische Spezialitäten und richtet ihre Menükarte danach aus, was die Fischer jeden Morgen anliefern oder der hauseigene Biogarten hergibt. Wer es noch puristischer mag, sollte bei Rafael Rosa essen: Der Manager der Anlage und zugleich ihr zweiter Maître serviert als wahrscheinlich einziger Küchenchef des Landes »raw living food«, ausschließlich rohe und naturbelassene Gerichte.

Buchtipp: »Herren des Strandes« von Jorge Amado

Un paradis caché

Le paradis n'a pas d'adresse – pas de rue, pas de numéro, pas de code postal. Pour le découvrir, les guides et les cartes ne servent à rien. Celui qui veut se rendre à la Vila Naiá doit se fier au sens de l'orientation du pilote d'avion, du chauffeur de voiture ou du capitaine de bateau. Le petit hôtel, ouvert seulement depuis septembre 2004, se trouve sur la côte atlantique près de Corumbau, en bordure du parc national de Monte Pascoal et d'une réserve maritime où seuls les autochtones ont le droit de pénétrer. La ville trépidante de Bahia semble à des années-lumière. Ici on entend le murmure du vent dans les palmiers et le grondement des vagues sur la plage, on respire l'air marin et l'on sent la caresse du soleil sur sa peau. Pendant dix ans, l'architecte Renato Marques et la propriétaire Renata Mellão ont travaillé sur le concept de la Vila Naiá, jusqu'à ce que les maisons soient aussi simples et authentiques que la nature environnante, sans tomber dans l'écologie à outrance mais en offrant assez de luxe pour les clients exigeants. Les quatre appartements et les quatre maisons habillés de bois sombre ont des lignes sobres et sont décorés sans exubérance – les chaises, hamacs et couvertures sont les seuls accents de couleur parmi les tons naturels. La cuisine est elle aussi dénuée de fioritures : à la Vila Naiá, Maria Alice Solimene prépare des spécialités typiquement brésiliennes en fonction des poissons que lui apportent les pêcheurs tous les matins ou en fonction des produits du jardin bio. Si vous êtes encore plus puriste, ne manquez pas d'aller manger chez Rafael Rosa : le gérant de l'hôtel, qui est en même temps le deuxième maître queux, est probablement le seul chef du pays à servir une « raw living food », des plats exclusivement crus et naturels.

Livre à emporter : « Capitaines des sables » de Jorge Amado

ANREISE	60 Kilometer südlich des Flughafens Porto Seguro gelegen. Transfer per Kleinflugzeug (20 Minuten, US$ 323), Landrover (4 Stunden, US$ 145) oder Landrover und Boot (2 Stunden 45 Minuten, US$ 340)
PREISE	Apartment US$ 260 für 2 Personen, Haus US$ 388 für 2 Personen. Mit Vollpension
ZIMMER	4 Apartments für max. 2 Personen, 4 Häuser für max. 3 Personen
KÜCHE	Brasilianische Gerichte und »raw living food«
GESCHICHTE	Nach zehnjähriger Entwicklung 2004 eröffnet
X-FAKTOR	Im Herzen der Natur

ACCÈS	Situé à 60 kilomètres au sud de l'aéroport de Porto Seguro. Transfert en petit avion (20 minutes, US$ 323), en Landrover (env. 4 heures, US$ 145) ou en Landrover et en bateau (2 heures 45 minutes, US$ 340)
PRIX	Appartement US$ 260 pour 2 personnes, maison US$ 388 pour 2 personnes. Pension complète
CHAMBRES	4 appartements pour 2 personnes au maximum, 4 maisons pour 3 personnes au maximum
RESTAURATION	Plats brésiliens et « raw living food »
HISTOIRE	Ouvert en 2004 après une conception de dix ans
LE « PETIT PLUS »	On ne saurait être encore plus proche de la nature

A room with a view...
La Posada del Faro, Maldonado

La Posada del Faro, Maldonado

A room with a view

East of Montevideo and Punta del Este lies the vacation capital of Uruguay: white sandy beaches lapped by the waves of the Atlantic and the River Plate, and small townships with all the necessary infrastructure of shops, restaurants, and clubs. Many are overrun in the high season – but one place that has so far remained relatively quiet is José Ignacio, about 30 kilometres or just under 20 miles from Punta del Este. The perfect retreat for a summer vacation is the Posada del Faro, with its gleaming white walls, awnings, and sun umbrellas. It's just 30 metres (100 feet) from the ocean, and the views it commands of the Atlantic would be fit for the cinema. The pool is the purest blue, and so (most days) is the sky; and if that's not enough blue for you, there are blue-painted doors or blue carpets here and there around the interior. Otherwise the ten rooms are cream-coloured, with a good deal of wood; every room is individually furnished, but they all have their own secluded terrace with recliners or hammocks. In the evenings when the barbecue is fired up for the typical "asado" and diners take their places at long tables, it's like eating with good friends. The Posada del Faro is an excellent base for local excursions – to bathing resorts such as Punta del Este or La Paloma, to the Isla de Lobos with its colony of sea lions, or to Cerro Catedral, which at 513 metres (just under 1,600 feet) is Uruguay's loftiest peak! **Book to pack: "Blood Pact & Other Stories" by Mario Benedetti**

La Posada del Faro	
Calle de la Bahia esquina Timonel	
Faro de José Ignacio	
Maldonado	
Uruguay	
Tel. (598) 4862110	
Fax (598) 4862111	
E-mail: informacion@posadadelfaro.com	
Website: www.posadadelfaro.com	
Booking: www.great-escapes-hotels.com	

DIRECTIONS	Situated 30 km/19 miles northeast of Punta del Este, on the Atlantic coast
RATES	Double rooms from US$ 105 for 2 persons. Breakfast included
ROOMS	10 individually furnished double rooms
FOOD	A small barbecue restaurant with a fine view of the ocean
HISTORY	A new retreat, alongside an old lighthouse dating from 1877
X-FACTOR	Like a private villa far from the madding crowd

Der Natur auf der Spur

Manchmal wünscht man sich ja auf diese fantastischen Abenteuerspielplätze zurück: Wo man im tiefsten Wald durchs Gebüsch pirschte und auf Hängebrücken gefährlich aussehende Schluchten überquerte, wo Blätter so groß wie Surfbretter grüne Dächer über den Wegen bildeten und wo am offenen Feuer Stockbrot geröstet werden konnte. Diese Sehnsucht kann gestillt werden – mit einer Reise zur Yacutinga Lodge, die sich im Dschungel an der Grenze zwischen Argentinien und Brasilien versteckt. In Harmonie mit der verwunschenen Natur wurden hier Häuser aus einheimischem Stein und dicken Holzplanken gebaut, jedes von Grün umhüllt wie von einem weichen Mantel und mit organisch geformten Möbeln sowie Stoffen in weichen Tönen ausgestattet. Yacutinga ist ein umfassendes Umweltprojekt und verspricht komfortablen Ökotourismus – es lässt seine Gäste nicht nur in der Natur, sondern mit der Natur leben. Rings um die Lodge dehnt sich ein 570 Hektar großes Privatreservat aus, das wiederum Teil eines 270.000 Hektar großen Schutzgebietes ist – hier darf im Gegensatz zu weiten Teilen der Region nicht gerodet werden. Mehr als 2.000 verschiedene Pflanzen- und rund 400 Tierarten profitieren davon; wer durch den Wald wandert, fühlt sich wie in einem überdimensionalen Dschungelbuch, entdeckt Schmetterlinge, Schlangen, Affen und Vögel. Professionelle Führer begleiten jede Exkursion – sei es zu Fuß, per Boot oder sogar während der Nacht, wenn die Geräusche und Gerüche weicher werden und dem Wald einen ganz besonderen Zauber verleihen. Mindestens drei Tage sollte man sich für die Lodge Zeit nehmen, doch die meisten Gäste bleiben ohnehin viel länger – denn auch darin ähneln sich ein Abenteuerspielplatz und Yacutinga: Ist man einmal dort, will man nie wieder weg.

Buchtipp: »Die Engel« von Rafael Alberti

Vacances vertes

Parfois on se surprend à avoir la nostalgie de ces fantastiques terrains de jeux d'aventure : on s'en allait courageusement à la chasse dans les taillis épais, on traversait des gorges dangereuses sur des ponts suspendus ; d'immenses feuilles vertes recouvraient les sentiers et on pouvait faire griller du pain sec sur des feux de camp. On peut retrouver tout cela au Yacutinga Lodge qui se dissimule dans la jungle à la frontière argentino-brésilienne.

Les quatre habitations construites ici en harmonie avec la nature avec la pierre locale et des planches épaisses, sont habillées de verdure et abritent des meubles aux formes organiques et des étoffes aux teintes pastelles. Yacutinga, projet écologique de vaste envergure, offre un refuge confortable aux adeptes du tourisme vert – les hôtes ne vivent pas seulement dans la nature, ils vivent avec la nature. Tout autour du Lodge se déploie une réserve naturelle privée de 570 hectares, elle-même faisant partie du « corridor vert » d'Iguazú, un secteur de 270.000 hectares dans lequel il est interdit de déboiser, contrairement à ce qui se passe dans de vastes zones de la région.

Plus de 2.000 espèces végétales et environ 400 espèces animales vivent ici : celui qui se balade en forêt découvre des papillons, des serpents, des singes et des oiseaux. Des guides naturalistes professionnels accompagnent toutes les excursions, qu'elles se fassent à pied, en bateau, ou la nuit quand les animaux sont actifs, quand les bruits et les odeurs se font plus lourds et donnent à la forêt un charme particulier. Il est recommandé de rester au moins trois jours au Lodge, mais la plupart des hôtes y séjournent beaucoup plus longtemps. C'est aussi le point commun entre Yacutinga et le terrain de jeux d'aventure – une fois que l'on y a pris goût, on ne veut plus le quitter.

Livre à emporter : « Marin à terre » de Rafael Alberti

ANREISE	Im äußersten Nordosten Argentiniens gelegen, 60 Kilometer von Iguazú entfernt. Transfer ab Puesto Tigre/Iguazú Wasserfälle per Auto und Boot wird organisiert	ACCÈS	Situé à l'extrême nord-est de l'Argentine, à 60 kilomètres d'Iguazú. Transfert en voiture et en bateau organisé à partir de Puesto Tigre/Chutes d'Iguazú
PREISE	Package (3 Tage/2 Nächte) ca. US$ 350 pro Person. Mit Vollpension und Exkursionen. Handling nicht über die Lodge selbst, sondern über ausgewählte Reiseveranstalter vor Ort	PRIX	Package (3 jours/2 nuits) environ US$ 350 par personne. Pension complète et excursions inclues. Pour réserver, il faut s'adresser à des tours-opérateurs sélectionnés sur place
ZIMMER	6 Doppelzimmer, 14 Dreibettzimmer	CHAMBRES	6 chambres doubles, 14 chambres à trois lits
KÜCHE	Frisches aus eigenem Anbau, Barbecues unter freiem Himmel	RESTAURATION	Avec des produits frais cultivés sur place (le Lodge a son propre potager). Barbecues en plein air
GESCHICHTE	Als Traumziel für moderne Ökotouristen konzipiert	HISTOIRE	Pour les touristes respectueux de l'environnement
X-FAKTOR	Alles im grünen Bereich	LE « PETIT PLUS »	Des vacances vertes

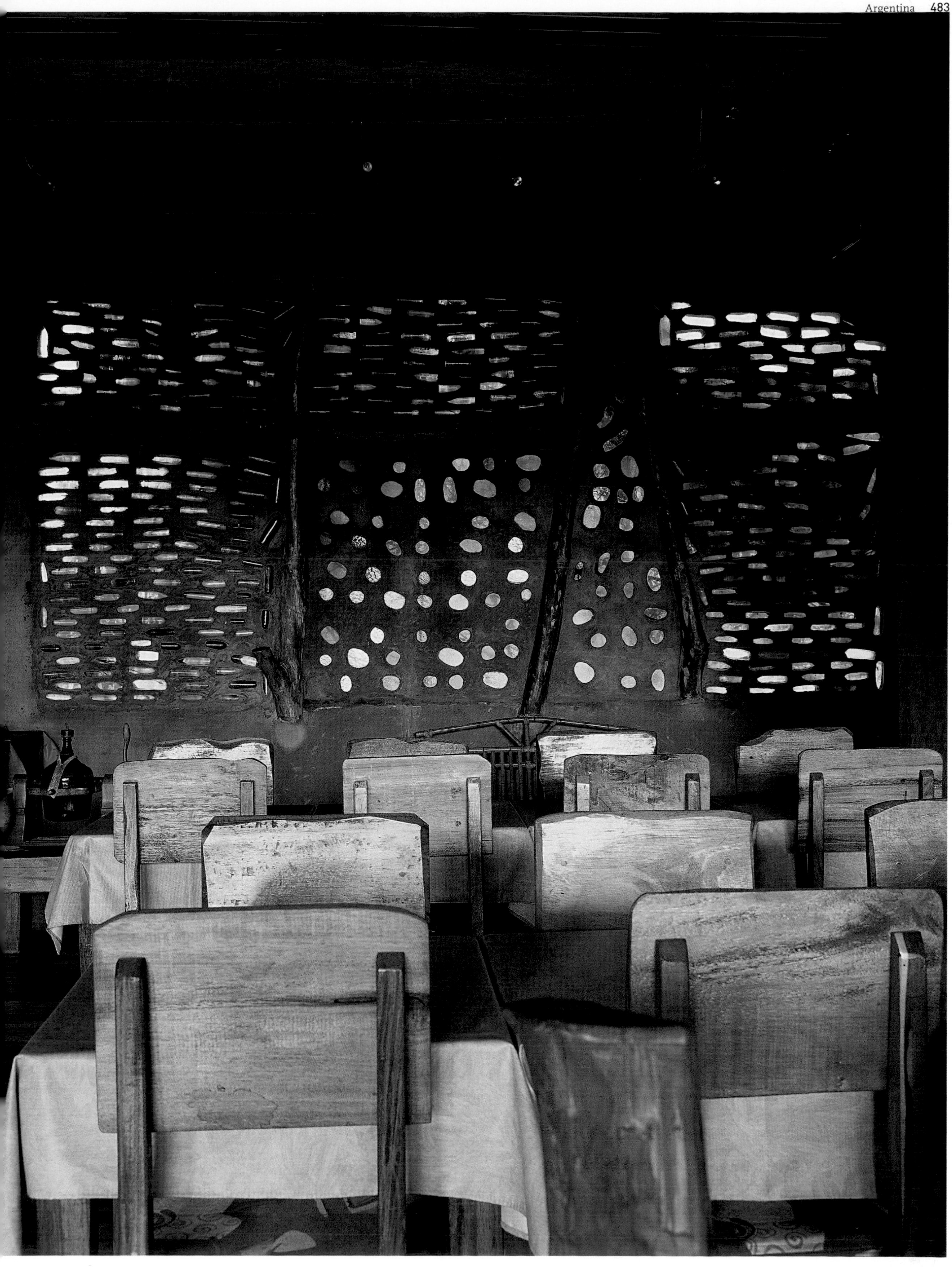

A remote world by the water
Pirá Lodge, Corrientes Province

Pirá Lodge, Corrientes Province

A remote world by the water

It's called the tiger of the rivers – *salminus maxillosus*, with its shimmering yellow scales, razor-sharp teeth, and powerful fins, which enable it to glide through the water at an extraordinary speed. The best place to go in pursuit of this salmon-like fish is the swamplands of Iberá, a region of crystal-clear rivers and shallow inlets, virtually untouched by humankind and almost twice the size of Florida's Everglades. For anglers and fly fishermen, this part of northern Argentina is still an insider's tip – as is the Pirá Lodge, in Corrientes Province. It is not remotely what you would normally expect a fishermen's hotel to be: there are no fusty odours, no rods to trip over, and the accommodation doesn't consist of four-bed dorms. Here, a maximum of ten guests reside comfortably in five well-appointed double rooms. They're light and airy, the furniture is hand-crafted, and a bath with a view is included in the price. The Pirá Lodge is country style of a sophisticated order, complete with a 20-metre (66 feet) pool and a barbecue restaurant, well-trained staff, and an angling store on the hotel premises. The season runs from September to April; but the Pirá is open outside this period too, and affords visitors at all times the opportunity to explore the countryside on horseback or in a kayak – or simply to enjoy the sun.

Book to pack: "The House of Bernarda Alba" by Federico Garcia Lorca

Pirá Lodge c/o Nervous Waters Av. Alicia Moreau de Justo 846 (Piso 4) C1107AAR, Buenos Aires Argentina Tel. (54) 11 4331 0444 E-mail: info@nervouswaters.com Website: www.piralodge.com Booking: www.great-escapes-hotels.com	**DIRECTIONS** Situated 640 km/400 miles north of Buenos Aires. The flight to Resistencia or Corrientes costs US$ 350 per person. The transfer to the Lodge takes about four hours and is organised for guests
	RATES One-week Fishing Package from US$ 2,625 per person in a double room. Includes full board. Non-Fishing Package US$ 1,260
	ROOMS 5 double rooms (each with en suite bath)
	FOOD Very good Argentine home cooking
	HISTORY One of the country's most recently established fishing lodges, small and select
	X-FACTOR An active vacation in first-class fishing country

Ferne Welt am Wasser

Er gilt als der »Tiger der Flüsse« – der *Salminus Maxillosus*
mit seinen gelb schimmernden Schuppen, seinen scharfen
Zähnen und seinen starken Flossen, die ihn im Rekordtem-
po durchs Wasser gleiten lassen. Wer auf die Jagd nach diesem lachsähnlichen Fisch gehen möchte, tut dies am besten
in den Sümpfen von Iberá, einem Marschland aus kristall-
klaren Flüssen und seichten Buchten, fast unberührt und
fast zweieinhalbmal so groß wie die Everglades in Florida.
Unter Sport- und Fliegenfischern gilt diese Region im Norden Argentiniens noch als Geheimtipp – genau so wie die
Pirá Lodge, die in der Provinz Corrientes ihre Pforten geöffnet hat. Sie ist weit entfernt von allem, was man sich im Allgemeinen unter einem Hotel für Angler vorstellt: Hier liegt
kein modriger Geruch in der Luft, man stolpert nicht stän-
dig über Ruten und schläft auch nicht in Vierbettzimmern –
hier logieren maximal zehn Gäste in fünf komfortablen
Doppelzimmern; viel Licht, handgefertigte Möbel und eine
Badewanne mit Aussicht inbegriffen. Ganz im Sinne des
gehobenen Countrystils gehören auch ein 20-Meter-Pool
und ein Grillrestaurant zur Lodge, und die fischenden
Gäste freuen sich über gut ausgebildetes Personal und einen
hoteleigenen Anglershop. Saison ist hier von September bis
April; doch Pirá hat auch außerhalb dieser Monate geöffnet
und empfängt dann vor allem Besucher, die die umliegende
Natur hoch zu Pferd oder im Kajak erkunden – oder einfach
nur die Sonne genießen.

Buchtipp: »Bernarda Albas Haus« von Federico Garcia Lorca

Ici l'on pêche

Avec ses écailles aux reflets jaunes, ses dents acérées et ses
nageoires puissantes qui lui permettent de glisser dans
l'eau à toute allure, le dorado *Salminus Maxillosus* est le
« tigre del rio ». Les amateurs peuvent pêcher ce poisson qui
ressemble au saumon dans les marais d'Iberá, un delta de
rivières cristallines et de baies peu profondes, pratiquement
vierges et deux fois et demie plus vaste que les Everglades
de Floride. Cette région du nord de l'Argentine n'est encore
connue que de quelques clubs de pêche et de pêcheurs à la
mouche – et c'est aussi le cas du Pirá Lodge qui a ouvert
ses portes dans la province de Corrientes.
Il ne ressemble pas à l'hôtel pour pêcheurs tels qu'on
l'imagine en général : ici pas d'odeur de vase, pas de
cannes à pêche où l'on se prend sans cesse les pieds et pas
de chambres à quatre lits. L'endroit peut loger dix personnes
dans cinq chambres doubles confortables. La lumière abondante, des meubles faits à la main et une baignoire avec vue
sont compris dans la location. Tout à fait dans l'esprit du
style Country élégant, une piscine de 20 mètres de long et
un restaurant à grillades font également partie du Lodge, et
les hôtes sont satisfaits du personnel aimable et compétent
et de la boutique offrant des articles de pêche qui appartient
à l'hôtel.
La saison de pêche débute au mois de septembre et s'achève
en avril, mais Pirá est ouvert toute l'année et accueille surtout des visiteurs qui veulent explorer la nature environnante à cheval ou en kayak, ou simplement profiter du soleil.

Livre à emporter : « La maison de Bernarda Alba » de Federico
Garcia Lorca

ANREISE	640 Kilometer nördlich von Buenos Aires gelegen. Flug nach Resistencia oder Corrientes US$ 350 pro Person. Rund vierstündige Weiterfahrt zur Lodge wird organisiert
PREISE	Einwöchiges »Fishing-Package« ab US$ 2.625 im Doppelzimmer (mit Vollpension). »Non-Fishing-Package« US$ 1.260
ZIMMER	5 Doppelzimmer. Mit je eigenem Bad
KÜCHE	Sehr gute argentinische Hausmannskost
GESCHICHTE	Eine der jüngsten Fishing-Lodges des Landes, klein und fein
X-FAKTOR	Aktivurlaub in einem erstklassigen Anglerrevier

ACCÈS	Situé à 640 kilomètres au nord de Buenos Aires. Vols à destination de Resistencia ou Corrientes US$ 350 par personne. Le trajet de quatre heures vers le Lodge est organisé
PRIX	Une semaine « Fishing-Package », a partir de US$ 2.650 par personne en chambre double. Pension complète. « Non-Fishing-Package » US$ 1.260
CHAMBRES	5 chambres doubles (avec salle de bains)
RESTAURATION	Excellente cuisine argentine
HISTOIRE	Un des plus récents Fishing-Lodges du pays
LE « PETIT PLUS »	Des vacances actives dans une zone de pêche de premier choix

Perfection of form...

La Escondida, Province Buenos Aires

La Escondida, Province Buenos Aires

Perfection of form

For Paul Pieres, memories of his childhood and youth in the pampas of Argentina are inseparable from polo. The moment he and his five siblings got out of school, they saddled their horses and rode out onto the pitch to thwack balls. "My father always had five or six horses in the stables and we kept those poor animals pretty busy," laughs Paul Pieres, looking back, "but they loved polo as much as we did!" Nowadays he shares his delight in Argentina's favourite sport with visitors from all around the world. Four years ago, with his wife Florencia, he opened the Estancia La Escondida. It is not only one of the best places for polo around Buenos Aires, it is also an architectural achievement of high interest. The sandstone-coloured building seems to have been set down amid the trees and greenery, clear and simple of line, wholly unornamented. The lofty interior spaces with their wooden ceilings and sparing, stylish furnishings convey an airy sense of spaciousness – and warm tones to offset the stone colours are provided by the open fire, colourful throws, and hides. Modern design is combined with nature without any sense of strain, and gives guests the experience of an all-in work of art – whether it's for a weekend escape from the city or for a whole month (La Escondida offers polo programmes up to four weeks). Of course the best place to relax after a day in the saddle is beside the pool, from where you can enjoy evening views of the most glorious sunsets Argentina has to offer.

Book to pack: "The Tunnel" by Ernesto Sabato

La Escondida		
Pilar/Buenos Aires	DIRECTIONS	Situated 60 km/39 miles (50 minutes by road) northwest of Buenos Aires
Argentina	RATES	Suite from US$ 140 to 200 for 2 people (depending on the number of guests, the season, and the length of stay). Full board included, but not polo programme
Tel. (54) 2322 420588		
E mail:	ROOMS	8 suites
paulpieres@estancialaescondida.com.ar and	FOOD	Home cooking using produce from the estate or region. Delicious "asados" (barbecues)
paulpieres@elsitio.net		
Website: www.estancialaescondida.com.ar	HISTORY	A country hotel in modern design, opened in 2000
Booking: www.great-escapes-hotels.com	X-FACTOR	For those who love active holidays and architecture

Formvollendet

Für Paul Pieres ist die Erinnerung an seine Kindheit und Jugend in der argentinischen Pampa untrennbar mit dem Polospiel verbunden: Sobald er und seine fünf Geschwister aus der Schule kamen, sattelten sie die Pferde, ritten aufs Feld und schlugen die Bälle um die Wette. »Mein Vater hatte immer fünf oder sechs Pferde im Stall, und wir hielten die armen Tiere ziemlich auf Trab«, lacht Paul Pieres heute, »aber sie mochten Polo genau so gern wie wir!« Den Spaß an Argentiniens beliebtester Sportart bringt er inzwischen auch Gästen aus aller Welt näher. Zusammen mit seiner Frau Florencia hat er vor vier Jahren die Estancia La Escondida eröffnet. Sie gehört nicht nur zu den besten Polo-Adressen rund um Buenos Aires, sondern ist zugleich ein architektonischer Höhepunkt: Der sandsteinfarbene Bau wurde wie ein Würfel aufs Grün und zwischen mächtige Bäume gesetzt; klar, einfach und schnörkellos inszeniert. Im Inneren vermitteln hohe Räume mit Holzdecken und sparsameleganter Möblierung viel Luft und Weite – für warme Akzente inmitten all der Steintöne sorgen Kaminfeuer, bunte Decken und Felle. Modernes Design soll sich hier wie selbstverständlich mit der Natur verbinden und Besucher in ein Gesamtkunstwerk entführen – sei es nur für ein Wochenende fern der Großstadt oder gleich für einen ganzen Monat (La Escondida bietet bis zu vierwöchige Polo-Programme an). Der schönste Platz nach einem Tag im Sattel ist übrigens ein Sessel am Pool: Von dort aus genießt man abends einen fantastischen Blick über das lang gezogene Becken mit offener Feuerstelle und hinein in einen der kitschig-schönsten Sonnenuntergänge, den Argentinien zu bieten hat.

Buchtipp: »Stefanos weite Reise« von Maria T. Andruetto

Un parcours sans fautes

Lorsque Paul Pieres évoque ses jeunes années dans la pampa argentine, le souvenir du polo lui vient immédiatement à l'esprit. À peine rentrés de l'école, les enfants sellaient leurs chevaux, galopaient sur le terrain et c'est à celui qui marquerait le plus de buts. « Mon père avait toujours cinq ou six chevaux à l'écurie et nous ne les ménagions pas, les pauvres », dit-il en riant, « mais ils aimaient cela autant que nous ! » Aujourd'hui, il tente de communiquer l'amour de ce sport, le plus apprécié en Argentine, à des hôtes venus du monde entier. Il y a quatre ans, avec son épouse Florencia, il a ouvert l'Estancia La Escondida, une des meilleures adresses des environs de Buenos Aires pour les amateurs de polo, mais aussi un triomphe architectural : le bâtiment couleur de sable est posé comme un dé sur la verdure entre des arbres imposants – une mise en scène claire, simple, sans fioriture. À l'intérieur, des pièces hautes dotées de plafonds de bois et de quelques meubles élégants génèrent une ambiance aérée et spacieuse – les flammes dans la cheminée, des plaids multicolores et des fourrures posent quelques accents chauds sur les teintes terreuses.

Le design moderne doit se marier ici à la nature comme si cela allait de soi et entraîner les visiteurs dans une œuvre d'art totale – pour le temps d'un week-end ou d'un mois (La Escondida offre des programmes de polo qui durent jusqu'à quatre semaines). Après une journée en selle, il fait bon se reposer sur un fauteuil près de la piscine. Le soir on jouit ici d'une vue fantastique sur le bassin qui s'étire en longueur et sur l'un des plus beaux couchers de soleil bigarrés que l'Argentine ait à offrir.

Livre à emporter : « Le tunnel », d'Ernesto Sabato

ANREISE	60 Kilometer (50 Fahrtminuten) nordwestlich von Buenos Aires gelegen
PREISE	Suite zwischen US$ 140 und 200 für 2 Personen (abhängig von Gästezahl, Saison und Dauer des Aufenthalts). Mit Vollpension, ohne Polo-Programm
ZIMMER	8 Suiten
KÜCHE	Hausgemachte Gerichte mit Zutaten aus eigenem Anbau oder der Region. Köstliche »asados« (Barbecues)
GESCHICHTE	Modern designtes Landhotel, 2000 eröffnet
X-FAKTOR	Für Aktivurlauber und Architekturliebhaber

ACCÈS	Situé à 60 kilomètres (50 minutes en voiture) au nord-ouest de Buenos Aires
PRIX	Suite entre US$ 140 et US$ 200 pour 2 personnes (selon le nombre d'hôtes, la saison et la durée du séjour). Pension complète, programme de polo non compris
CHAMBRES	8 suites
RESTAURATION	Plats cuisinés sur place avec produits du jardin ou de la région. «Asados» (barbecues) succulents
HISTOIRE	Hôtel de campagne au design moderne, ouvert en 2000
LE « PETIT PLUS »	Pour les amateurs d'exercice et d'architecture

Willkommen im Märchen

Der Park besitzt mehr Grüntöne, als auf der Palette eines professionellen Malers Platz hätten. Bäume, Büsche und Rasen leuchten in Dunkel- und Hellgrün, in Lind- und Smaragdgrün, in Zart- und Giftgrün. Mit rund 40 Hektar Fläche ist das Anwesen eine der größten Estancias der Region – und in jedem Fall das märchenhafteste: Inmitten des grünen Gartens nämlich thront das Haupthaus von Santa Rita, ein Palast in Rosé und Crème, mit Bögen, Säulen und Türmchen reich verziert und eine Hommage an die spanisch geprägte Kolonialzeit. 1790 errichtete die Familie Ezcurra die ersten Gebäude auf einer Art Verteidigungslinie um Buenos Aires, später ging Santa Rita an den Provinzsenator Antonio Carboni über, der seine Besitzansprüche mehr als deutlich manifestierte und vier Kilometer vom Landsitz entfernt das Dörfchen Carboni gründete. Heute gehört das Anwesen dem Ehepaar Isabel Duggan und Franklin Nüdemberg sowie seinen sechs Töchtern – und ist seit 1996 ein verwunschenes Countryhotel. In seinem Inneren regiert ein fantastischer Stilmix. Da gibt es reich mit Stuck, fließenden Stoffen und Himmelbetten ausgestattete Salons, Zimmer mit unverputztem Mauerwerk, dunklen Holzdecken und offenen Kaminen und sparsam möblierte Wintergärten, in denen nichts vom Blick in die Natur ablenkt. Kein Raum gleicht dem anderen, und jeder erzählt mit Details, die man oft erst nach Tagen entdeckt, seine eigene Geschichte. Den Zaubergarten von Santa Rita entdeckt man am besten zu Fuß oder im Pferdesattel und lässt sich abends bei Kerzenschein und Klassik mit argentinischen Menüs verwöhnen – alle Zutaten stammen soweit möglich aus eigenem Anbau.
Buchtipp: »Der Kuss der Spinnenfrau« von Manuel Puig

Bienvenue au royaume des fées

Le parc offre plus de tons de vert que ne pourrait en présenter la palette d'un peintre. Les arbres, les arbustes et la pelouse sont resplendissants dans leurs coloris vert foncé, vert clair, vert émeraude et vert tilleul. Avec ses quarante hectares la propriété est l'une des plus grandes Estancias de la région, et en tous cas la plus enchanteresse de toutes : au milieu de ce parc verdoyant trône le bâtiment principal de Santa Rita, un palais rose et crème aux ornements nombreux, avec ses arcs, ses colonnes et ses petites tours, un hommage à l'époque coloniale espagnole. C'est en 1790 que la famille Ezcurra fit construire les premiers bâtiments comme une sorte de ligne de défense tout autour de Buenos Aires. Plus tard Santa Rita fut remise à Antonio Carboni, le sénateur de la province, qui manifesta très clairement ses droits de propriétaire et fonda à quatre kilomètres de là le village de Carboni. Aujourd'hui la propriété appartient au couple Isabel Duggan et Franklin Nüdemberg ainsi qu'à leurs six filles, et est devenue depuis 1996 un hôtel enchanteur. Un mélange fantastique de styles règne à l'intérieur : chambres ornées de stuc, avec leurs étoffes artistement drapées et leurs lits à baldaquin, pièces aux murs sans crépi, avec leurs plafonds en bois sombre et leurs cheminées, jardins d'hiver meublés sobrement où rien ne vient détourner le regard de la nature. Aucune pièce ne ressemble à une autre et chacune nous conte sa propre histoire avec des détails que l'on ne remarque parfois qu'au bout de quelques jours. On ira à la découverte du parc enchanté à pied ou à cheval et le soir, à la lueur des chandelles, on savourera les menus argentins dont la plupart des produits proviennent de la propriété.
Livre à emporter : « Le baiser de la femme-araignée » de Manuel Puig

ANREISE	120 Kilometer südwestlich von Buenos Aires gelegen (90 Minuten Fahrtzeit)	ACCÈS	Situé à 120 kilomètres au sud-ouest de Buenos Aires (90 minutes en voiture)
PREISE	Doppelzimmer US$ 290 für 2 Personen. Mit Vollpension und allen Aktivitäten	PRIX	Chambre double US$ 290 pour 2 personnes. Pension complète et activités comprises
ZIMMER	9 Doppelzimmer	CHAMBRES	9 chambres doubles
KÜCHE	Argentinische und internationale Spezialitäten; viele Zutaten aus eigenem Anbau	RESTAURATION	Spécialités argentines et internationales ; beaucoup de produits sont « maison »
GESCHICHTE	1870 erbaut und seit 1996 ein kleines Hotel	HISTOIRE	Construit en 1870 et transformé en petit hôtel depuis 1996
X-FAKTOR	Schönster Stilmix mitten im Grünen	LE « PETIT PLUS »	Le plus beau mélange de styles au milieu d'une nature verdoyante

Patagonia and nothing but...
explora en Patagonia, Patagonia

explora en Patagonia, Patagonia

Patagonia and nothing but

It is the end of the world. A raw, rugged landscape where once colonial powers competed for the upper hand, and whalers and sealers made a living out of their bloody pursuit. But it is also country of almost unreal beauty: Patagonia, in southern Chile. Rarely will your loungs breathe so bracing an air. Rarely will you see such emerald-green lakes or such breathtaking mountain chains. In the very heart of the region is the Torres del Paine National Park, a region of granite needles, glacial waters, forests, and vast mosses, which is under UNESCO protection. It was there that explora Hotels opened their first establishment in 1993, the explora en Patagonia, which looks very much as if it were an immense liner lying at anchor on the shoreline of Lago Pehoé. Chilean designer Germán de Sol has cast the architecture in an entirely marine mould, with a wood-cladding façade, a landing stage, a reception area resembling a canin, and model ships in the lobby. As on a ship's deck, the rooms lie along seemingly endless passageways, and are fitted out in natural materials such as wood, hides, or stone. The philosophy of the house calls for purist quality, as evidenced in accessories such as hand-woven bed linen, rough-cut cakes of soap in the bathroom, or an entire ham on the breakfast buffet – it is an experience that involves all the senses and affords the purest encounter with nature. This is also true of the bath-house with its panoramic view of the lake and mountains, and of the expeditions on offer every day – when professional guides lead visitors into the secret heart of Patagonia.

Book to pack: "In Patagonia" by Bruce Chatwin

explora en Patagonia	
Sector Salto Chico S/N, Comuna Torres del Paine	
Casilia 57, Puerto Natales	
Patagonia, Chile	
Tel. (56) 2 2066060	
Fax (56) 2 2284655	
E-mail: reservexplora@explora.com	
Website: www.explora.com	
Booking: www.great-escapes-hotels.com	

DIRECTIONS	Situated 200 km/125 miles northwest of Punta Arenas (domestic flights from Santiago). Transfer by minibus is organised
RATES	Package of 3 nights from US$ 1,234 per person in double rooms (7 nights from US$ 2,323), includes airport transfer, full board, and excursions
ROOMS	26 Cordillera Paine double rooms, 4 Exploradores suites
FOOD	First-rate, purist cuisine using fresh fish, vegetables, and fruit. There is also a bar
HISTORY	Opened in October 1993
X-FACTOR	Discover the end of the world!

Patagonien pur

Es ist das Ende der Welt; eine raue Landschaft, in der einst Kolonialmächte um die Vorherrschaft stritten und Wal- und Robbenjäger mit blutigen Methoden um ihren Lebensunterhalt kämpften – doch es ist auch eine Landschaft von fast unwirklicher Schönheit: Patagonien im Süden Chiles. Selten atmet man eine so kristallklare Luft wie hier, blickt auf smaragdgrün schimmernde Seen und auf Bergketten wie überdimensionale Fototapeten. Im Herzen dieser Region liegt der Nationalpark Torres del Paine, von der Unesco geschützt und geprägt von Granitnadeln, Gletscherwasser, Wäldern sowie Moosflächen. Hier haben die explora-Hotels 1993 ihr erstes Haus eröffnet: das explora en Patagonia, das wie ein riesiger Dampfer am Ufer des Lago Pehoé vor Anker zu liegen scheint. Der chilenische Designer Germán de Sol setzt ganz auf eine bootartige Architektur – mit einer holzverkleideten Fassade, einem Zutrittssteg, einer kajütenähnlichen Rezeption und Schiffsmodellen in der Halle. Wie auf einem Deck liegen die Zimmer entlang scheinbar endloser Flure und sind mit natürlichen Materialien wie Holz, Fell oder Stein eingerichtet. Dass die Philosophie des Hauses der edle Purismus ist, merkt man an Accessoires wie handgewebter Bettwäsche, groben Seifestücken im Bad oder einem ganzen Schinken auf dem Frühstücksbuffet – hier soll man alle Sinne einsetzen und die Natur in ihrer reinsten Form erleben. Das gilt auch für Besuche im Badehaus mit Panoramablick auf See und Berge sowie für die Expeditionen, die jeden Tag angeboten werden – geführt von professionellen Guides kommen die Gäste so den Geheimnissen Patagoniens auf die Spur.

Buchtipp: »In Patagonien« von Bruce Chatwin

Purisme en Patagonie

La Patagonie, c'est au bout du monde, une terre sauvage qui a vu les luttes d'influence entre les puissances coloniales et les chasseurs de baleines et de phoques se battre pour survivre dans un environnement aussi rude qu'eux. Mais sa beauté est presque irréelle. L'air y est d'une pureté cristalline, les lacs chatoient, couleur d'émeraude, au pied de la cordillère spectaculaire. C'est au cœur de cette région que se trouve le parc national Torres del Paine, protégé par l'Unesco, avec ses tours granitiques, ses glaciers, ses chutes d'eau, ses forêts et sa steppe. En 1993, la chaîne explora-Hotels a ouvert ici son premier hôtel, l'explora en patagonia, qui semble amarré, tel un gigantesque vapeur, sur les rives du Lago Pehoé.

Le designer chilien Germán de Sol a misé sur une architecture navale – façade habillée de bois, passerelle, « cabine » de réception – et décoré le hall de maquettes de bateau. Les chambres, disposées comme sur un pont dans de longs corridors, sont décorées de matériaux naturels comme le bois, la fourrure ou la pierre.

L'ambiance est imprégnée de purisme, on le remarque par exemple dans la literie tissée à la main, les morceaux de savon « grossiers » dans la salle de bains ou le jambon entier que propose le buffet du petit-déjeuner. Ici, tous les sens doivent entrer en action et percevoir la nature dans sa forme la plus pure. Le même souci de noble simplicité règne dans la maison de bains qui offre un panorama splendide sur le lac et les montagnes ainsi que sur les expéditions proposées tous les jours. Accompagnés par des guides professionnels, les hôtes s'en vont percer les mystères de la Patagonie.

Livre à emporter : « En Patagonie » de Bruce Chatwin

ANREISE	200 Kilometer nordwestlich von Punta Arenas gelegen (dorthin Inlandsflüge ab Santiago), Transfer im Minibus wird organisiert
PREISE	Package mit 3 Nächten ab US$ 1.234 pro Person im Doppelzimmer (7 Nächte ab US$ 2.323). Mit Flughafentransfer, Vollpension und Exkursionen
ZIMMER	26 Doppelzimmer Cordillera Paine, 4 Suiten Exploradores
KÜCHE	Erstklassig und ebenfalls dem Purismus verpflichtet – mit frischem Fisch, Gemüse und Obst. Außerdem eine Bar
GESCHICHTE	Im Oktober 1993 eröffnet
X-FAKTOR	Entdecken Sie das Ende der Welt!

ACCÈS	Situé à 200 kilomètres au nord-ouest de Punta Arenas (là-bas, vols intérieurs à partir de Santiago), un transfert en minibus est organisé
PRIX	3 nuits à partir de US$ 1.234 par personne en chambre double (7 nuits à partir de US$ 2.323), transfert de l'aéroport, pension complète et excursions inclus
CHAMBRES	26 chambres doubles Cordillera Paine, 4 suites Exploradores
RESTAURATION	De premier choix, avec également des accents puristes – poisson frais, légumes et fruits. Et un bar
HISTOIRE	Ouvert en octobre 1993
LE « PETIT PLUS »	Pour découvrir le bout du monde !

Hotel Antumalal, Araucanía

A question of style

In October 1938 a young couple fleeing the impending Second World War, Guillermo and Catalina Pollak from Prague, arrived in Pucón with dreams of making a new life for themselves in Chile. But at first their chosen home at the other side of the world proved full of obstacles. A volcanic eruption and a fire destroyed the Pollakstet club and hotel. Ten years later, however, all was well and things were on the up at last – literally so. High on a rocky plateau above Lake Villarrica, together with Chilean architect Jorge Elton, the couple created what has remained to this day one of the most unusual hotels in all South America: a long, flat building in the Bauhaus style. Antumalal ("sunshine court" in the language of the Mapuche people) commands views across a garden of flowers, far across the water, to the volcano, the snow-capped summit of which looks as if it had been powdered with icing sugar. No wonder the rooms don't trouble with such profane distractions as televisions – the view from the panoramic windows is far better than any movie. The design focusses on native wood and Chilean country style; every room has its own fireplace as standard. An entertaining mixture of Czech and South American dishes is served in the restaurant, and the proprietors are especially proud of their bar counter, which measures 3.99 metres (about 13 feet) and was fashioned from a single piece of timber. The splendid Chilean wines should not be over-indulged in, though – it would be a pity to spoil your delight in nearby Huerquehue National Park by visiting with a hang-over!

Book to pack: "Memoirs" by Pablo Neruda

Hotel Antumalal	DIRECTIONS	Situated 125 km/80 miles southeast of Temuco airport, which is reached by domestic flight from Santiago. 90-minute transfer to hotel on request
Casilia 84		
Pucón	RATES	Double rooms from US$ 140 for 2 people, suite from US$ 190 for 2, Royal Chalet from US$ 380 for 4. Breakfast included
Chile		
Tel. (56) 45 441011		
Fax (56) 45 441013	ROOMS	11 double rooms, 1 suite, 1 family suite, 1 Royal Chalet
E-mail: hotel@antumalal.com	FOOD	"Restaurant del Parque" serving Czech-Chilean cuisine. Also, "Don Guillermo's Bar"
Website: www.antumalal.com		
Booking: www.great-escapes-hotels.com	HISTORY	Opened in 1950, the hotel was built in the Bauhaus style
	X-FACTOR	Unique architecture, unique views

Auf Salz gebaut

Es gibt Hotels, die betten ihre Gäste auf Holzplanken, Strohsäcke oder Eisblöcke – und es gibt ein Hotel, in dem man sogar auf Salz schläft. Mehr noch: Man sitzt auf Salzstühlen an Salztischen und blickt durch in Salzwände gehauene Fenster auf endlose Salzflächen – willkommen im Hotel de Sal. Bei Atulcha, im Salar de Uyuni von Bolivien, haben Marinko und Rita Ayaviri eine der ungewöhnlichsten Unterkünfte Südamerikas geschaffen; ohne elektrisches Licht, ohne Telefon und Minibar, aber mit unglaublicher Gastfreundschaft, Umweltbewusstsein und beinahe ganz aus dem reichhaltigsten Rohstoff der Region. Der Salar de Uyuni ist die größte Salzwüste der Anden, 12.000 Quadratkilometer groß und knapp 3.700 Meter hoch zwischen der Ost- und Westkordillere gelegen. »Weißes Meer« oder »Alaska von Bolivien« nennen die Einheimischen dieses Gebiet auch – hier oben ist die Luft dünn, das Licht gleißend und die Salzkruste bis zu zehn Meter dick. Während der Trockenzeit bekommt sie skurrile Risse und erinnert an gefrorene Bienenwaben, während der Regenfälle zwischen November und März kann sie sich in einen tückischen Sumpf verwandeln – vor allem in diesen Monaten sind Fremde hier verloren und sollten nur im Allradjeep mit Navigationssystem und in Begleitung eines bolivianischen Guides durch die Wüste fahren. Vor Ort bieten diverse Agenturen und Veranstalter mehrtägige Ausflüge durch den Salar an, die für eine Nacht auch im Hotel de Sal Station machen. Nach der holprigen Fahrt genießt man hier ein Abendessen bei Kerzenschein und an mit bunten Stoffen geschmückten Tischen, träumt nachts von den Schönheiten der unwirklichen Landschaft und weiß spätestens bei der Abreise, dass das Paradies auch aus Salz sein kann.

Buchtipp: »Das Fest des Ziegenbocks« von Mario Vargas Llosa

Édifié sur du sel

Certains hôtels font coucher leurs clients sur des planches de bois, des balles de paille ou des blocs de glace – et il y en a un où l'on dort même sur du sel. Mais cela ne s'arrête pas là car on est assis sur des chaises en sel à une table, elle aussi, en sel et à travers les fenêtres percées dans les murs en sel, la vue donne sur des immensités de sel : bienvenue à l'Hotel de Sal. C'est près d'Atulcha, dans le Salar de Uyuni de Bolivie, que Marinko et Rita Ayaviri ont créé l'un des hôtels les plus insolites d'Amérique du Sud ; sans lumière électrique, téléphone ou minibar, mais extrêmement chaleureux, écologique et construit presque exclusivement avec la ressource naturelle la plus abondante de la région. Le Salar de Uyuni est le plus grand désert de sel des Andes. D'une surface de 12.000 kilomètres carrés, il est situé à près de 3.700 mètres d'altitude entre la Cordillère de l'est et celle de l'ouest. Les habitants de cette région le surnomment la « mer blanche » et l'« Alaska de Bolivie » – ici l'air se raréfie, la lumière est éblouissante et la croûte de sel peut atteindre dix mètres d'épaisseur. Pendant la saison sèche, le désert de sel présente des failles d'aspect bizarre qui évoque une ruche gelée tandis que pendant la saison des pluies, entre novembre et mars, il se transforme en un dangereux marécage. C'est surtout durant ces mois que des étrangers se sont perdus. Si l'on désire s'aventurer dans le désert, il est conseillé de le faire dans une jeep équipée d'un système de navigation et en compagnie d'un guide bolivien. Diverses agences proposent des excursions de plusieurs jours à travers le Salar, avec une nuit passée à l'Hotel de Sal. Après une route cahotante, vous serez ravi de savourer un dîner aux chandelles à une table joliment décorée d'étoffes colorées. La nuit vous rêverez des beautés de ce paysage irréel et au moment du départ, vous saurez que le paradis peut être aussi en sel.

Livre à emporter : « La fête au bouc » de Mario Vargas Llosa

ANREISE	300 Kilometer nordwestlich von Uyuni gelegen. Das Hotel wird im Rahmen mehrtägiger, organisierten Touren durch den Salar de Uyuni angefahren	ACCÈS	Situé à 300 kilomètres au nord-ouest d'Uyuni. Les excursions de plusieurs jours à travers le Salar prévoient un arrêt à l'hôtel
PREISE	Doppelzimmer US$ 15 für 2 Personen. Mit Abendessen und Frühstück	PRIX	Chambre double US$ 15 pour 2 personnes. Dîner et petit-déjeuner compris
ZIMMER	20 Doppelzimmer	CHAMBRES	20 chambres doubles
KÜCHE	Einfache bolivianische Gerichte	RESTAURATION	Plats boliviens simples
GESCHICHTE	Eines von zwei Salzhotels im Salar de Uyuni – das schönere!	HISTOIRE	L'un des deux hôtels de sel dans le Salar de Uyuni – celui-ci est le plus beau !
X-FAKTOR	Alles ist Salz	LE « PETIT PLUS »	Tout est en sel

Wandeln auf historischen Wegen

Als die Inka im 15. Jahrhundert die ersten Häuser von Cuzco errichteten, gründeten sie weit mehr als eine einfache Hauptstadt – Cuzco war ihr Heiligtum und das Zentrum ihrer Welt. Die Stadt behielt ihren Stolz auch während der spanischen Kolonialherrschaft und gehört als Unesco-Weltkulturerbe heute zu den wichtigsten und vielfältigsten Stätten Südamerikas. Wer hier, auf 3.300 Metern Höhe und vor einer beeindruckenden Andenkulisse, in die Historie eintauchen möchte, zieht am besten ins Hotel Monasterio. Aus dem 1592 erbauten Kloster ist das vielleicht schönste bewohnbare Museum in Peru geworden – man lebt hinter altehrwürdigen Mauern, die so dick sind, als müssten sie ihre Gäste vor der Außenwelt schützen, wandelt durch von Rundbögen gesäumte Kreuzgänge und ist beinahe enttäuscht, wenn einem hinter der nächsten Ecke kein Mönch entgegenkommt. Der Grundriss der einstigen Zellen, der Versammlungsräume und der Kapelle wurde kaum verändert – die spartanische Ausstattung aber ist Vergangenheit. Im Hotel Monasterio gleicht kein Raum dem anderen; hier thront ein plüschiger Sessel, dort prangt ein goldumrahmtes Gemälde; es gibt wertvolle Antiquitäten, blitzblank geputzte Spiegel und Kristallleuchter. Vom Kabelfernsehen bis zur Minibar sind die Zimmer mit allem modernen Komfort ausgestattet und können seit neuestem sogar mit Sauerstoff angereichert werden, um der unangenehmen Höhenkrankheit vorzubeugen. Nach einer Nacht unter der »Sauerstoffdusche« kann man sich ganz ohne Beschwerden von der Magie Cuzcos verzaubern lassen oder einen Ausflug nach Machu Picchu unternehmen – die »verlorene Stadt der Inka« liegt nur eine dreieinhalbstündige Zugfahrt entfernt.

Buchtipp: »Tod in den Anden« von Mario Vargas Llosa

Suivre les chemins de l'histoire

Lorsque les Incas bâtirent au 15e siècle les premières maisons de Cuzco, ils ne fondèrent pas seulement une capitale – Cuzco était pour eux un lieu sacré et le centre de leur univers. La ville qui garda toute sa fierté même sous la domination des Espagnols, est classée aujourd'hui au patrimoine mondial de l'Unesco. Elle fait partie des sites les plus importants et les plus pittoresques d'Amérique du Sud. Celui qui désire remonter dans le temps, résidera à l'hôtel Monasterio, situé à 3.300 mètres d'altitude dans le décor imposant de la cordillère des Andes. Cet ancien monastère datant de 1592 est peut-être le plus beau musée habitable du Pérou. Protégé du monde extérieur par d'épaisses murailles, l'hôte se promène à travers les arcades du cloître et il est presque déçu de ne rencontrer aucun moine au détour de son chemin. Si le plan des cellules, des salles communes et de la chapelle n'a pratiquement pas subi de modifications, l'équipement spartiate fait lui bien partie du passé. À l'hôtel Monasterio, aucune pièce ne ressemble à une autre. Ici trône un fauteuil en peluche, là resplendit le cadre doré d'un tableau. Chaque pièce recèle des antiquités précieuses. Les chambres sont équipées du confort moderne, qui va du câble au minibar, et depuis peu, elles sont même alimentées en oxygène afin d'éviter les effets indésirables de l'altitude. Après une nuit sous la « douche à oxygène » on pourra alors succomber sans problèmes à la magie de Cuzco ou entreprendre une excursion jusqu'à Machu Picchu – la « ville perdue des Incas » n'est en effet qu'à trois-quarts d'heure de train.

Livre à emporter : « Lituma dans les Andes »
de Mario Vargas Llosa

ANREISE	Im Zentrum von Cuzco gelegen, 10 Fahrminuten vom Flughafen entfernt		ACCÈS	Situé dans le centre de Cuzco, 10 min. de l'aéroport
PREISE	Doppelzimmer US$ 303, Junior Suite US$ 396, Deluxe Suite US$ 589, Präsidenten-Suite US$ 721, Royal Suite US$ 897. Preise für 2 Personen mit Frühstück		PRIX	Chambre double US$ 303, suite junior US$ 396, suite de luxe US$ 589, suite présidentielle US$ 721, suite royale US$ 897. Prix sont pour 2 personnes, petit-déjeuner compris
ZIMMER	109 Doppelzimmer, 12 Junior Suiten, 1 Deluxe Suite, 3 Präsidenten-Suiten, 2 Royal Suiten		CHAMBRES	109 chambres doubles, 12 suites junior, 1 suite de luxe, 3 suites présidentielles, 2 suites royales
KÜCHE	3 Restaurants mit peruanischer und internationaler Küche. Am schönsten ist »El Tupay« mit seinem festlichen Inka-Dinner		RESTAURATION	3 restaurants proposant une cuisine péruvienne et internationale. Le plus beau est « El Tupay » avec son dîner inca
GESCHICHTE	1592 als Kloster erbaut, seit 1995 ein Hotel		HISTOIRE	Monastère construit en 1592, hôtel depuis 1995
X-FAKTOR	Wo man Historie hautnah erlebt		LE « PETIT PLUS »	Un lieu où l'on peut revivre le passé

Spiegelbild einer fremden Kultur

Sie versteckt sich mitten im Regenwald, die einzige »Straße«, die zu ihr führt, ist ein Wasserweg, und zur nächsten größeren Stadt sind es zehn Tagesmärsche: Die Kapawi Ecolodge liegt am Ende unseres räumlichen Vorstellungsvermögens. Wer hierher reist, erlebt im Dschungel Ecuadors Naturschauspiele, wie er sie nicht einmal von den Fotos im »National Geographic« her kannte, und bekommt eine Ahnung von der Welt der Achuar. Denn die Lodge wurde vom Privatunternehmen Canodros zusammen mit den Eingeborenen erbaut und wird ihnen im Jahr 2011 ganz gehören – als einzigartiges Öko- und Communityprojekt, das den Achuar neuen Lebensraum sichern soll, ohne dass sie ihren traditionellen aufgeben müssen. Die 20 Hütten zwischen dichtem Grün und der Kapawi Lagune sind nach überlieferter Art auf Stelzen gebaut, damit der Boden nicht mehr als nötig belastet wird, mit Stroh gedeckt und mit Solarenergie versorgt. Man wohnt überraschend komfortabel (wenn auch von Zeit zu Zeit in Gesellschaft tierischer Dschungel»gäste«), hat aber bei aller Annehmlichkeit immer das Gefühl, ein echtes Abenteuer zu bestehen. Zum Beispiel, wenn es morgens um sechs Uhr zum Birdwatching am Ufer des Capahuari-Flusses geht, mittags eine Trekkingtour mit Picknick in tropischer Kulisse auf dem Programm steht oder nachts die Kaimane auftauchen. Je nach Kondition der Gäste bietet die Lodge leichte, mittlere oder anspruchsvolle Exkursionen an – inbegriffen ist immer auch ein Besuch bei den Achuar. In ihren Dörfern und in ihrer Gesellschaft lässt man sich von einer fremden Lebensart in einer fremden Welt faszinieren – und versteht die Philosophie von Kapawi anschließend noch ein bisschen besser.

Buchtipp: »Jivaro« von Jörgen Bitsch

Retour aux sources

Difficile de se représenter l'emplacement du Kapawi Lodge, dissimulé au cœur de la forêt, et auquel on n'accède que par voie d'eau, la grande ville la plus proche se trouvant à dix jours de marche. Celui qui séjourne ici dans la jungle écuadorienne peut contempler des spectacles naturels que même « National Geographic » n'a pas photographiés, et découvrir l'univers des Achuar. En effet, le Lodge a été construit par l'entrepreneur Canodros en collaboration avec les autochtones et il leur appartiendra complètement en 2011. Ce projet communautaire et écologique unique en son genre doit assurer aux Achuar un nouvel espace vital sans qu'ils doivent renoncer à leur mode de vie traditionnel.

Les vingt huttes édifiées entre la végétation luxuriante et la lagune de Kapawi sont construites sur pilotis comme le veulent les traditions Achuar, cette méthode évitant que le sol soit trop chargé. Elles sont couvertes de paille et ravitaillées en énergie solaire. On y vit de manière étonnamment confortable (quoique les animaux de la jungle n'hésitent pas à s'inviter sans façons) sans toutefois perdre la sensation de vivre une aventure authentique et de devoir faire ses preuves. C'est le cas le matin à six heures quand on part observer les oiseaux sur les rives de la Capahuari, le midi pendant la randonnée avec pique-nique dans un décor tropical et la nuit quand les caïmans se réveillent.

Le Lodge offre des excursions adaptées à la forme physique de chacun – faciles, moyennes et difficiles – mais elles comportent toujours une visite chez les Achuar. Dans leur village et en leur compagnie on est fasciné par un mode de vie qui nous est étranger dans un monde qui nous est tout aussi peu familier. Ensuite on comprend mieux encore la philosophie de Kapawi.

Livre à emporter : « Les Jivaros » de Michael J. Harner

ANREISE	300 Kilometer südöstlich von Quito gelegen. Der Transfer per Flugzeug und Kanu wird organisiert
PREISE	Package 4 Tage/3 Nächte ab US$ 600 pro Person im Doppelzimmer (8 Tage/7 Nächte ab US$ 1.100). Mit Vollpension und allen Exkursionen
ZIMMER	20 Doppelzimmer in Hütten; mit Bad und Veranda
KÜCHE	Ecuadorianische und internationale Küche, mit Produkten aus der Region. Auch für Vegetarier
GESCHICHTE	1993 gemeinsam mit den Achuar erbaut. 2011 werden die Eingeborenen die Lodge ganz besitzen
X-FAKTOR	Ökotourismus erster Klasse

ACCÈS	Situé à 300 kilomètres au sud-est de Quito. Le transfert en avion et en canot est organisé
PRIX	Package 4 jours/3 nuits à partir de US$ 600 par personne (8 jours/7 nuits à partir de US$ 1.100). Pension complète et toutes les excursions incluses
CHAMBRES	20 chambres doubles dans des huttes ; avec salle de bains et véranda
RESTAURATION	Cuisine écuadorienne et internationale avec des produits de la région. Menus végétariens
HISTOIRE	Construit avec les Achuar en 1993. En 2011, le Lodge entrera en possession des autochtones
LE « PETIT PLUS »	Tourisme vert de première classe

Pictures of paradise...
Hotel San Pedro de Majagua, Islas del Rosario

Hotel San Pedro de Majagua,
Islas del Rosario

Pictures of paradise

In 1955, off the coast of Columbia, French artist Pierre Daguet found his very own personal paradise: the Isla Grande, where the trees stood so close that the canopy of their crowns was a heaven of green. where the beaches were of white sand, and where the crystal-clear sea all around was rifted with brightly-coloured coral reefs. Diving beneath the waves, Daguet seemingly found not only exotic fish but also mysterious "Ondinas" – shimmering water nymphs that he immortalised in his paintings. Today, where once there were easels in his erstwhile studio, there are now surfboards and sailboats – for the humble cabin now serves as a boat-house for the Hotel San Pedro de Majagua. The accommodation is in 17 pretty *cabanas*, the all-natural roofs of which look as if over-long fringes were curtaining their faces. On their terraces you can relax in striped hammocks, deep wooden armchairs, or bright red sofas. Inside, the cottages are appointed with purist simplicity, with clear lines, select dark pieces of furniture, and fabrics in light colours – but there's fun too, with amusing notes struck by a stone tortoise on the floor, or an orange starfish on the wall. You could easily pass the days here walking the island, gazing out upon the glittering sea, and dreaming of Daguet's nymphs... The artist's memory is preserved not only in his lively paintings but also in testimony to his capacity for drink: just a few metres off the beach, all the wine bottles he emptied in the course of well-nigh 30 years with friends and in high carousals are submerged under the waves – they have now become a coral reef in their own right, known to the locals as the "Bajo de las Botellas de Daguet".

Book to pack: "The Story of a Shipwrecked Sailor"
by Gabriel García Márquez

Hotel San Pedro de Majagua	
Isla Grande	
Islas del Rosario	
Colombia	
Tel. (57) 16228246	
Fax (57) 16228290	
E-mail:	
majagua.bovedas@hotelsantaclara.com	
Website: www.hotelmajagua.com	
Booking: www.great-escapes-hotels.com	

DIRECTIONS	Situated on Isla Grande (Islas del Rosario National Park), 45 minutes by boat southwest of Cartagena de Indias
RATES	Cabana Suite US$ 117 for 2 people, Cabana Playa US$ 83 for 2 people, Cabana Laguna US$ 59 for 2 people. Breakfast included
ROOMS	4 Cabanas Suite, 10 Cabanas Playa, 3 Cabanas Laguna
FOOD	Restaurant serving first-class seafood
HISTORY	Centred on the former studio of artist Pierre Daguet
X-FACTOR	For latter-day Crusoes and enthusiastic divers

North America

Canada • Wisconsin • Massachusetts • Florida
Texas • New Mexico • Arizona
California • Colorado • Utah • Wyoming

Photos by Don Freeman   *Text by* Daisann McLane   *Edited by* Angelika Taschen

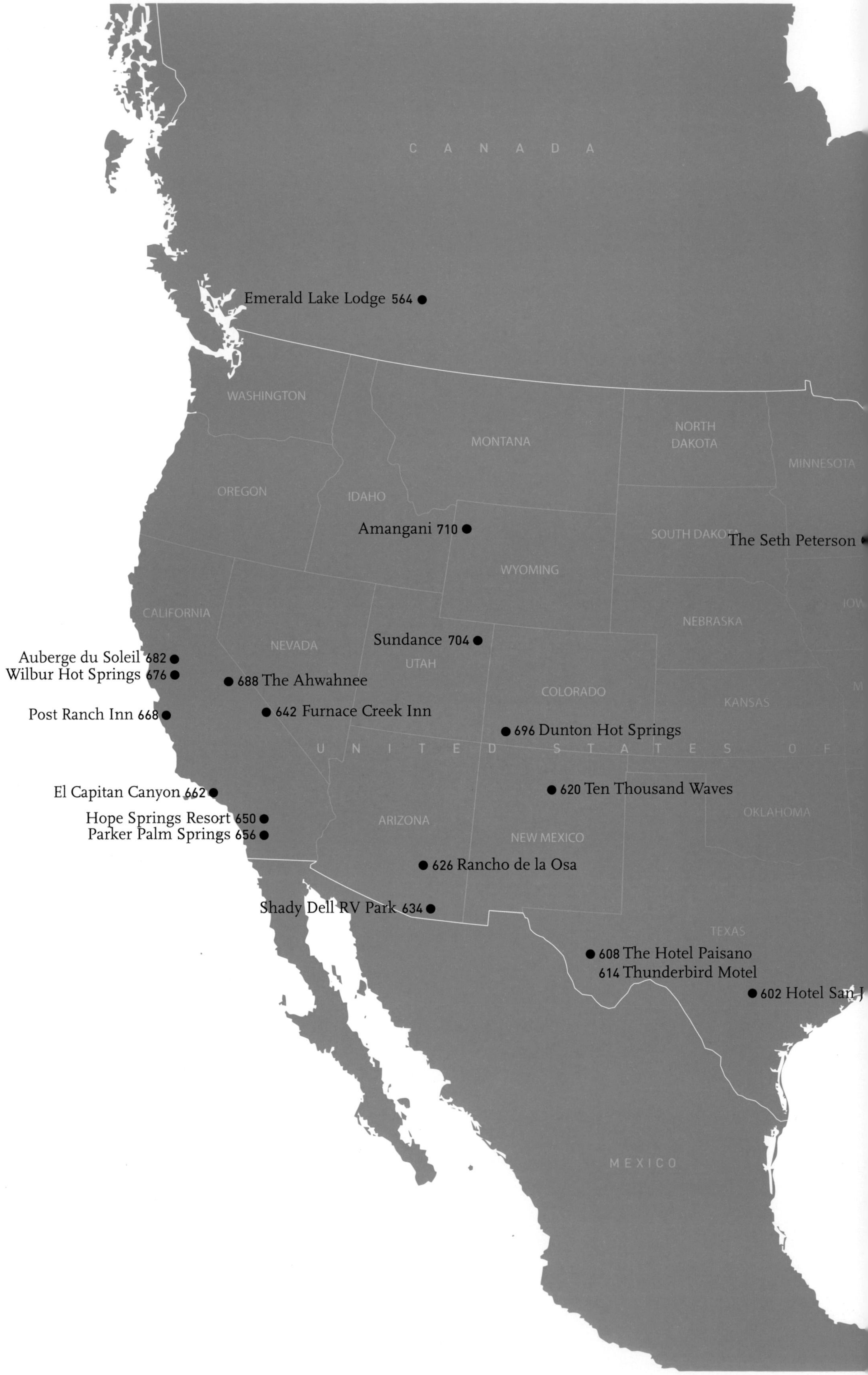
CANADA
Emerald Lake Lodge 564
WASHINGTON
MONTANA
NORTH DAKOTA
MINNESOTA
OREGON
IDAHO
Amangani 710
SOUTH DAKOTA
The Seth Peterson
WYOMING
CALIFORNIA
NEBRASKA
NEVADA
Sundance 704
UTAH
Auberge du Soleil 682
Wilbur Hot Springs 676
688 The Ahwahnee
COLORADO
KANSAS
Post Ranch Inn 668
642 Furnace Creek Inn
696 Dunton Hot Springs
UNITED STATES OF
El Capitan Canyon 662
620 Ten Thousand Waves
Hope Springs Resort 650
Parker Palm Springs 656
ARIZONA
NEW MEXICO
OKLAHOMA
626 Rancho de la Osa
Shady Dell RV Park 634
TEXAS
608 The Hotel Paisano
614 Thunderbird Motel
602 Hotel San J
MEXICO

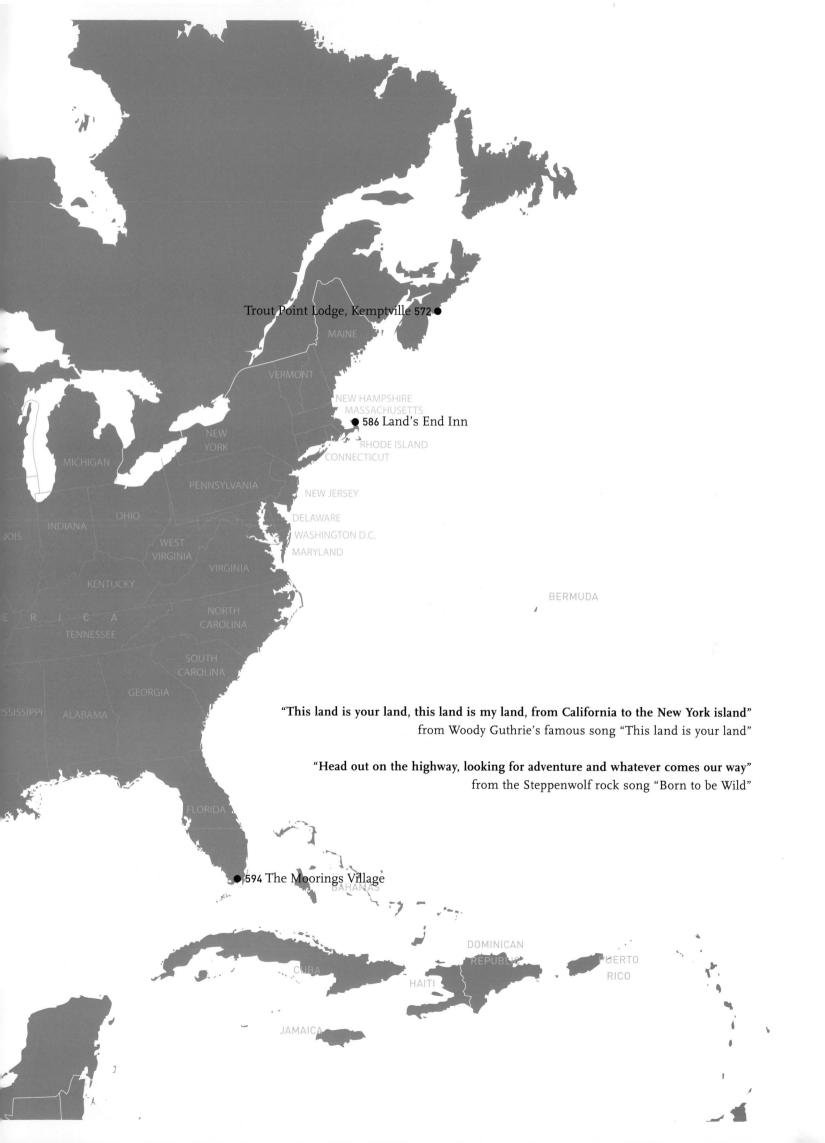

Trout Point Lodge, Kemptville **572** ●

● **586** Land's End Inn

● **594** The Moorings Village

"This land is your land, this land is my land, from California to the New York island"
from Woody Guthrie's famous song "This land is your land"

"Head out on the highway, looking for adventure and whatever comes our way"
from the Steppenwolf rock song "Born to be Wild"

Canadian Jewel...
Emerald Lake Lodge, Field, British Columbia

Emerald Lake Lodge, Field, British Columbia

Canadian Jewel

Sometimes nature startles us with a display of color that seems almost unreal, too stunning not to be a mirage or digitally enhanced. But the intense, opaque aquamarine green of Emerald Lake, high in the Canadian Rockies, is real, just as real now as it was in the late 19th century, when the Canadian Railroad company's workers were pushing the rails westward through this challenging mountain terrain. The Canadian Railroad company built grand hotels and lodges along the rail lines, to lure tourists out to the wilds of western Canada. Nearly 100 years later, these marvellous buildings, great examples of Canadian vernacular architecture, still continue to welcome visitors to Canada's wilderness. Emerald Lake Lodge is one of the more remote of the railroad lodges; until it was restored and expanded in the 1980s, it was just a couple of cabins by the lake surrounded by white-capped mountains. The eco-sensitive renovation and expansion has not disturbed the impressive isolation and beauty of the area–visitors must leave their cars a distance away, and take a shuttle bus to the lodge. Inside your log cottage room, a warm stone fireplace awaits; ski trails and hiking trails begin right outside your door. But after hiking to high mountain meadows thick with wildflowers, you can return to civilization (and to dinner in the lodge's fine restaurant). Step out onto the wooden porch, relax in a cushioned chair under a blanket, snug against the chill, and take a deep breath of this crisp, clean Canadian air. The lake spreads before you, reflecting mountains and fir trees in splendid stillness.

Book to Pack: "Call of the Wild" by Jack London.
Famous novel about life in the far north woods.

Emerald Lake Lodge	
P.O. Box 10	
Field, British Columbia V0A 1G0	
Canada	
Tel. +1 403 410 7417	
Fax +1 403 410 7406	
Email: info@crmr.com	
Website: www.crmr.com	
Booking: www.great-escapes-hotels.com	

DIRECTIONS	In Yoho National Park, 25 miles (40 km) west of Lake Louise; about 125 miles (200 km) west of Calgary airport.
RATES	From $188.
ROOMS	100 rooms in 24 log chalets.
FOOD	Fine dining (California and "mountain" cuisine with local wild game) in Mount Burgess Dining Room; casual meals in Kicking Horse Lounge.
HISTORY	Originally built by the Canadian Pacific Railroad in 1902; renovated and expanded in 1986.
X-FACTOR	A cozy stay in the most breathtaking natural setting in Canada.

Ein bisschen Frieden

Die Natur stellt sich manchmal kitschiger dar als ein digital bearbeitetes Farbfoto. So als würde man in einem Werbeprospekt blättern oder unter heftigen Sinnestäuschungen leiden. Wie etwa beim Anblick des milchig-aquamarinen Grüns des »Emerald Lake« in den kanadischen Rocky Mountains. Der auffällige See wurde im späten 19. Jahrhundert von Bahnarbeitern entdeckt, als sie sich während des Baus einer Bahnlinie über die Rockies abrackerten. Um Touristen in die unberührte Natur des Westens zu locken, ließ die kanadische Eisenbahngesellschaft entlang dieser Bahnlinien Grand Hotels und Lodges bauen. Fast hundert Jahre später kommen immer noch Touristen in die wunderschöne Landschaft und übernachten in den Hotels beispielhafter kanadischer Alltagsarchitektur. »Emerald Lake Lodge« ist eine dieser Eisenbahn-Lodges und wohl am weitesten von der Zivilisation entfernt. Ein paar Hütten vor schneebedeckten Bergen waren bis zur öko-verträglichen Renovierung in den Achtzigern alles, was hier stand. Diese brachte zwar mehr Komfort, änderte aber nichts an der Unberührtheit, Stille und Schönheit der umliegenden Natur. Die Anlage ist autofrei – die Gäste lassen ihre Autos ein Stück weiter draußen auf einem Parkplatz und werden per Shuttle-Bus zur Lodge gefahren. In den Zimmern der Blockhütten flämmelt ein wärmendes Feuer im Steinkamin, Ski- und Wanderwege führen direkt bis vor die Haustür. Nach einer ausgiebigen Wanderung durch die mit Wildblumen übersäten Bergwiesen kann man sich auf der Holzveranda bei kristallklarer Luft, eingekuschelt in Decken und Kissen, schön entspannen.

Buchtipp: »Der Ruf der Wildnis« von Jack London. Berühmter Roman über das Leben in den Wäldern von Alaska.

Joyau du Canada

Parfois la nature nous coupe le souffle avec ses couleurs presque surnaturelles, si incroyables qu'on croirait un mirage ou une photo retouchée. Mais le bleu-vert opaque d' « Emerald Lake », haut perché dans les Rocheuses canadiennes, est tout aussi réel aujourd'hui qu'à la fin du 19e siècle, quand les ouvriers de la compagnie des chemins de fer progressaient péniblement vers l'Ouest, posant les rails dans les montagnes. La compagnie construisit de grands hôtels et des gîtes le long de la voie pour attirer les touristes. Près de 100 ans plus tard, ces merveilleux bâtiments, belles illustrations de l'architecture canadienne, continuent d'accueillir les visiteurs en pleine nature. Jusqu'à ce qu'elle soit restaurée et agrandie dans les années quatre-vingt, « Emerald Lake Lodge » ne comptait que quelques cabanes au bord du lac ceint de sommets enneigés. Les modifications respectueuses de l'environnement n'ont pas détruit l'isolement et la beauté du lieu. Les visiteurs doivent laisser leurs voitures à une certaine distance et emprunter une navette. À l'intérieur de votre cabane en bois, une cheminée en pierre vous attend. Les pistes de ski et les sentiers de randonnée démarrent sur le pas de votre porte. Après une ballade dans les prés montagneux envahis de fleurs sauvages, vous retrouverez la civilisation (et un bon dîner) dans l'excellent restaurant de la lodge. Détendez-vous sous une couverture dans un fauteuil douillet ou sortez sur votre porche en bois pour inspirer un grand bol de l'air pur du Canada. Le lac s'étend à vos pieds, reflétant les massifs et les pins dans un calme splendide.

Livre à emporter : « L'Appel de la forêt » de Jack London. Célèbre roman sur la vie dans les forêts du Grand Nord.

ANREISE	Im Yoho National Park, 40 km westlich von Lake Louise; rund 200 km westlich vom Flughafen Calgary.
PREISE	Ab 150 €.
ZIMMER	100 Zimmer in 24 Chalets.
KÜCHE	Elegante kalifornische Küche im »Mount Burgess Dining Room«, auf der Karte stehen auch Wild-Gerichte; einfache Menüs in der »Kicking Horse Lounge«.
GESCHICHTE	1902 von der Canadian Pacific Railroad gebaut, 1986 renoviert und erweitert.
X-FAKTOR	Gemütliche Unterkunft in atemberaubend schöner Naturlandschaft im Westen Kanadas.

ACCÈS	Dans le parc national Yoho, à 40 km à l'ouest de Lake Louise; environ 200 km à l'ouest de l'aéroport de Calgary.
PRIX	À partir de 150 €.
CHAMBRES	100 chambres dans 24 chalets.
RESTAURATION	Menus gastronomiques dans la « Mount Burgess Dining Room » ; repas plus simples dans la « Kicking Horse Lounge ».
HISTOIRE	Construit par le Canadian Pacific Railroad en 1902 ; rénové et agrandi en 1986.
LE « PETIT PLUS »	Un séjour douillet dans le décor naturel le plus époustouflant du Canada.

Cajun Roots...
Trout Point Lodge, Kemptville, Nova Scotia

Trout Point Lodge, Kemptville, Nova Scotia

Cajun Roots

A bitter history links the Canadian island of Nova Scotia with the state of Louisiana, far to the south: in 1755, the French settlers in the northeastern part of Canada were forcibly expelled by the British army, and they had to flee south to Louisiana which was then a French colony. The expulsion – called "le grand dérangement"– uprooted thousands of people, and nearly erased the French Acadian culture from the Nova Scotia area. Nearly 250 years later, three successful restauranteurs and gourmets from New Orleans travelled to Nova Scotia in search of their French Acadian ("Cajun") roots. They found roots, and more. The trip through Nova Scotia's fishing villages inspired a best selling cookbook, and it also inspired the trio to open a lodge, cooking school, and gourmet restaurant in the backwoods of Nova Scotia. Trout Point Lodge is somewhat like an overgrown cabin, made of local wood, with a long second story porch; the beds, chairs and tables are handmade from saplings. Here you can learn to cook a courtbouillon with seafood recently plucked from the ocean, or go fishing or hiking. Or, you can just hang out and relax on the porch with a glass of fine French wine, and celebrate the triumphant Canadian return of these food-loving Louisiana Cajuns.

Book to Pack: "Evangeline" by Henry Wadsworth Longfellow. Classic American poem about the migration of the French Acadian settlers from Nova Scotia to New Orleans.

Trout Point Lodge		
189 Trout Point Road off the East Branch Road	DIRECTIONS	23 miles (37 km) northeast of Yarmouth, Nova Scotia.
East Kemptville, Yarmouth County, Nova Scotia	RATES	From $125 for a room to $450 for an entire lodge.
B0W 1Y0	ROOMS	13 rooms and suites, a two bedroom cottage, and a 12 bed lodge.
Canada		
Tel. +1 902 749 7629	FOOD	The Dining Room restaurant serves Creole and Cajun inspired gourmet dishes, emphasis on fresh seafood; cooking seminars are also regularly held at Trout Point.
Email: info@foodvacation.com		
Website: www.troutpoint.com	HISTORY	Founded by three cookbook authors from New Orleans.
Booking: www.great-escapes-hotels.com	X-FACTOR	Explore the roots of French New World (Cajun and Creole) cuisine in a rustic woodsy retreat.

Zurück zu den Wurzeln

Die kanadische Insel Nova Scotia und der US-Staat Louisiana verbindet ein unrühmliches Stück Geschichte. Nachdem die französische Krone 1755 ihre kanadischen Besitzungen an die Briten abtreten mussten, wurden die französischen Siedler unverzüglich von der Armee des Landes verwiesen. Die heimatlos gewordenen Menschen flohen Richtung Süden nach Louisiana, damals noch unter französischer Herrschaft. Der Landesverweis, »le grand dérangement« genannt, entwurzelte tausende von Menschen und löschte die französische Kultur in Nova Scotia beinahe ganz aus. Rund 250 Jahre später machten sich drei erfolgreiche französischstämmige Gastronome und Feinschmecker aus New Orleans, Louisiana, auf die Suche nach ihren Wurzeln in Nova Scotia. Die Reise durch die Fischerdörfer von Nova Scotia inspirierte das Trio zu einem Kochbuch über kreolische Küche und ihre französischen Ursprünge, das schnell zu einem Bestseller wurde. Der nächste Schritt war naheliegend: Die erfolgreichen Kochbuchautoren eröffneten im Hinterland von Nova Scotia eine Gäste-Lodge mt einem Gourmetrestaurant und einer Kochschule. »Trout Point Lodge« ist eine gemütliche Blockhütte mit zweistöckiger Veranda, umgeben von einem Pflanzendschungel. Die Betten, Stühle und Tische sind alle aus jungen Zweigen handgefertigt. Mitten im Grünen kann man hier etwas über die Ursprünge der Cajun-Küche erfahren und dabei lernen, wie man eine Court Bouillon mit Fischen und Meeresfrüchten zubereitet.

Buchtipp: »Evangeline« von Henry Wadsworth Longfellow.
Klassisch amerikanisches Gedicht über französische Siedler, die Nova Scotia verließen, um nach New Orleans auszuwandern.

Racines acadiennes

Une histoire cruelle lie l'île de Nouvelle-Écosse à l'état de la Louisiane : en 1755, les colons français du nord-est canadien furent expulsés manu militari par l'armé britannique et se réfugièrent tout au sud, parmi leurs compatriotes de Louisiane. Ce « grand dérangement » déracina des milliers de personnes et faillit anéantir la culture acadienne la Nouvelle-Écosse. Près de 250 ans plus tard, trois restaurateurs de talent et fins gourmets de la Nouvelle-Orléans firent le périple inverse à la recherche de leurs racines. Ils y trouvèrent bien plus que cela : les villages de leurs ancêtres leur inspirèrent un livre de recettes qui fit un tabac et les convainquirent d'ouvrir un gîte, une école de cuisine et un restaurant gastronomique dans l'arrière-pays de l'île. Construite en rondins de bois, « Trout Point Lodge » ressemble à une cabane démesurée avec son long porche à l'étage. Les chaises, les lits et les tables artisanales ont été réalisés dans de jeunes arbres locaux. Ici, on peut apprendre à préparer un court-bouillon avec des fruits de mer frais du jour même, aller à la pêche ou en randonnée. À moins qu'on préfère se détendre sur le porche avec un verre de bon vin français et célébrer le retour triomphal au Canada de ces trois Cajuns de Louisiane amateurs de bonne chère.

Livre à emporter : « Evangeline » d'Henry Wadsworth Longfellow.
Classique de la poésie américaine sur l'exode des colons acadiens de la Nouvelle-Écosse à la Nouvelle-Orléans.

ANREISE	37 km nordöstlich von Yarmouth, Nova Scotia.
PREISE	Zwischen 100 € für ein Zimmer und 360 € für eine Lodge.
ZIMMER	13 Zimmer und Suiten, ein Cottage mit zwei Schlafzimmern, eine Lodge mit 12 Betten.
KÜCHE	Im Restaurant »Dining Room« gibt's kreolische Küche und Cajun-Food – auf der Menükarte stehen viele Fischgerichte; in der »Trout Point Lodge« werden zudem Kochkurse durchgeführt.
GESCHICHTE	Von drei Kochbuchautoren aus New Orleans eröffnet.
X-FAKTOR	Kreolisches Essen und Cajun-Food in rustikaler Umgebung.

ACCÈS	À 37 km au nord-est de Yarmouth, en Nouvelle-Ècosse.
PRIX	À partir de 100 € pour une chambre, jusqu'à 360 € pour une cabane entière.
CHAMBRES	13 chambres et suites, un cottage avec deux chambres à coucher et une cabane de 12 lits.
RESTAURANT	Le « Dining Room » sert une cuisine gastronomique d'inspiration créole et cajun. Des séminaires de cuisine sont régulièrement organisés.
HISTOIRE	Fondé par les trois auteurs d'un livre de cuisine originaires de la Nouvelle-Orléans.
LE « PETIT PLUS »	Explorez les racines de la cuisine française du nouveau monde dans une retraite au fond des bois.

The Wright Stuff...
The Seth Peterson Cottage, Lake Delton

The Seth Peterson Cottage, Lake Delton

The Wright Stuff

It is a rare and special thing to be able to spend a vacation retreat inside a work of art. The Seth Peterson Cottage was one of Frank Lloyd Wright's last commissions as an architect, in 1958, and today it is the only one of his houses available for rental by the general public. Staying here is a total immersion in his revolutionary design principles – the house has been described as "having more architecture per square foot than any other building he ever designed." From outside the cottage is a beautifully realized structure made of wood and natural sandstone that harmonizes with the wooded terrain of the remote Wisconsin state park where it is located. Light floods inside through floor to ceiling windows that embody Wright's principle of blending the exterior and interior. Inside, Wright's trademark massive stone fireplace is the center of an open living space that is furnished with custom-built furniture. The vacation cottage, designed for a local businessman who died before it was completed, had languished and fallen into disrepair until it was rediscovered by a community activist. Together with a group of citizens concerned about preservation, she formed a nonprofit trust to renovate the cottage strictly according to Wright's original vision. At the Seth Peterson Cottage Wright's ideas come alive for the lucky guests who can spend a lazy weekend here, sitting on Wright-designed chairs, gazing through his wall of glass at the beautiful woods beyond.

Book to Pack: "An Autobiography" by Frank Lloyd Wright. Written by the master architect of the 20th century while in seclusion in a cabin in Minnesota.

The Seth Peterson Cottage	
E9982 Fern Dell Road	
Mirror Lake State Park	
Lake Delton, WI USA 53940	
Contact: Sand County Service Company	
Box 409, Lake Delton, WI USA 53940	
Tel. +1 608 254 6551 Fax +1 608 254 4400	
Email: spccmlk@dellsnet.com	
Website: www.sethpeterson.org	
Booking: www.great-escapes-hotels.com	

DIRECTIONS	About 50 miles (80 km) northwest of Madison, Wisconsin.
RATES	From $225 a night.
ROOMS	The cottage holds up to 4 overnight guests.
FOOD	Self-catering.
HISTORY	Designed by Wright for Wisconsin native Seth Peterson in 1958; restored in 1992.
X-FACTOR	The only Frank Lloyd Wright house available for rental to the general public.

Architekturlegende

Ganz, ganz selten ist es möglich, in einem Kunstwerk zu leben. Eine der großen Ausnahmen ist das »Seth Peterson Cottage« – das letzte Auftragswerk von Frank Lloyd Wright aus dem Jahr 1958. Das Cottage kann man heute mieten und damit die revolutionären Architektur-Prinzipien Wrights hautnah erleben. Bewunderer des Baus meinen, in keinem anderen Werk Wrights gäbe es so viel Architektur wie in diesem. Das Cottage aus Holz und Sandstein schmiegt sich in die bewaldete Umgebung des Wisconsin State Park perfekt ein. Riesige Panoramafenster lassen reichlich Licht ins Innere und verkörpern so Wrights Grundsatz, die Grenzen zwischen Innen und Außen aufzulösen. In der Mitte des offenen Wohnraums mit maßgefertigen Möbeln steht, typisch für Wright, ein massiver Steinkamin. Wright erhielt den Auftrag für den Bau des Feriencottages vom Geschäftsmann Seth Peterson. Doch noch bevor der Bau fertig gestellt war, segnete dieser das Zeitliche, und lange kümmerte sich niemand darum. Ein Bewohner der Gemeinde entdeckte dann das halb zerfallene Werk des legendären Architekten und tat sich mit einer Gruppe von Leuten zusammen, die sich für die Erhaltung bedeutender Bauwerke einsetzt. Zusammen gründeten sie einen Non-Profit-Fonds. Mit diesem Geld wurde das Cottage ganz genau nach den Vorstellungen Wrights in Stand gesetzt und die Ideen des Architekten damit zu neuem Leben erweckt.

Buchtipp: »Frank Lloyd Wright« von Bruce Brooks Pfeiffer. Ein Überblick über die Werke des bedeutenden amerikanischen Architekten.

Vivre dans l'art

On n'a pas tous les jours l'occasion de passer ses vacances dans une œuvre d'art. Le « Seth Peterson Cottage », dernière commande de Frank Lloyd Wright en 1958, est aujourd'hui sa seule demeure que l'on peut louer. Y séjourner constitue une immersion complète dans ses principes architecturaux révolutionnaires. La maison a été décrite comme « possédant plus d'architecture au mètre carré que n'importe quelle autre de ses créations ». De dehors, c'est une superbe structure en bois et en grès naturel qui s'harmonise avec le paysage boisé du parc de l'état du Wisconsin. La lumière inonde les pièces grâce aux baies vitrées, Wright ayant toujours cherché à fondre l'intérieur et l'extérieur. L'espace de séjour ouvert est dominé par une cheminée centrale massive et aménagé de meubles sur-mesure. Cette ancienne résidence d'été, construite pour un homme d'affaires de la région mort avant son achèvement, tombait en ruines quand elle a été redécouverte par la militante d'une association locale. Avec d'autres citoyens soucieux du patrimoine, ils ont créé un trust à but non lucratif pour la restaurer conformément à la vision originale de l'architecte. Au « Seth Peterson Cottage », les idées de Wright prennent vie pour les heureux élus qui y passent un week-end paresseux, assis dans les fauteuils qu'il a dessinés, contemplant la belle forêt environnante à travers son mur de verre.

Livre à emporter : « Autobiographie » de Frank Lloyd Wright. Écrite par le maître architecte du 20e siècle alors qu'il était reclus dans une cabane du Minnesota.

ANREISE	Etwa 80 km nordwestlich von Madison, Wisconsin.
PREISE	Ab 180 € pro Nacht.
ZIMMER	Im Cottage können bis zu vier Personen übernachten.
KÜCHE	Für das Essen muss man selber sorgen.
GESCHICHTE	Von Architekturlegende Frank Lloyd Wright im Auftrag von Seth Peterson 1958 entworfen; 1992 restauriert.
X-FAKTOR	Das einzige Haus von Frank Lloyd Wright, das man mieten kann.

Accès	À environ 80 km au nord-ouest de Madison, dans le Wisconsin.
Prix	À partir de 180 € la nuit.
Chambres	Le cottage peut loger 4 personnes à la fois.
Restauration	Cuisine équipée pour préparer ses repas.
Histoire	Conçu par Wright pour un natif du Wisconsin, Seth Peterson, en 1958 ; restauré en 1992.
Le « petit plus »	La seule maison de Frank Lloyd Wright que le grand public peut louer.

Sand's End...
Land's End Inn, Provincetown

Land's End Inn, Provincetown

Website: www.landsendinn.com

Sand's End

Provincetown, Massachusetts, is a small town built on a skinny finger of sand that sticks out like a hook in the Atlantic Ocean. It is one of the places in America – Key West in Florida is the other – where the road comes to an end at the sea, where the only way to leave (besides sailing away) is to turn around and go back. "A man may stand there and put all America behind him," Henry David Thoreau wrote about Provincetown in 1865. End-of-the-road towns are magnets for free spirits. Thoreau was just one of a legion of writers, artists, intellectuals and thinkers who have made Provincetown their home. The town, indeed, is a genuine bohemian colony, with a well-regarded local theater, art galleries, writer's workshops, and a big and lively gay community. Eugene O'Neill produced plays here; Norman Mailer retired here. The Land's End Inn, which sits atop a hill overlooking the Atlantic at the far end of town, is the embodiment of Provincetown's free spirit. It is a strange folly of a building, with a rounded main section that looks like the prow of a ship heading out to sea. Inside are quirky rooms – a few, like the domed "Tower Room" are circular, with sweeping views of shoreline. All are decorated with an explosion of Victoriana and fine European linens and fabrics. There are decks and porches where you balance a cocktail on the flat arm of an Adirondack chair and admire the sunset; or scramble down the stairway that leads to the beach. The shops and galleries, and the free spirits who make Provincetown such a unique place, are just a short stroll away from the Land's End Inn. And America? When you're ready you can turn around and go back there.

Book to Pack: "Land's End: A Walk in Provincetown" by Michael Cunningham.
Travel essays on Provincetown by the Pulitzer Prize winning author of "The Hours".

Land's End Inn
22 Commercial Street
Provincetown, MA 02657
USA
Tel. +1 508 487 0706
Fax +1 508 487 0755
Email: info@landsendinn.com
Website: www.landsendinn.com
Booking: www.great-escapes-hotels.com

DIRECTIONS	120 miles drive (195 km) from Boston Logan International Airport.
RATES	$165 to $495.
ROOMS	16 rooms and suites.
FOOD	Continental breakfast only; no restaurant (but lots of choices in Provincetown).
HISTORY	House was built as a summer cottage by a Boston hatmaker in 1904; later it was converted to an inn which opened in 1926.
X-FACTOR	Windswept folly of a house, the perfect place to soak up Provincetown's artsy, bohemian mood.

Am Ende der Welt

Die schmale Sandbank ragt wie ein Haken hinaus in den Atlantik. Zuvorderst an der Spitze liegt das Städtchen Provincetown, Massachusetts, dessen Hauptstraße direkt ins Meer mündet. Ausufernde Straßen gibt es sonst nur noch in Key West, Florida. Will man von da weg, hat man nicht gerade viel Möglichkeiten. Entweder man kehrt um – oder man segelt auf dem Meer davon. »An diesem Ort lässt man Amerika ganz hinter sich«, schrieb der Dichter Henry David Thoreau 1865 über Provincetown. Thoreau war nur einer von vielen Schriftstellern, Künstlern, Intellektuellen und Denkern, die von Provincetown magisch angezogen wurden und daraus eine Künstlerkolonie gemacht haben. Es gibt ein angesehenes Theater, Kunstgalerien, Schriftsteller-Workshops und eine lebendige Schwulenszene. Der Bühnendichter und Nobelpreisträger Eugene O'Neill ließ hier seine Stücke aufführen, und Schriftsteller Norman Mailer setzte sich in Provincetown zur Ruhe. Das »Land's End Inn«, eine skurrile Anhäufung verschiedener Häuser, liegt auf einem Hügel hoch über dem Altantik, am Ende der Stadt. Und wie ein Schiffsbug ragt das Hauptgebäude zum Ozean hinaus. Die Zimmer sind eigenwillig und mit viktorianischer Opulenz eingerichtet, zum Teil haben sie wie im »Tower Room« abgerundete Decken, und die Wäsche ist aus feinstem europäischen Leinen. Abends kann man auf den Terrassen und Veranden des Hotels bei einem Cocktail den Sonnenuntergang genießen. Und wer ein Stück echtes Provincetown erleben möchte, klettert die Treppe hinunter zum Strand oder stöbert durch die typischen Läden und Galerien.

Buchtipp: »Land's End« von Michael Cunningham.
Reise-Essays über Provincetown des Pulitzer-Preisträgers und Autoren von »Die Stunden« (»The Hours«).

Au bout du monde

Provincetown, dans le Massachusetts, est bâtie sur une fine langue de sable qui pointe dans l'Atlantique. C'est l'un de ces endroits des États-unis (comme Key West, en Floride) où la route s'arrête sur l'océan. Le seul moyen d'en repartir est de faire demi-tour (ou de mettre les voiles). « L'homme qui se tient là a toute l'Amérique derrière lui », a écrit Henry D. Thoreau en 1865. Ces villes du bout du monde attirent les libres penseurs. Outre Thoreau, des légions d'artistes, d'écrivains et d'intellectuels se sont établies ici. Une vraie colonie bohème s'y épanouit, avec un théâtre renommé, des galeries d'art, des ateliers d'écriture et une communauté gay très active. Eugène O'Neill y a écrit des pièces, Norman Mailer s'y est retiré. Le « Land's End Inn », perché sur une colline qui domine l'océan, est l'incarnation de l'esprit libre de « Provincetown ». Cette étrange folie au corps arrondi évoque la proue d'un navire mettant le cap vers le large. Certaines chambres, telle que la « Tower Room », circulaire et surmontée d'un dôme, jouissent d'une vue panoramique sur le rivage. Toutes sont décorées à la victorienne avec du beau linge et des étoffes d'Europe. Depuis les terrasses et les porches, on peut poser son cocktail sur l'accoudoir plat d'un fauteuil de l'Adirondack pour admirer le coucher de soleil, à moins qu'on préfère descendre les quelques marches qui mènent à la plage. Les boutiques, les galeries et l'ambiance qui font de « Provincetown » un lieu unique ne sont qu'à un jet de pierre. Et l'Amérique ? Quand vous sentirez prêt, vous n'aurez qu'à pivoter sur vos talons et y retourner.

Livre à emporter : « La Maison du bout du monde » de Michael Cunningham.
Chronique de la vie de deux marginaux dans les années 1980 à la recherche d'un refuge, par l'auteur de « Les Heures », lauréat du prix Pulitzer.

ANREISE	195 km vom internationalen Flughafen Boston Logan.
PREISE	Zwischen 130 € und 395 €.
ZIMMER	16 Zimmer und Suiten.
KÜCHE	Kontinentales Frühstück; kein Restaurant (aber eine große Auswahl an Restaurants in Provincetown).
GESCHICHTE	1904 als Sommer-Cottage von einem Hutmacher aus Boston erbaut, ab 1926 ein Gasthaus.
X-FAKTOR	Das etwas skurrile Hotel ist der perfekte Ort, um die Künstlerseele von Provincetown zu entdecken.

ACCÈS	À 195 Km de l'aéroport international Boston Logan.
PRIX	De 130 € à 395 €.
CHAMBRES	16 chambres et suites.
RESTAURATION	Petit-déjeuner continental uniquement ; pas de restaurant (mais il n'en manque pas à Provincetown).
HISTOIRE	Ancienne résidence d'été construite par un chapelier de Boston en 1904 ; convertie en auberge en 1926.
LE « PETIT PLUS »	Folie battue par les vents ; l'endroit idéal pour tremper dans l'ambiance bohème et artistique de Provincetown.

Long, Lazy Days...
The Moorings Village, Islamorada

The Moorings Village, Islamorada

Long, Lazy Days

This is what Florida used to be like, before the tourists arrived in force, before real estate speculators turned vast stretches of beach into concrete walls of condominums. At Moorings Village, an 18 acre compound of little cottages and houses small and grand in Islamorada, Florida, things are kept deliberately simple. There is no fancy restaurant – each of the homes is self-contained, with a kitchen and in many cases a washer and dryer. There are no "activities" scheduled, but a 1,100 foot (333 metre) long private white sand beach is at the guest's disposal for kayaking, windsurfing, swimming, or just lazing around. Moorings Village has a variety of lodgings; some are modest bungalows with screened porches that look like the setting for a scene in a crime thriller by famous Florida authors Carl Hiassen or Elmore Leonard; others are neat two-story colonial houses with pillars and gingerbread and wraparound porches. All are placed well away from the beach, ensuring its quiet and beauty. Islamorada is the US capital of the sport of bonefishing, which has nothing to do with bones, but rather involves chasing one of the most difficult to catch and vigorously aggressive deep sea fish in North America. Here in the peaceful, sleepy Moorings Village, the bonefish are probably the most rambunctious creatures you'll encounter.

Book to pack: "Tourist Season" by Carl Hiaasen.
Biting satire about Florida life, full of local color and characters.

The Moorings Village	
123 Beach Road	
Islamorada, FL 33036	
USA	
Tel. +1 305 664 4708	
Fax +1 305 664 4242	
Website: www.themooringsvillage.com	
Booking: www.great-escapes-hotels.com	

DIRECTIONS	80 miles (130 km) south of Miami International Airport.
RATES	From $225 a night for the simplest cottage, up to $7000 a week for a house.
ROOMS	18 cottages and houses, ranging from one to three bedrooms.
FOOD	Self-catering: the houses and cottages have fully-equipped kitchens.
HISTORY	Originally built in 1936 as a private estate. Opened as a resort in 1989.
X-FACTOR	Discover a rare bit of old Florida, before the real estate and tourism boom.

Nichts als Faulenzen

»Moorings Village« ist ein Stück Florida, wie es früher einmal war. Bevor Touristenströme einfielen, Immobilienspekulanten Wohnsiedlungen hinklotzten und Betonwüsten aus Stränden machten. Die 7,2 Hektar große Siedlung auf Islamorada besteht aus kleinen Cottages und verschiedenen größeren und kleineren Häusern. Der Lifestyle ist bewusst einfach, ein schickes Restaurant sucht man hier vergebens. Jedes der Häuser ist aber mit einer Küche ausgestattet, und die meisten verfügen auch über eine Waschmaschine und einen Wäschetrockner. »Moorings Village« bietet den Gästen auch kein ausgeklügeltes Programm mit Aktivitäten an, doch langweilig wird hier niemandem. Am über 300 Meter langen, weißen Privatstrand kann man kajakfahren, surfen, schwimmen oder ganz einfach faulenzen. Die Unterkünfte sind sehr unterschiedlich: hier die bescheidenen Bungalows mit Veranden und Storen, die an Szenerien erinnern, wie sie Floridas bekannteste Krimiautoren, Carl Hiaasen und Elmore Leonard, beschreiben. Dort die schmucken zweistöckigen Kolonialhäuser mit säulenverzierten Veranden. Alle liegen, lauschig und ruhig, etwas weiter weg vom Strand. Islamorada ist übrigens das Mekka einer sehr exklusiven Sportart: dem »Bonefishing«. Hier wird Jagd nach aggressiven Riesenbarschen gemacht. Ein bisschen Aufregung kann auch im sonst friedlichen und verschlafenen »Moorings Village« nicht schaden.

Buchtipp: »Miami-Terror« von Carl Hiaasen.
Bissige Satire über das Leben in Florida mit viel Lokalkolorit.

De longues journées de paresse

C'est à cela que ressemblait la Floride avant l'arrivée en masse des touristes, quand les spéculateurs immobiliers n'avaient pas encore bétonné de vastes étendues de plages pour y construire des immeubles d'appartements. À Islamorada, « Moorings Village » est un domaine de plus de sept hectares où la vie est maintenue délibérément simple. Ici, pas de restaurant branché. Chacune des maisons est autosuffisante, avec sa cuisine et, dans la plupart des cas, tout l'équipement ménager nécessaire. Il n'y pas d'activités prévues, rien qu'une plage privée de sable blanc de plus de 300 mètres de long, où l'on peut faire du kayac, de la planche à voile, nager ou rien du tout. « Moorings Village » possède tout un éventail de logements : du modeste bungalow avec son porche et sa moustiquaire, semblant tout droit sorti d'un polar des célèbres auteurs Carl Hiassen ou Elmore Leonard (tous deux de Floride), à la demeure coloniale avec ses balcons ouvragés, ses colonnes et sa galerie ouverte qui court tout autour de la maison. Tous les bâtiments sont construits en retrait de la plage pour préserver son calme et sa beauté. Islamorada est la capitale américaine de la pêche à la banane de mer, ou « bonefishing », qui n'a rien à voir avec le fruit du bananier mais avec la chasse de l'un des poissons de haute mer les plus vigoureux et agressifs d'Amérique du Nord. À « Moorings Village », la banane de mer est sans doute la créature la plus énervée que vous croiserez.

Livre à emporter : « Miami Park » de Carl Hiaasen.
Satire acerbe de la vie en Floride, remplie de personnages hauts en couleurs.

ANREISE	130 km südlich vom internationalen Flughafen in Miami.
PREISE	Ab 180 € pro Nacht für ein einfaches Cottage, ein Haus kostet bis zu 5660 € pro Woche.
ZIMMER	Insgesamt 18 Cottages und Häuser mit ein bis drei Schlafzimmern.
KÜCHE	Selbstversorgung; die Häuser und Cottages verfügen über eine Küche.
GESCHICHTE	1936 als Privatanlage gebaut. Seit 1989 ein Resort.
X-FAKTOR	Florida wie es früher war.

ACCÈS	À 130 km au sud de l'aéroport international de Miami.
PRIX	À partir de 180 € la nuit pour le bungalow le plus simple, jusqu'à 5660 € la semaine pour une maison.
CHAMBRES	18 bungalows et maisons, comptant de une à trois chambres à coucher.
RESTAURATION	Les maisons et les bungalows ont des cuisines entièrement équipées.
HISTOIRE	Construit en 1936 comme un domaine privé. Converti en complexe hôtelier en 1989.
LE « PETIT PLUS »	Découvrez un des rares vestiges de la Floride d'autrefois, avant le boom du tourisme et de l'immobilier.

Texas Modern...
Hotel San José, Austin

Hotel San José, Austin

Texas Modern

For Americans, Austin has a reputation as the best place in Texas to have fun – the state capital is home to a big university, lots of intellectuals and artists, quirky bohemians and hipsters young and old. Every year the city hosts a major film festival, and an international music-business convention, South by Southwest. Speaking of music, Austin probably has more live musicians per capita than any other city in America, from country to rock to classical, and you can happily spend an entire week cruising nightclubs and concert halls. But if you stay in the Hotel San José, Austin's coolest hotel, you may not make it out of the parking lot. The San José Hotel is one of those happy little accidents of a hotel where a structure with bones and history fell into the hands of an owner with taste and style. Built in the 1930s as a classic American motor hotel, it fell into disrepair over the years. It was a flophouse, then a Bible school. Then native Texan Liz Lambert bought it in the 1990s, and saved up until she could afford to renovate it exactly as she wanted: as a mimimalist-inspired funky retreat. Rooms are simply furnished with red Eames chairs and platform beds; the floors are cool, polished concrete. By contrast, the grounds and common areas are lush with bamboo, cactus and vine covered arbors; you gravitate, automatically, to the main courtyard, where metal lawn chairs and a little swimming pool tempt you to linger over coffee or wine. But what will make you most happy about staying at the Hotel San José are the details. For instance, the breakfast that comes in a handmade Japanese bento box, and the vintage Remington typewriter and Polaroid camera available from the front desk. Borrow it now, and take a picture of your room in the Hotel San José, to remember the best fun you had in Austin.

Book to Pack: "The Last Picture Show" by Larry McMurtry.
Novel about life in a small Texas town by the Pulitzer Prize winning Texas novelist.

Hotel San José	
1316 South Congress Street	
Austin, TX 78704	
USA	
Tel. +1 512 444 7322	
Fax +1 512 444 7362	
Website: www.sanjosehotel.com	
Booking: www.great-escapes-hotels.com	

DIRECTIONS	In downtown Austin, 9 miles (15 km) northwest of Austin-Bergstrom International Airport.
RATES	Rooms from $85-$290.
ROOMS	40 guest rooms.
FOOD	Free continental breakfast served in room; Jo's, a coffeeshop across the parking lot, serves BBQ sandwiches and salads.
HISTORY	1930's era motor court motel, renovated in 1998.
X-FACTOR	The hippest place to stay in Austin, Texas.

»Texas modern«

Austin, die Hauptstadt von Texas, ist eine äußerst lebendige Stadt. Wie in jeder Universitätsstadt tummeln sich hier Intellektuelle, Künstler und Hipster. Austin kann sogar mit einem alljährlichen Filmfestival aufwarten. Auch die internationale Musikindustrie pilgert regelmäßig in die Stadt, um sich am Kongress »South by Southwest« auszutauschen. Den Ort hätte man für einen solchen Anlass nicht besser erfinden können: Austin hat mehr Live-Musiker – Country, Rock und Klassisch – pro Einwohner als jede andere Stadt Amerikas. Hier kann man eine ganze Woche lang durch Nachtclubs und Konzerthallen ziehen, ohne sich auch nur eine Sekunde zu langweilen. Doch aufgepasst, wer im coolsten Hotel der Stadt, dem »San José«, absteigt, wird es kaum weiter als bis zum Parkplatz schaffen. Das »San José Hotel« hatte das Glück, an eine Besitzerin zu geraten, die für die Architektur und die Geschichte des ehemaligen Motels aus den Dreißigern das richtige Gespür hatte. Lange eine billige Absteige, dann eine Bibelschule, kaufte es die Texanerin Liz Lambert in den Neunzigern, ohne allerdings das Geld zu haben, das baufällige Motel instand zu setzen. Lambert sparte so lange, bis sie sich die Renovierung leisten konnte, die ihr vorschwebte. Die Zimmer mit polierten Betonböden sind schlicht-minimalistisch mit roten Eames-Stühlen und Plattform-Betten eingerichtet. Der Innenhof mit Swimmingpool setzt mit üppigem Bambus, Kakteen und weinumrankten Lauben einen Kontrapunkt. Lamberts Sinn für Stil zeigt sich auch in den Details: Das Frühstück wird zum Beispiel in einer handgefertigten japanischen Bento-Box gereicht.

Buchtipp: »Die letzte Vorstellung« von Larry McMurtry. Roman über das Leben in einer texanischen Kleinstadt vom Pulitzer-Preisträger.

« Texas modern »

Pour les Américains, Austin est la ville du Texas où l'on s'amuse : elle héberge une grande université, une multitude d'intellectuels, d'artistes, d'excentriques et de branchés de tous âges. Chaque année s'y tiennent un grand festival du cinéma et un salon international du disque. De fait, elle compte un nombre impressionnant de musiciens. Country, rock ou classique, on peut passer une semaine à écumer night-clubs et salles de concert. Mais si vous logez à l'« Hotel San José », le plus cool d'Austin, vous n'aurez pas envie de sortir. C'est l'un de ces petits accidents heureux où une structure avec une histoire tombe entre les mains d'une femme de goût. Construit dans les années 30 comme un motel classique, il devint asile de nuit puis école de catéchisme avant d'être ramené à la vie dans les années 1990 par la Texane Liz Lambert, qui épargna jusqu'à pouvoir le restaurer exactement tel qu'elle le voulait : minimaliste et moderne. Les chambres sont meublées de chaises rouges de Eames et de lits sur plateformes. Les sols sont en béton poli. En revanche, jardins et parties communes débordent de bambous, de cactus et de tonnelles envahies par la vigne. On gravite autour de la cour principale, où des transats en métal et une petite piscine invitent à s'attarder pour un café ou un verre de vin. Mais ce qui vous ravira le plus, ce sont les détails. Les petits déjeuners sont servis dans des boîtes artisanales en bentonite ; une vieille Remington et un Polaroïd sont disponibles à la réception. Empruntez-le pour photographier votre chambre en souvenir du bon temps passé à Austin.

Livre à emporter : « La dernière séance » de Larry McMurtry. Roman sur la vie dans une petite ville du Texas par un auteur texan lauréat du prix Pulitzer.

ANREISE	Im Stadtzentrum von Austin, rund 15 km nordwestlich vom internationalen Flughafen Austin-Bergstrom.
PREISE	Zimmer zwischen 70 € und 235 €.
ZIMMER	40 Gästezimmer.
KÜCHE	Ein kontinentales Frühstück ist im Preis inbegriffen und wird direkt aufs Zimmer gebracht. Im Coffeeshop »Jo's« gibt es BBQ Sandwiches und Salate.
GESCHICHTE	Motel aus den Dreißigern, 1998 renoviert.
X-FAKTOR	Das angesagteste Hotel in Austin, Texas.

ACCÈS	Au centre d'Austin, à 15 km au nord-ouest de l'aéroport international d'Austin-Bergstrom.
PRIX	Chambres entre 70 € et 235 €.
CHAMBRES	40 chambres.
RESTAURATION	Petit-déjeuner continental gracieusement offert et servi dans les chambres. De l'autre côté du parking, le café «Jo's» sert des sandwichs au barbecue et des salades.
HISTOIRE	Motel des années 1930, rénové en 1998.
LE « PETIT PLUS »	L'hôtel le plus branché d'Austin, au Texas.

Cowtown Cool...
The Hotel Paisano, Marfa

The Hotel Paisano, Marfa

Cowtown Cool

Marfa, population 2,424, sits on the high desert plateau of West Texas, a good three hours drive from anywhere. Marfa got its start as a "cowtown" in 1883; it was a railroad hub for the local ranchers to ship their cattle up north. But even back then, this was a one-horse town with a touch of class – the wife of the railroad boss who founded the town named it "Marfa" after a character in Dostoevsky's "Brothers Karamazov". The original builders of the Hotel Paisano also seem to have had a premonition that big things were in store for little Marfa – the announcement for their grand, faux-Spanish style hotel, constructed just before the 1929 stock market crash proclaimed it "the most elegant hotel between El Paso and San Antonio." In the 1950s, the Paisano, which resembles a cross between a wedding cake and The Alamo, served as the headquarters for the actors and crew of "Giant", an epic film about Texas history starring the late cinema icon James Dean. There's a room filled with Dean memorabilia now at the hotel, which was gently renovated in 2001, but still feels like a place where you could make a deal in the lobby for 1,000 head of cattle over whiskey and cigars. But the hip travellers who keep Hotel Paisano's 33 rooms fully-booked year round are not here to pay homage to Dean, Dostoyevsky, nor cows. They are here to visit the Chinati Foundation, artist Donald Judd's museum of site-specific sculpture, and the engine behind the Hotel Paisano's – and Marfa's – unexpected renaissance.

Book to Pack: "Giant" by Edna Ferber.
The book from which the James Dean movie was made; a sweeping tale of Texas history by a famous 1920's American novelist.

The Hotel Paisano P.O. Box Z Marfa, TX 79843 USA Tel. +1 432 729 3669 Fax +1 432 729 3779 Email: frontdesk@hotelpaisano.com Website: www.hotelpaisano.com Booking: www.great-escapes-hotels.com	**DIRECTIONS** 190 miles (300 km) southeast of El Paso International Airport. **RATES** Rooms and suites from $79 to $200. **ROOMS** 33 rooms. **FOOD** Jett's Grill-named after James Dean's character in "Giant": steaks, ribs, chops, live music on weekends. **HISTORY** Originally built as a grand hotel in 1929; renovated and reopened in 2001. **X-FACTOR** Historic Spanish stucco hotel with a dash of old Hollywood glamour.

Im Schatten der Giganten

Marfa liegt hoch auf einem Wüstenplateau im Westen von Texas – im Niemandsland. Die nächste größere Stadt, El Paso, ist etwa drei Autostunden entfernt. Marfa hat gerade mal 2424 Einwohner. Der Ort wurde 1883 gegründet und war auch damals nicht viel größer als ein »Kuhdorf«. Die Haupttätigkeit der Rancher bestand darin, Vieh in Bahnwaggons zu verfrachten und es Richtung Norden transportieren zu lassen. Ein Hauch von Klasse brachte die Gattin des Eisenbahn-Chefs in den gottverlassenen Ort. Sie nannte ihn »Marfa« nach einer Figur aus Dostojewskis »Die Brüder Karamasow«. Kurz vor dem großen Börsencrash 1929 wurde in Marfa das »Hotel Paisano« im spanischen Kolonialstil eröffnet und stolz als »elegantestes Hotel zwischen El Paso und San Antonio« beworben. Vielleicht eine kleine Vorahnung auf eine größere Zukunft. Das Hotel, das aussieht wie eine Kreuzung aus einer Hochzeitstorte und der Festung »The Alamo«, stand zum ersten Mal in den Fünfzigern im Rampenlicht. Die Crew von »Giant«, einem Film über die Geschichte von Texas, hatte sich hier einquartiert. Darunter Hollywood-Ikone James Dean. Eines der Hotelzimmer dient heute als Dean-Museum. Das »Paisano« wurde 2001 sanft renoviert, aber noch immer kann man sich vorstellen, wie in der Lobby bei Whisky und Zigarren ein Kuhhandel nach dem anderen abgeschlossen wurde. Heute sind die Hotelgäste allerdings weder an Kühen noch an James Dean interessiert. Sie kommen der Chinati Foundation wegen. Das Museum mit Skulpturen und Installationen des Künstlers Donald Judd ist heute der Grund, nach Marfa zu reisen.

Buchtipp: »Giganten« von Edna Ferber.

Eine Erzählung aus dem historischen Texas. Das Buch, in den 1920ern verfasst, diente als Vorlage für den gleichnamigen Film mit James Dean.

Dans l'ombre des géants

Marfa, 2 424 habitants, est perchée sur un haut plateau dans le désert de l'ouest texan, à trois bonnes heures de nulle part. Elle a vu le jour en 1883 comme gare d'où les ranchers venaient envoyer leurs troupeaux vers le nord. Mais, même alors, c'était un bled perdu avec un petit quelque chose en plus : la femme du chef des chemins de fer qui fonda le bourg le baptisa « Marfa » en hommage à un personnage des « Frères Karamazov » de Dostoïevski. Les bâtisseurs du « Paisano » devaient avoir pressenti l'avenir grandiose du petit bourg : la publicité de leur grand hôtel au style hispanisant, construit juste avant le krach de 1929, le proclamait « l'établissement le plus élégant entre El Paso et San Antonio ». Dans les années cinquante, le Paisano, un hybride entre une pièce montée et « l'Alamo », servit de Q. G. aux acteurs et à l'équipe « de Géants », film à grand spectacle qui retrace une partie de l'histoire du Texas avec le légendaire James Dean. Une chambre abrite aujourd'hui tous les souvenirs de la star. L'hôtel a été restauré en 2001 mais, dans le hall, on peut encore s'imaginer troquant 1 000 têtes de bétail contre du whisky et des cigares. Toutefois, les voyageurs éclairés qui remplissent l'hôtel toute l'année ne viennent ni pour Dean, ni pour Dostoïevski ni pour les vaches. Ils sont là pour visiter la fondation « Chinati », le musée de sculptures contextuelles créé par Donald Judd, le moteur derrière la renaissance inattendue de l'« Hotel Paisano » et de Marfa.

Livre à emporter : « Géant » d'Edna Ferber.

Le livre qui a inspiré le film avec James Dean, tout un pan de l'histoire du Texas par la célèbre romancière américaine des années vingt.

ANREISE	300 km südöstlich vom internationalen Flughafen El Paso.
PREISE	Zimmer und Suiten zwischen 60 € und 160 €.
ZIMMER	33 Zimmer.
KÜCHE	Der »Jett's Grill« ist nach der von James Dean gespielten Figur im Film »Die Giganten« benannt. Hier gibt's Steaks, Ribs, Chops und am Wochende wird Live-Musik gespielt.
GESCHICHTE	1929 als Grand-Hotel gebaut, 2001 renoviert und wiedereröffnet.
X-FAKTOR	Historisches Hotel im spanischen Kolonialstil mit einem Hauch Hollywood-Glamour.

ACCÈS	À 300 km au sud-est de l'aéroport international d'El Paso.
PRIX	Chambres et suites entre 60 € et 160 €.
CHAMBRES	33 chambres.
RESTAURATION	Le « Jett's Grill », baptisé d'après le personnage de James Dean dans « Géant »: steaks, côtes de bœuf, côtelettes ; musique live les week-ends.
HISTOIRE	Construit comme un « grand hôtel » en 1929, restauré et rouvert en 2001.
LE « PETIT PLUS »	Hôtel historique rococo avec une pointe de vieux glamour hollywoodien.

Cowboy Minimalist...
Thunderbird Motel, Marfa

Thunderbird Motel, Marfa

Cowboy Minimalist

Until artist Donald Judd discovered this dusty but picturesque West Texas cowtown in the 1970s, Marfa's main attraction was the "Marfa Mystery Lights" an eerie, unexplained display of flashing lights that, if you were lucky, sometimes illuminated the town's inky-black star-filled sky after midnight. Nowadays, there is a lot more activity in Marfa, since Judd's famed Chinati Foundation draws art enthusiasts from all over the world to visit the installation of site-specific large-scale artworks on a former military base on Marfa's outskirts. The newcomers have brought their big-city culture to the small town, and nowadays Marfa is a place where you can, in the same day, drink a long-necked Budweiser with a guy in cowboy boots, and, eat grilled raddichio and gorgonzola appetizers with a New York art gallery manager. The Thunderbird Motel, on the surface, would seem to be a place that caters to the latter customer – it exudes the hip confidence of an owner who understands that old American 1950s motels are the quintessence of minimalist hip, especially when outfitted with fine cotton sheets from India, custom-built pecan-wood furniture, and Broadband internet connections. But the Thunderbird Motel, like the Chinati museum, is an upstart with a sense of place; it may bring new ideas to Marfa, but it embraces its surroundings and its West Texas roots. The motel's pale blue façade blends into the big sky of Texas; its jasmine-covered trellises are made from salvaged oil pipeline, and in the courtyard, there's a big slab of mesquite wood for a table. City slickers and cowboys should feel equally at home in this outpost of the new Marfa.

Book to Pack: "Complete Writings 1959-1975" by Donald Judd. Reviews, essays and criticism by the American artist and Chinati Foundation founder.

Thunderbird Motel
600 West San Antonio
Marfa, TX 79843
USA
Tel. +1 432 729 1984
Fax +1 432 729 1989
Email: info@thunderbirdmarfa.com
Website: www.thunderbirdmarfa.com
Booking: www.great-escapes-hotels.com

DIRECTIONS	On Highway 90, 190 miles (300 km) southeast of El Paso International Airport.
RATES	Rooms and suites from $95 to $125.
ROOMS	24 rooms.
FOOD	Restaurant planned for 2008.
HISTORY	Renovated classic American motel, originally built 1959, opened 2005.
X-FACTOR	Cowboy minimalist motel from the proprietor of Austin's Hotel San José.

Minimalistisches Cowboy-Motel

Bevor der Künstler Donald Judd in den Siebzigern die zwar pittoreske, aber staubige Kleinstadt Marfa im Westen von Texas entdeckte, war hier nicht viel los. Als einzige Attraktion machten die »Marfa Mystery Lights« von sich reden, ein unerklärliches Phänomen, das sich nachts bei schwarzem, sternenbehangenem Himmel als strahlende, leuchtende Punkte am Horizont zeigt. Die öden Zeiten sind für Marfa ein für allemal vorbei. Judds Chinati Foundation lockt eine ganze Heerschar von Kunstfans aus aller Welt zu den riesigen, permanenten Installationen, die auf einer ehemaligen Militärbasis am Rande Marfas stehen. Der frische Wind hat etwas Großstadtkultur in die Kleinstadt gebracht, und heute kann man in Marfa mit einem Kerl in Cowboy-Boots ein Bier trinken und dann mit einem New Yorker Galeristen Raddichio mit Gorgonzola verspeisen. Das »Thunderbird Motel« wirkt auf den ersten Blick urban – eine Ikone des Minimalismus der Fünfziger Amerikas, kombiniert mit Baumwollwäsche aus Indien, handgefertigten Möbeln aus Pekanholz und Breitband-Internetanschluss. Doch das »Thunderbird Motel« hat, genau wie das »Chinati Museum«, seine texanischen Wurzeln nicht vergessen. Die hellblauen Fassaden des Motels und der weite Himmel von Texas fließen ineinander, der Jasmin wächst über ein Geflecht von alten Öl-Rohrleitungen und im Hinterhof wurde eine Mesquite-Holzplatte zu einem Tisch umfunktioniert. Hier fühlen sich Landeier genau so wohl wie Stadt-Cowboys.

Buchtipp: »Donald Judd« von Donald Judd und Nicholas Serota. Würdigung des einflussreichen amerikanischen Künstlers und Gründer der Chinati Foundation in Marfa.

Western minimaliste

Jusqu'à ce que l'artiste Donald Judd découvre ce bourg poussiéreux mais pittoresque dans l'ouest du Texas dans les années soixante-dix, la principale attraction de Marfa était ses « lumières mystérieuses », des éclairs inexpliqués et inquiétants qui, parfois, illuminent le ciel étoilé après minuit. Il s'y passe beaucoup plus de choses depuis que la fondation « Chinati » ouverte par Judd attire des amateurs d'art venus des quatre coins du monde pour visiter l'installation de grandes œuvres contextuelles sur une ancienne base militaire à la lisière de Marfa. Les nouveaux venus ont importé leur culture métropolitaine et, dans la petite ville tranquille, on peut, dans la foulée, siroter une bière avec un cow-boy en santiags puis déguster des « raddichio et gorgonzolas grillés » avec un galeriste new-yorkais. En apparence, le « Thunderbird Motel » semble avoir été créé pour cette seconde catégorie de clients. Il dégage la suave assurance d'un propriétaire qui sait que les motels des années cinquante sont la quintessence du minimalisme branché, surtout équipés de draps en fin coton indien, de meubles sur-mesure en pacanier et de connexions Internet à haut débit. Mais, à l'instar du musée « Chinati », le motel est un lieu ambitieux qui sait s'intégrer. S'il apporte de nouvelles idées à Marfa, il a également fait siennes les racines de l'Ouest. Sa façade bleu pâle se fond dans le grand ciel texan, ses treillis couverts de jasmin sont faits de vieux pipelines et, dans la cour, une planche en proposis massif fait office de table. Citadins et cow-boys se sentent chez eux dans cet avant-poste de la Nouvelle Marfa.

Livre à emporter : « Écrits 1963-1990 » de Donald Judd. Critiques et essais de l'artiste américain, créateur de la fondation Chinati.

ANREISE	300 km auf dem Highway 90 südöstlich vom internationalen Flughafen El Paso.	ACCÈS	Sur le Highway 90, à 300 km au sud-est de l'aéroport international d'El Paso.
PREISE	Zimmer und Suiten zwischen 75 € und 100 €.	PRIX	Chambres et suites entre 75 € et 100 €.
ZIMMER	24 Zimmer.	CHAMBRES	24 chambres.
KÜCHE	Ein Restaurant ist für 2008 geplant.	RESTAURATION	Ouverture d'un restaurant prévue pour 2008.
GESCHICHTE	Renoviertes, klassisch amerikanisches Motel von 1959, 2005 wiedereröffnet.	HISTOIRE	Motel américain classique construit en 1959 et rénové en 2005.
X-FAKTOR	Minimalistisches »Cowboy-Motel«.	LE « PETIT PLUS »	« Motel cow-boy minimaliste », appartenant au même propriétaire que l'«Hotel San José» d'Austin.

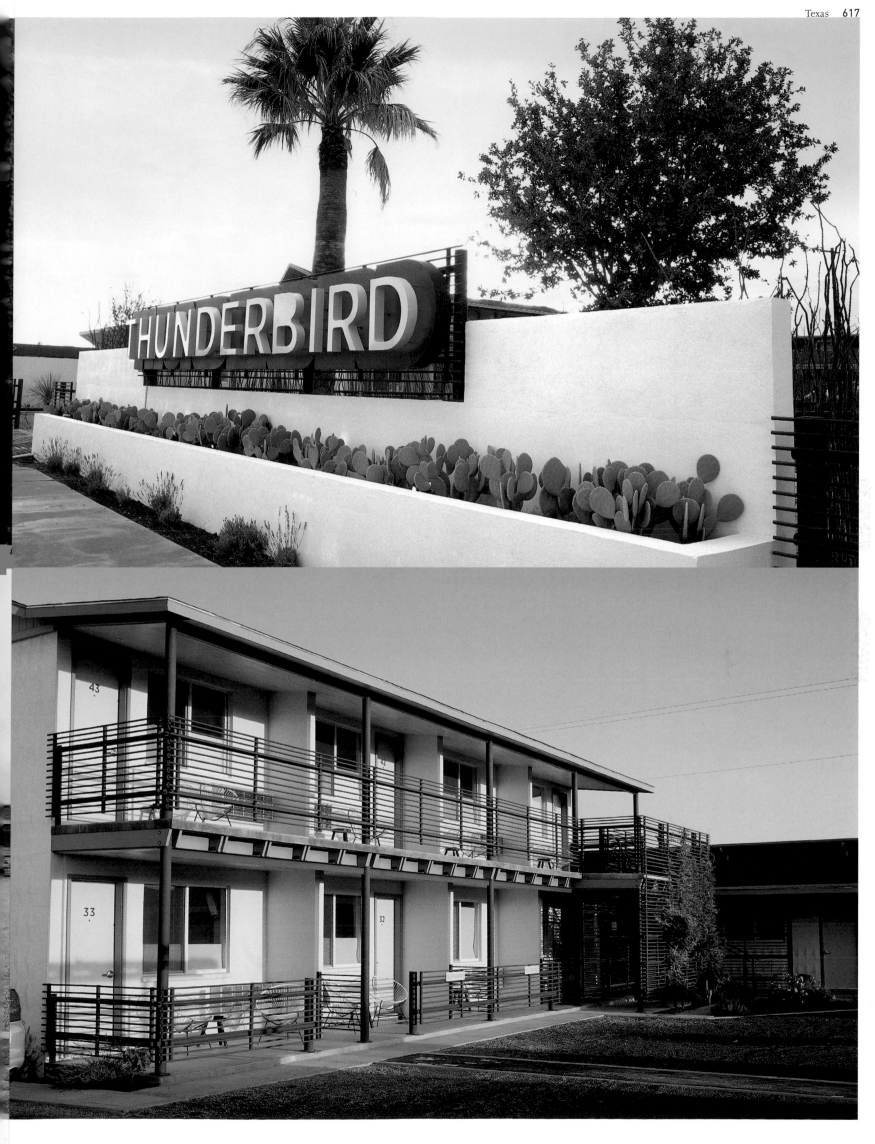

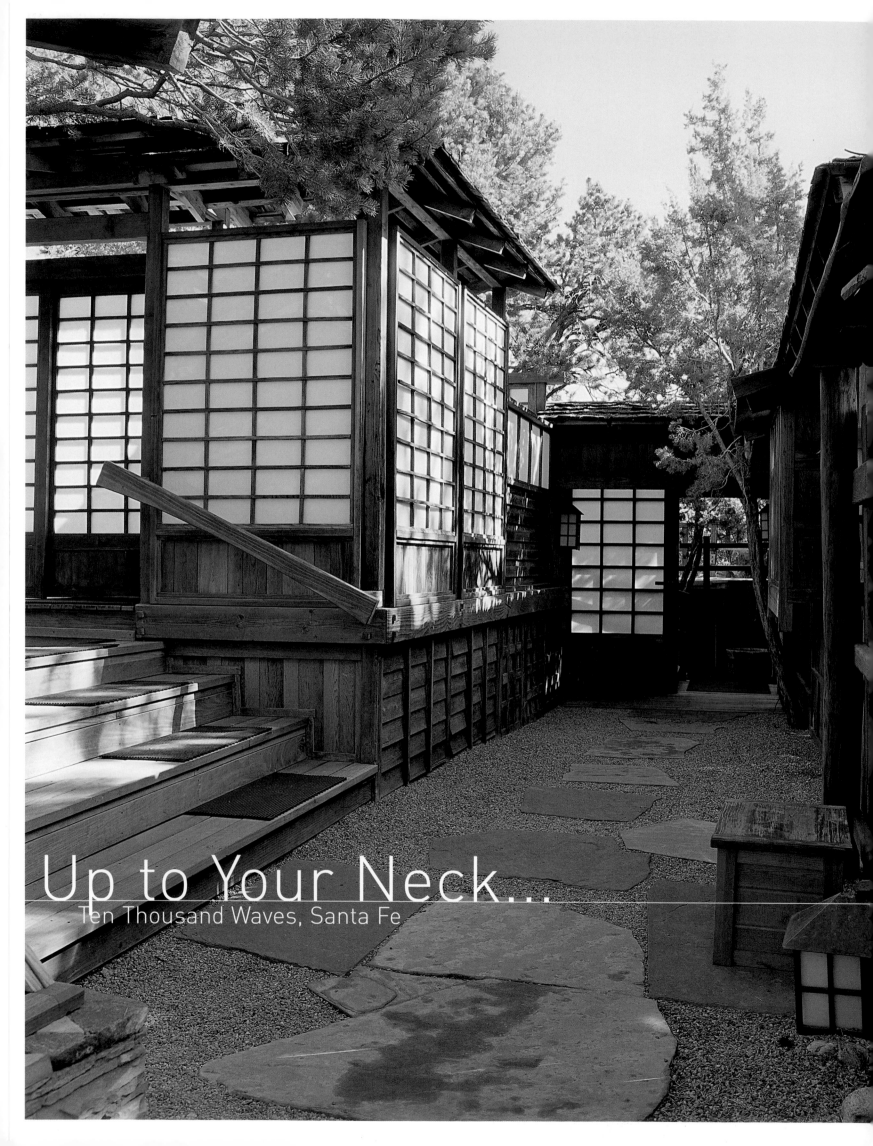

Up to Your Neck...
Ten Thousand Waves, Santa Fe

Ten Thousand Waves, Santa Fe

Up to Your Neck

There's an argument to be made that water-specifically mineral-rich spring water that bubbles naturally from deep inside the earth-is the most potent drug on the planet. It is an argument that seems especially compelling after about twenty minutes soaking in a deep tub of intensely hot, steaming water. The Japanese understand the power of water, and they have created a whole culture around the act of hot springs bathing, and raised it to an aesthetic experience. Few places in the U.S. understand the subtleties of the Japanese bath, but at Ten Thousand Waves the onsen culture has been transplanted almost intact from the Japanese woods to the American high desert. The centrepieces of Ten Thousand Waves, as in Japan, are the two outdoor communal tubs, or "ofuro". One is for both sexes, the other for women only, and both are built in harmony with the outdoors; tiny rock gardens hold small iron lanterns, the railings are rough-hewn timbers, and bathing areas are separated by traditional Shoji screens. Ten Thousand Waves was originally a hot springs spa for day guests, but some years ago the owners decided to add some suites so that the completely unwound and de-stressed customers wouldn't have to worry about finding their way home after the bath. The suites are decorated in the same satisfyingly rustic Southwest-meets-Mt. Fuji style as the pool areas. Slip into the hot water on a cool, dry desert night, lean back, look up, and wonder: Do the stars shine so brightly in Tokyo?

Book to pack: "Memoirs of a Geisha" by Arthur Golden
Historical novel about Japanese geishas and their lifestyle.

Ten Thousand Waves
3451 Hyde Park Road
Santa Fe, NM 87504
USA
Tel. +1 505 992 5052
Fax +1 505 989 5077
Email: askus@tenthousandwaves.com
Website: www.tenthousandwaves.com
Booking: www.great-escapes-hotels.com

DIRECTIONS	3.5 miles (5 km) west of Santa Fe.
RATES	From $190 to $260 a night.
ROOMS	12 guest suites.
FOOD	No food; some guest suites have hibachi grills.
HISTORY	Originally only a hot tub spa retreat; guest suites were added in 1997.
X-FACTOR	For authentic Japanese hot springs bathing under the New Mexico desert sky.

Einfach eintauchen und entspannen

Wasser ist eines der wirksamsten Heilmittel überhaupt. Erst recht, wenn es reich an Mineralien ist und aus einer Quelle aus dem tiefen Inneren der Erde sprudelt. Nach zwanzig Minuten in der heiß-dampfenden Wanne fängt man an, die Wohltaten zu spüren. Die Japaner haben eine ganze Kultur rund ums heiße Bad entwickelt und sie zum ästhetischen Erlebnis erhoben. Nur wenige Spas in den Vereinigten Staaten verstehen die Feinheiten der japanischen Badekultur. Zu den Ausnahmen gehört »Ten Thousand Waves«, ein Spa, das die Rituale des heißen Quellbades in die Wüste New Mexicos gebracht hat. Zwei gemeinschaftlich genutzte »Ofuro«-Becken (das eine für Frauen und Männer, das andere nur für Frauen) bilden nach japanischem Vorbild das Herzstück. Sie liegen harmonisch in der freien Natur. Miniatur-Steingärten verankern kleine Eisenlaternen, die Geländer sind aus grob gehobelten Holzbalken gezimmert, und die Badezonen sind mit traditionellen »Shoji«-Wandschirmen abgetrennt. »Ten Thousand Waves« war zunächst ausschließlich als Spa konzipiert. Damit die Gäste nach dem Bad nicht aus ihrer wohligen Entspannung herausgerissen werden, haben die Besitzer vor ein paar Jahren Suiten hinzugebaut. Sie sind im ansprechenden Dekor des Spas gehalten - ein Mix aus rustikalem Western-Stil und Fuji-Ästhetik. Am schönsten ist ein nächtliches Bad unter klarem Sternenhimmel. Denn nirgendwo strahlen die Sterne so hell wie hier.

Buchtipp: »Die Geisha« von Arthur Golden
Historischer Roman über das Leben der Geishas in Japan.

Jusqu'au cou

D'aucuns soutiennent que l'eau de source riche en sels minéraux qui jaillit directement des entrailles de la terre est la drogue la plus puissante de la planète. On est tenté de le croire après avoir trempé vingt minutes dans une profonde cuve fumante. Les Japonais comprennent le pouvoir de l'eau au point d'avoir créé toute une culture autour du bain dans des sources chaudes, l'érigeant en expérience esthétique. Peu d'endroits aux États-Unis comprennent les subtilités du bain japonais mais, à « Ten Thousand Waves », la tradition « onsen » des forêts du Japon a été transplantée quasi intacte dans le haut désert américain. Ici, les pièces maîtresses sont les deux « ofuro », des bassins collectifs en plein air. L'un est mixte, l'autre réservé aux femmes et tous deux s'harmonisent avec la nature. De minuscules jardins de pierres sont éclairés par de petites lanternes en fer, les balustrades sont en bois brut et les bains sont séparés par des écrans traditionnels « Shoji ». À l'origine, « Ten Thousand Waves » n'accueillait les thermalistes que pendant la journée, jusqu'à ce que les propriétaires n'ajoutent quelques suites pour que leurs clients complètement relaxés n'aient pas à s'inquiéter de devoir reprendre la route. Le décor des chambres témoigne du même mariage heureux entre l'ouest américain et le style du mont Fuji que les thermes. Glissez-vous lentement dans l'eau chaude par une fraîche nuit dans le désert, détendez-vous et admirez le ciel : les étoiles ont-elles autant d'éclat à Tokyo ?

Livre à emporter : « Geisha » de Arthur Golden
Roman historique sur la vie des geishas japonaises.

ANREISE	5 km westlich von Santa Fe.
PREISE	Zwischen 150 € und 210 € pro Nacht.
ZIMMER	12 Gästesuiten.
KÜCHE	Keine Verpflegungsmöglichkeiten. In einigen Suiten steht ein »Hibachi«-Grill.
GESCHICHTE	Ursprünglich nur ein Spa; Gästesuiten wurden 1997 dazugebaut.
X-FAKTOR	Authentische Badekultur aus Japan unter dem Wüsten-Himmel New Mexicos.

ACCÈS	5 km à l'ouest de Santa Fe.
PRIX	Entre 150 € et 210 € la nuit.
CHAMBRES	12 suites.
RESTAURATION	Pas de restaurant ; certaines suites sont équipées de grills hibachi.
HISTOIRE	Initialement un spa de sources chaudes auquel des suites ont été ajoutées en 1997.
LE « PETIT PLUS »	Des bains de sources chaudes à la japonaise en plein air dans le désert du Nouveau Mexique.

Mi Adobe Hacienda…
Rancho de la Osa, Tucson

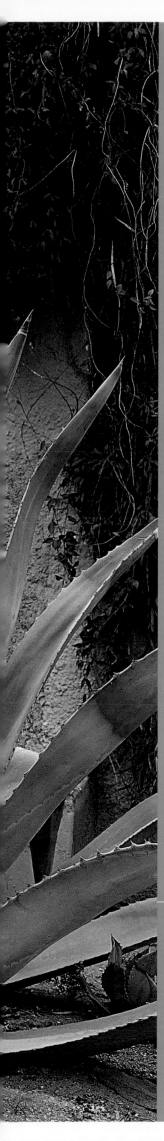

Rancho de la Osa, Tucson

Mi Adobe Hacienda

We are in the United States, but not quite. Once upon a time, this piece of beautiful high desert land in southern Arizona, where Rancho de la Osa sits, was part of Mexico. Before that it belonged to Spain, and still before that, the Navajo Indians made this place their home. Like all borderlands, the rugged valley between the Baboquivari peak and the Sierra Mountains retains an unexpected mix of cultures and folkways. You can taste them in the Rancho's daily menu, where ancient ingredients like Navajo corn and beans blend with Latin spices and servings of succulent meat (the big business here, until recently, was cattle ranching) roasted on mesquite wood chips. Rancho de la Osa is a place to immerse yourself in this unique American borderland culture; here, you can wander among old adobe buildings, sit under shady eucalyptus trees, listen to the gentle sounds of ranch life: the ring of the mission bell, voices chattering in both English and Spanish, the hoofbeats of horses. The horses, of course, are one of the Rancho's biggest attractions – it is a working dude ranch, where horses have been raised and trained for more than 300 years (In the 1920s and 1930s, Western movies were shot here, and the singing cowboy Tom Mix was a regular guest). There's a staff of vaqueros – that's cowboys to you – who will help you saddle up and ride into the surrounding grasslands and hills (the room rate includes two rides a day). If you are not a seasoned cowboy, at Rancho you can take riding lessons, and you can even borrow cowboy boots ("Shake them out before using," warns the Rancho guest manual.) Good advice, in any language.

Book to pack: "The Milagro Beanfield War" by John Nichols. Novel about the history of the American-Mexican borderlands; made into a Robert Redford movie.

Rancho de la Osa P.O. Box 1 Tucson/Sasabe, AZ 85633 USA Tel. +1 520 823 4257 Fax +1 520 823 4238 Email: osagal@aol.com Website: www.ranchodelaosa.com Booking: www.great-escapes-hotels.com	**DIRECTIONS** Located about 92 miles (150 km) southwest of the Tucson, Arizona airport. **RATES** From $215 per person, incl. all meals and scheduled activities, 3 nights minimum stay. **ROOMS** 19 mountain-view guest rooms, most with fireplaces; each one is different and filled with Mexican antiques. **FOOD** Modern Southwestern American-style meals – tortilla soup, mesquite grilled meats – are served in the ochre-walled dining room in the main hacienda building. **HISTORY** The ranch is more than three hundred years old, and dates back to the time of the Spanish missions. **X-FACTOR** Stunning desert nights, old Spanish Southwest culture.

Fiesta Mexicana

Die Heimat der »Rancho de la Osa« im Süden Arizonas ist anders als der Rest der Vereinigten Staaten. Kein Wunder: Das Gebiet gehörte einst zu Mexiko und zuvor der spanischen Krone. Bevor die Kolonialmacht Besitzansprüche stellte, hatten hier allerdings die Navajo-Indianer das Sagen. Im rauen Tal zwischen dem »Baboquivari Peak« und den »Sierra Mountains« vermischen sich Kulturen und Traditionen. In der Küche werden zum Beispiel traditionelle Zutaten wie Navajo-Mais und Bohnen genauso verwendet wie lateinamerikanische Gewürze. Eine Spezialität ist Kakteenfleisch, das über dem wohlriechendem Mesquite-Holz gebraten wird, und der Anbau und Handel von Kakteen hat sich hier zu einem blühenden Geschäft entwickelt. Wer die amerikanisch-mexikanische Grenzkultur erleben möchte, ist auf der »Rancho de la Osa« genau richtig. Hier kann man an traditonellen Lehmziegel-Häusern vorbeispazieren, unter schattigen Eukalyptusbäumen sitzen und dabei dem Leben auf der Ranch zuhören: hier das Läuten einer alten Kirchenglocke, da ein Stimmengewirr zwischen Englisch und Spanisch und dort Pferdehufschlag. Seit über 300 Jahren werden hier Pferde gezüchtet und trainiert, und trotz Gästen wird noch richtig gearbeitet. In den Zwanzigern und Dreißigern wurden hier auch einige Western-Filme gedreht. Die Pferde sind die größte Attraktion der Ranch. Die Vaqueros, der spanische Ausdruck für Cowboys, helfen den Gästen gerne für den Ausritt in den Sattel. Ein erfahrener Reiter braucht man allerdings nicht zu sein – es gibt Reitstunden. Und die passenden Cowboy-Boots kann man sich dazu auch noch ausleihen.

Buchtipp: »Milagro« von John Nichols.
Das Buch zum Film von Robert Redford. Eine Geschichte aus dem amerikanisch-mexikanischen Grenzgebiet.

Mon hacienda en adobe

On est aux États-Unis mais pas tout à fait. Autrefois, cette partie du désert au sud de l'Arizona était mexicaine. Avant cela, elle fut espagnole et, plus loin encore, terre des Navajos. Comme toutes les régions frontalières, cette vallée sauvage blottie entre le pic « Baboquivari » et la « Sierra Mountains » abrite un surprenant mélange de cultures et de coutumes. On le sent dans la cuisine du Rancho, où des ingrédients comme le maïs et les haricots navajos s'associent aux épices latino-américaines pour accompagner les viandes succulentes (jusqu'à récemment, l'élevage était l'activité principale du ranch) grillées sur des copeaux de prosopis. « Le Rancho de la Osa » est le lieu rêvé pour baigner dans cette ambiance unique. Promenez-vous parmi les vieilles bâtisses en adobe, asseyez-vous à l'ombre des eucalyptus, laissez-vous bercer par les bruits familiers : la cloche de la mission, les bribes de conversation en anglais et en espagnol, le martèlement des sabots de chevaux. Ces derniers, naturellement, sont la grande attraction de l'établissement, qui les dresse depuis plus de 300 ans (dans les années vingt et trente, on tournait ici des westerns, et le cow-boy chanteur Tom Mix était un habitué). Une équipe de « vaqueros » vous aidera à grimper en selle pour un galop dans les prairies et les collines environnantes (le prix de la chambre inclut deux balades par jour). Si vous n'êtes pas un cavalier chevronné, le Rancho offre des cours. Vous pouvez même emprunter des bottes de cow-boy (le guide du Rancho met en garde « Secouez-les bien avant de les enfiler.» Un bon conseil, dans toutes les langues).

Livre à emporter : « Milagro ou la guerre des haricots » de John Nichols.
Roman sur l'histoire de la frontière américano-mexicaine, adapté à l'écran par Robert Redford.

ANREISE	Etwa 150 km südwestlich vom Flughafen Tucson, Arizona.
PREISE	Ab 175 € pro Person, Mahlzeiten und Aktivitäten eingeschlossen. Mindestaufenthalt von drei Nächten.
ZIMMER	19 Zimmer mit Sicht auf die Berge, die meisten mit Kamin, und alle mit mexikanischen Antiquitäten eingerichtet.
KÜCHE	Spezialitäten des amerikanischen Südwestens wie Tortillasuppe oder Grilladen auf Mesquite-Holz werden im ockerfarbenen Speisesaal der Hacienda serviert.
GESCHICHTE	Die Ranch wurde vor mehr als 300 Jahren während der spanischen Kolonialzeit gegründet.
X-FAKTOR	Atemberaubend schöne Wüstennächte; amerikanisch-mexikanische Kultur des Südwestens.

ACCÈS	Situé à 150 km au sud-ouest de l'aéroport de Tucson, dans l'Arizona.
PRIX	À partir de 175 € par personne, en pension complète et incluant toutes les activités. Séjour minimum de 3 nuits.
CHAMBRES	19 chambres avec vue sur la montagne, la plupart avec cheminée.
RESTAURATION	Cuisine américaine moderne typique du Sud-Ouest. Les repas sont servis dans la salle à manger ocre dans le bâtiment principal de l'hacienda.
HISTOIRE	Vieux de plus de 300 ans, le ranch date de l'époque des missions espagnoles.
LE « PETIT PLUS »	Nuits somptueuses sous le ciel du désert.

Silver Boxes...
Shady Dell RV Park, Bisbee

Shady Dell RV Park, Bisbee

Silver Boxes

In the 1950s, decades before Motel 6 and Days Inns turned America's budget motels into a standardized, fast-food experience, this is how Americans travelled on the cheap. Families packed up and headed out on the highway in a car with a silver box trailing behind it. These yachts of the road had evocative names – Airstream, Manor, Royal Mansion – and sleek, aerodynamic shapes that hinted speed, open spaces, and freedom. The tourism slogan of the period was "See America First", and there probably never was a time when travelling overland across America's deserts and farmlands was more carefree or romantic. The Shady Dell RV Park is a tiny enclave that preserves 1950s trailer travelling in all its glory for contemporary travellers. Situated behind a gas station and next to a cemetery, about a mile away from the famous "Ghost Town" of Bisbee, Arizona, the trailer park is home to 10 vintage aluminium trailers and one beached wooden yacht that have been painstakingly restored into 1950s time capsules, down to the tiniest detail. Bedspreads are chenille, phonographs come with Elvis Presley 45rpm discs, and the cupboards hold antique Martini glasses and shakers. You can sip your Martini while staring out at the desert, then take a drive into nearby Bisbee, an abandoned copper mining town that's found a second life as a community for hippies, artisans and bohemians of all types. Or you can escape across the Mexican border, just a few miles down the highway. From inside a shiny silver box with wheels, anything and everything seems possible.

Book to pack: "Airstream, The History of the Land Yacht" by Bryan Burkhart and David Hunt.
An illustrated cultural history of American vintage trailers.

Shady Dell RV Park	
1 Old Douglas Road	
Bisbee, AZ 85603	
USA	
Tel. +1 520 432 3567	
Email: shadydell@lycos.com	
Website: www.theshadydell.com	
Booking: www.great-escapes-hotels.com	

DIRECTIONS	Located about 92 miles (150 km) southeast of the Tucson, Arizona airport.
RATES	Individual trailers rent from $40 a night; a 38 foot Chris Craft yacht rents for $125.
ROOMS	Ten vintage aluminium travel trailers from the 1940s and 1950s, and one beached Chris Craft Yacht.
FOOD	Dot's Diner, a 10-stool American diner, serves breakfasts and lunches between 7am and 2pm, Wednesday to Sunday.
HISTORY	An American roadside trailer park, opened in 1927, restored and re-fitted with vintage aluminum trailers in 1995 by a couple of former antique dealers.
X-FACTOR	The freedom and romance of Roadside America, circa 1950.

Silberne Schmuckkästchen

Im Amerika der fünfziger Jahre hatten Budget-Unterkünfte noch Stil. Billighotel-Ketten wie »Motel 9« oder »Days Inns« – mit dem Charme von Fast-Food-Restaurants – existierten noch nicht. Die typische amerikanische Familie packte ganz einfach ihre Siebensachen ins Auto und fuhr los. Hinten angehängt glitzerte ein silberner Wohnwagen. Es waren richtige Straßen-Yachten mit aerodynamischen Formen und so klingenden Namen wie »Airstream«, »Manor« oder »Royal Mansion«. Sie evozierten Träume von Geschwindigkeit, unendlich weiten Landschaften und der großen Freiheit. Nie war das Reisen quer durch Amerikas Wüsten und Felder unbeschwerter und romantischer. Der »Shady Dell RV (Recreational Vehicle) Park« hat ein Stück dieser gloriosen Fünfziger-Trailer-Romantik bewahrt. Er liegt keine zwei Kilometer außerhalb der Geisterstadt Bisbee in Arizona, gleich hinter einer Tankstelle und neben einem Friedhof. Zehn Wohnwagen aus Aluminium und eine gestrandete Holz-Yacht wurden bis ins letzte Detail restauriert und stehen hier als Zeitinsel der Fünfziger. Bettdecken aus Chenille, Elvis-Presley-Vinylplatten und klassische Martini-Gläser und -Shaker ergänzen das Stilbild stimmig. Mit dem Martini-Glas an den Lippen lässt sich der Blick auf die Wüstenlandschaft besonders gut genießen. Unbedingt empfiehlt sich ein Ausflug nach Bisbee, einer verlassenen Kupferminen-Stadt, die heute als Kommune für Hippies, Künstler und Bohemiens eine Renaissance erlebt. Oder man fährt kurz ein paar Meilen auf dem Highway über die Grenze nach Mexiko. Hat man eine glänzende Silber-Box auf Rädern als Zufluchtsort, scheint plötzlich alles möglich.

Buchtipp: »Airsteam, **The History of the Land Yacht**« von Bryan **Burkhart und David Hunt.**
Illustrierte Kulturgeschichte amerikanischer Trailer.

Des écrins d'argent

Dans les années cinquante, bien avant que des chaînes telles que « Motel 9 » et « Days Inn » ne transforment les motels bon marché américains en produits standardisés et aseptisés, c'est ainsi que les Américains voyageaient à peu de frais. Les familles prenaient la route avec la caravane accrochée à l'arrière de la voiture. Ces yachts sur roues aux noms suggestifs – « Airstream », « Manor », « Royal Mansion » – avaient des lignes aérodynamiques symboles de vitesse, de grands espaces et de liberté. La devise de l'époque était « voir l'Amérique d'abord ». Jamais voyager à travers les déserts et les champs des États-Unis n'avait fleuré aussi bon l'insouciance et le romantisme. Le « Shady Dell RV Park » est une minuscule enclave qui préserve ces joyaux pour le plus grand bonheur des voyageurs d'aujourd'hui. Situé entre une pompe à essence et un cimetière, à moins de deux kilomètres de la « ville fantôme » de Bisbee, en Arizona, il accueille dix caravanes en aluminium et un yacht en bois à sec, tous des années cinquante et minutieusement restaurés jusque dans leurs moindres détails : couvre-lits en chenille, phonographes équipés de vieux vinyles d'Elvis Presley, verres à martini et shakers d'époque. Vous pouvez sirotez votre cocktail tout en admirant le désert, puis faire un saut à Bisbee, qui, une fois les mines de cuivre désertées, est devenue une communauté de hippys, d'artisans et de marginaux de tous poils. Vous pouvez aussi fuir au Mexique, dont la frontière se trouve à deux pas. Douillettement blotti à l'intérieur d'un étincelant écrin d'argent monté sur roues, tout paraît possible.

Livre à emporter : « Airstream, **The History of the Land Yacht** » de Bryan Burkhart et David Hunt.
Une histoire illustrée de la culture de la caravane aux États-Unis.

ANREISE	Rund 150 km südöstlich vom Flughafen in Tucson, Arizona.
PREISE	»Alu-Trailer« ab 32 €/Nacht. »Chris Craft Yacht«, etwa 12 Meter lang, 101 €/Nacht.
ZIMMER	Zehn »Vintage-Aluminium-Wohnwagen« aus den 1940ern und 1950ern und eine gestrandete »Chris Craft Yacht«.
KÜCHE	»Dot's Diner«, ein typisch amerikanischer Diner mit zehn Plätzen, für Frühstück und Mittagessen, Mittwoch bis Sonntag zwischen 7 und 15 Uhr geöffnet.
GESCHICHTE	Amerikanischer Trailerpark aus dem Jahr 1927 von einem ehemaligen Antiquitätenhändler-Paar 1995 restauriert und mit Vintage-Aluminium-Wohnwagen bestückt.
X-FAKTOR	Freiheit und Romantik im Amerika der Fünfziger Jahre.

ACCÈS	Situé à environ 150 km au sud-est de l'aéroport de Tucson, dans l'Arizona.
PRIX	Location d'une caravane individuelle à partir de 32 € la nuit; le yacht « Chris Craft » de 12 mètres de long se loue 100 €.
CHAMBRES	Dix caravanes en aluminium des années 1940 et 1950 et un yacht « Chris Craft » échoué.
RESTAURATION	« Dot's Diner » sert le petit-déjeuner et le déjeuner entre 7h et 15h, du mercredi au dimanche
HISTOIRE	Un village de caravanes ouvert en 1927, restauré et rééquipé avec des caravanes d'époque en 1995.
LE « PETIT PLUS »	La liberté et le romantisme de la route américaine.

Hot Hot Hot...
Furnace Creek Inn, Death Valley

Furnace Creek Inn, Death Valley

Hot Hot Hot

Sometimes the numbers say it all. 65 meters below sea level. Rainfall less than 5mm a year. Average temperature in June, 48 C. The desert in Death Valley, which straddles the state borders of California and Nevada, is the lowest, driest, hottest place in the United States. Despite its forbidding climate, is is also astonishingly lush and beautiful: strange salt formations rise from its pulverized soil, which changes color from white to grey to shades of brown and purple as the relentless sun makes its way across the sky. When it does rain, purple and gold wildflowers magically sprout from the dust. The Furnace Creek Inn dates back to 1927. It's opening was a bit of a gamble – the property owners, a mining company, were hoping to lure tourists to the area to buffer the fluctuating market demand for their product, borax. While tourists didn't exactly flock to vacation under the white hot sun, they came often enough for the hotel to remain operation for more than 75 years. It's Death Valley National Park's only resort hotel, an oasis of cool adobe, shady palms, and a 70 foot natural spring-fed swimming pool. The desert begins right outside your hotel room door, and you can admire it from a shady white wicker chair over breakfast. If the landscape seems strangely familiar, that's because it is: Death Valley has served the backdrop for dozens of Hollywood and international movies, from Stanley Kubrick's "Spartacus", to Antonioni's "Zabriskie Point".

Book to pack: "The White Heart of Mojave: An Adventure with the Outdoors of the Desert" by Edna Brush Perkins.
The author's amazing tale of her 1920 journey into the Mojave desert seeking to escape civilization and secure voting rights for women.

Furnace Creek Inn Highway 190 Death Valley, CA 92328 USA Tel. +1 760 786 2345 Fax +1 760 786 2514 Website: www.furnacecreekresort.com Booking: www.great-escapes-hotels.com	

DIRECTIONS	Located about 120 miles (195 km) northwest of the Las Vegas, Nevada airport.
RATES	From $250 to $390 per night.
ROOMS	66 rooms in the original historic Inn, only available in season, from mid-October to mid-May.
FOOD	Breakfast, lunches, and dinners (California-style eclectic menu) served in the Inn Dining Room; afternoon tea in the lobby.
HISTORY	The original Mission-style Inn was designed by LA architect Albert C. Martin, and opened for business in 1927.
X-FACTOR	A cool retreat in the middle of one of the starkest, lowest most desolate landscapes on earth.

In Hot Water, Chilled Out...

Hope Springs Resort, Desert Hot Springs

Hope Springs Resort, Desert Hot Springs

In Hot Water, Chilled Out

Drive twenty minutes north of Palm Springs, and you reach the town of Desert Hot Springs, a completely opposite style of desert oasis. If the signature drink of Palm Springs is the dry martini, then Desert Hot Springs' preferred libation is the glass of mineral water, preferably one drawn from one of the town's dozens of wells that bubble and burble with health-giving, healing natural spring water. The Agua Caliente Indians were the first settlers in the area around Desert Hot Springs, and you can still feel their spirits in the dry air here, and at the end of streets that suddenly, abruptly, turn into wild desert brush. It was never a particularly fashionable place – the dozens of little courtyard motels that dot the area were built mostly in the 1950s and 1960s to serve the needs of health enthusiasts taking the waters. Almost unchanged over the years, they now are like vintage canvases, waiting to be restored by a new generation of hoteliers who have come to Desert Hot Springs enchanted by the water, the high desert, and the nearby Joshua Tree National Park. Hope Springs is one of those loving renovations – out front the owner has even kept the original trapezoidal neon sign that proclaims the property, incorrectly, as "Cactus Springs". Inside, in a spacious courtyard dotted with cacti and desert palms, cozy 1940s-style padded lounge chairs invite you to nap by one of the three thermal bathing pools, each one heated to a slightly higher temperature. The rooms, with their simple neutral linens and platform beds, have a Japanese feel, and most of them open onto a small patio made private by clever landscaping. No room phones, no tv. Throw open the French doors, toddle out to the hot pool, soak, rinse, repeat.

Book to pack: "Cathedrals of the Flesh: My Search for the Perfect Bath" by Alexia Brue.

The adventures of an English woman who recently traveled the world in search of the ultimate hot spring spa.

Hope Springs Resort	
68075 Club Circle Drive	
Desert Hot Springs, CA 92240	
USA	
Tel: +1 760 329 4003	
Fax: +1 760 329 4223	
Email: manager@hopespringsresort.com	
Website: www.hopespringsresort.com	
Booking: www.great-escapes-hotels.com	

DIRECTIONS	8 miles (13 km) north of Palm Springs Airport.
RATES	Rooms start at $135 incl. breakfast.
ROOMS	10 rooms; four have kitchens.
FOOD	Continental buffet breakfast only, included in room rate.
HISTORY	Vintage mid-century motel converted to hip haven.
X-FACTOR	Unwind in hot water, in a laid-back vintage mid-century motel.

Chill-out in heissen Quellen

Zwanzig Autominuten nördlich vom kalifornischen Palm Springs liegt eine weitere Wüstenoase, »Desert Hot Springs«. Während Palm Springs das mondäne Leben und den Dry Martini liebt, bevorzugt »Desert Hot Springs« gesundes Mineralwasser, das hier aus dutzenden von Quellen hervorblubbert. Die ersten Bewohner der Gegend waren Indianer des Agua-Caliente-Stammes. Noch immer ist ihr Geist in der trocken-flirrenden Luft zu spüren, besonders dort, wo die Straßen abrupt in der Trockenholz-Wüste enden. »Desert Hot Springs« war nie besonders schick – in den Fünfzigern und Sechzigern reisten vor allem Gesundheitsfanatiker zu den Heilquellen und übernachteten in den kleinen Motels mit den typischen Innenhöfen. Über Jahre hinweg blieben sie praktisch unverändert. Dann zog die Vintage-Welle eine neue Generation von Hoteliers an, die die Motels renovierten und auch von den Heilquellen, der Wüstenlandschaft und dem nahegelegenen Joshua Tree National Park begeistert waren. »Hope Springs« ist eines dieser liebevoll renovierten Motels: Der Besitzer hat sogar das dreieckige Original-Neonschild draußen stehenlassen, obschon darauf der alte Name »Cactus Springs« steht. Im großräumigen Innenhof stehen Wüstenpalmen und kusch-lig-gepolsterte Lounge-Sessel, die zum Faulenzen einladen. Drei Thermalbecken mit unterschiedlichen Temperaturen sorgen für Entspannung. Vertiefen kann man sie nach dem Bad in den Gästezimmern: Mit direktem Zugang auf die Terrasse, einfachen Plattform-Betten und heller Wäsche strahlen sie zen-buddhistische Ruhe aus.

Buchtipp: »Cathedrals of the Flesh: My Search for the Perfect Bath« von Alexia Brue.

Die Erzählungen einer Engländerin auf der Suche nach dem ultimativen heißen Quellbad.

Un bain de jouvence

À vingt minutes de voiture au nord de Palm Springs, « Desert Hot Springs » est une oasis radicalement différente. Ici, la boisson de prédilection n'est pas le martini dry mais l'eau minérale thérapeutique qui gargouille dans les nombreux puits de la ville. Les Indiens d'« Agua Caliente » furent les premiers à s'y installer. Leurs esprits hantent encore l'air sec, errant dans ces rues qui s'interrompent abruptement sur le désert de broussailles. L'endroit ne fut jamais très mondain : la plupart des dizaines de petits motels de la région furent construits dans les années ciquante et soixante pour les fans de médecine naturelle venus prendre les eaux. Restés dans leur jus au fil des ans, ils attendent d'être restaurés par la nouvelle génération d'hôteliers attirés à « Desert Hot Springs » par son eau, le désert et le parc national du Joshua Tree voisin. « Hope Springs » est un exemple de ces relookages inspirés. À l'extérieur, son propriétaire a même conservé l'enseigne d'origine avec l'ancien nom « Cactus Springs ». À l'intérieur, dans une cour spacieuse plantée de cactus et de palmiers, des transats capitonnés style années quarante invitent à la sieste au bord d'une des trois piscines thermales, chacune d'une température différente. Les chambres, avec leur linge neutre et leurs lits juchés sur des plates-formes, baignent dans une atmosphère japonisante. La plupart donnent sur un patio auquel un paysagisme astucieux confère une allure privative. Elles n'ont ni téléphone ni télévision. Ouvrez la baie vitrée, traînez-vous jusqu'à un bassin, trempez-vous, rincez-vous, recommencez.

Livre à emporter : « Cathedrals of the Flesh: My Search for the Perfect Bath » de Alexia Brue.

Les aventures d'une Anglaise qui a récemment sillonné le monde en quête du nec plus ultra en matière de thermes.

ANREISE	Etwa 13 km nördlich vom Flughafen Palm Springs.
PREISE	Zimmer ab 110 € inkl. Frühstück.
ZIMMER	Zehn Zimmer, davon haben vier eine Küche.
KÜCHE	Frühstücksbüffet, im Zimmerpreis eingeschlossen.
GESCHICHTE	Motel der Moderne, heute schicker Hippie-Hangout.
X-FAKTOR	Entspannung in ultramoderner Umgebung. Eintauchen in warme Heilquellen.

ACCÈS	À 13 km au nord de l'aéroport de Palm Springs.
PRIX	À partir de 110 € avec petit-déjeuner.
CHAMBRES	10 chambres, dont quatre avec cuisine.
RESTAURATION	Buffet continental pour le petit-déjeuner uniquement, inclus dans le prix de la chambre.
HISTOIRE	Hôtel des années cinquante converti en refuge branché.
LE « PETIT PLUS »	Décompressez dans l'eau chaude, dans un cadre décontracté et rétro.

Five-star Luxury Kitsch.
Parker Palm Springs, Palm Springs

Parker Palm Springs, Palm Springs

Five-star Luxury Kitsch

In the 1960s and 1970s, US television was in its prime, and so was TV style – the futuristic, bordering on kitsch home décor of the living rooms of popular TV comedies and talk shows like "The Brady Bunch" and "The Merv Griffin Show". The Parker Palm Springs is the perfect retro-retreat for that generation of American baby boomers who grew up doing their homework in front of the tube, by the light of a Lava Lamp. Step behind the lobby entrance – a striking mid-century "bris soile" wall of latticed concrete, the signature architectural motif of the 1950s Holiday Inn this property once was-and you're suddenly in a luxe, grown-up reinvention of your favorite 70s TV program. The set designer of the show is ceramicist and furniture designer Jonathan Adler, who believes that "minimalism is a bummer", and that "handcrafted tchotchkes are life-enhancing". The public spaces and rooms in the Parker Palm Springs, which is part of the international Le Meridien group, quote diverse sources – there's a touch of the cartoon "The Flintstones" in the floor-to-ceiling freeform concrete room dividers, while the almost-not-quite-tacky blue, green, and olive geometric prints on the chairs of the in-house restaurant "Mister Parker's" work beautifully with mirrored ceilings and chandeliers to create a setting that's Liberace-esque. Adler's playful interiors contrast with the old-fashioned service-intensive ethic of Palm Springs' only 5 star resort – the staff's been ordered, for instance, to immediately offer a picnic lunch to any guest who lazes in one of the resort's hammocks. But will they serve TV dinners?

Book to pack: "Do You Remember TV? The Book That Takes You Back" by Michael Gitter, Sylvie Anapol and Erika Glazer. Kitchy and informative pictorial guide to American classic tv shows from the 1960s and 1970s.

Parker Palm Springs	DIRECTIONS	3.5 miles (6 km) south of Palm Springs International Airport.
4200 East Palm Canyon Drive	RATES	Rooms from $245 to $5,000 for the Gene Autry Residence.
Palm Springs, CA 92264	ROOMS	131 Rooms, 12 private one bedroom villas, and the Gene Autry Residence, a home with two bedrooms, living room, dining room, kitchen, two baths and lawn area.
USA		
Tel. +1 760 770 5000		
Fax +1 760 324 2188	FOOD	Norma's: A five-star diner that serves high-end American "comfort food". Mister Parker's, a 65-seat restaurant with no menus, and a daily changing prix fixe dinner.
Email: reservations@theparkerpalmsprings.com		
Website: www.theparkerpalmsprings.com	HISTORY	Built in the 1950s as a Holiday Inn, it was Merv Griffin's Givenchy Resort and Spa. The Parker Palm Springs was reopened in 2004.
Booking: www.great-escapes-hotels.com		
	X-FACTOR	Retro chic for grownup American baby-boomers.

Luxus-Kitsch

Das amerikanische Fernsehedekor erlebte in den Sechzigern und Siebzigern einen Höhepunkt. Komödien und Talk-Shows glänzten mit Studiowohnzimmern, die haarscharf am Kitsch vorbei steuerten. Für die Generation der Baby Boomer, die als Kinder vor der Glotze und neben einer blubbernden Lava-Lampe ihre Hausaufgaben zu erledigen pflegten, ist das »Parker Palm Springs« der perfekte Retro-Rückzugsort. Eine riesige frei stehende Betonwand mit durchbrochenem Muster markiert den Eingang. Sie ist ein Relikt aus den Fünfzigern, als das Hotel der »Holiday-Inn«-Gruppe angeschlossen war und solche Wände zur Corporate Identity gehörten. Von hier gelangt man in die Lobby – eine zeitgemäße und luxuriöse Version eines Siebziger-Jahre-Fernseh-Dekors. Inszeniert hat dieses Bühnenbild der New Yorker Keramik- und Möbeldesigner Jonathan Adler im Auftrag der Meridien-Gruppe, der Besitzerin des »Parker Palm Springs«. Von Minimalismus scheint Adler offensichtlich nicht viel zu halten. Das ganze Hotel ist ein einziger gigantischer Stilmix: Ein skurriler Freestyle-Wandtrenner erinnert an den Einrichtungsstil der »Familie Feuerstein«, und das Restaurant »Mister Parker's« mit blau, grün, oliv gemusterten, leicht billig wirkenden Polsterstühlen, verspiegelten Decken und Lüstern würde selbst Liberace alle Ehre machen. Einzig beim Service kennt das Haus keinen Spaß. Das einzige 5-Sterne-Resort in Palm Springs betreibt ihn auf höchstem Niveau.

Buchtipp: »Do You Remember TV? The Book That Takes You Back« von Michael Gitter, Sylvie Anapol und Erika Glazer. Kitschiges und informatives Bilderbuch über die amerikanischen TV-Shows der 1960er und 1970er.

Luxe kitsch cinq étoiles

Dans les années soixante et soixante-dix, la télévision américaine était dans la fleur de l'âge, tout comme son esthétique illustrée par le look futuriste frôlant le kitsch des séries populaires et des talk-shows comme le « Brady Bunch » ou le « Merv Griffin Show ». Le « Parker Palm Springs » est la retraite rétro idéale pour cette génération de « baby-boomers » qui a grandi en faisant ses devoirs devant le poste, à la lueur de la lampe à bulles d'huile. Dès que l'on franchit l'entrée, un surprenant mur en dentelle de béton, motif architectural typique des « Holiday Inn » des années cinquante dont l'hôtel faisait autrefois partie, on se croirait dans la version luxe d'un plateau d'émission à succès des années soixante-dix. Le céramiste et designer Jonathan Adler a signé le décor, fidèle à sa devise « le minimalisme, ça craint » et convaincu de « l'effet revigorant des bibelots artisanaux ». Les espaces communs et les chambres de l'hôtel, aujourd'hui propriété de la chaîne du Méridien, renvoient à diverses sources : il y a une touche de la « Famille Pierrafeu » dans les lignes libres des cloisons en béton des chambres, tandis que les motifs géométriques bleus, verts et olive – pas tout à fait ringards mais presque – sur les chaises du restaurant « Mr. Parker's » s'accordent parfaitement avec le plafond en miroirs et les lustres pour créer une ambiance à la Liberace. Les intérieurs pleins d'humour d'Adler contrastent avec l'éthique rigoureuse du seul cinq étoiles de Palm Springs : tous les clients surpris à lézarder dans un des hamacs de l'hôtel se voient aussitôt proposés un repas pique-nique. Sert-on aussi des plateaux-télé ?

Livre à emporter : « Séries télé : De Zorro à Friends, 60 ans de téléfictions américaines » de Martin Winckler. Le romancier américain nous dévoile les coulisses des séries télé passées, présentes et futures.

ANREISE	6 km südlich vom internationalen Flughafen Palm Springs.
PREISE	Zimmer ab 200 € pro Nacht, die Gene-Autry-Residenz kostet etwa 4.050 € pro Nacht.
ZIMMER	131 Zimmer, 12 Privatvillen. Gene-Autry-Residenz: zwei Schlafräume, Wohnraum, Esszimmer, Küche und Privatgarten.
KÜCHE	»Norma's«, ein 5-Sterne-Restaurant mit einfach-luxuriösen amerikanischen Gerichten. »Mister Parker's« mit 65 Plätzen und täglich wechselnden Prix-Fixe-Angeboten.
GESCHICHTE	In den Fünfzigern ein »Holiday Inn«, später das »Merv Griffin Givenchy Resort and Spa«. Im Oktober 2004 als »Parker Palm Springs« wiedereröffnet.
X-FAKTOR	Retro-Schick für Baby Boomer.

ACCÈS	À 6 km au sud de l'aéroport de Palm Springs.
PRIX	Chambres à partir de 200 € la nuit ; jusqu'à 4050 € pour la « Gene Autry Residence »,
CHAMBRES	131 chambres, 12 villas individuelles avec une chambre à coucher, et la « Gene Autry Residence », une maison individuelle avec jardin.
RESTAURATION	« Norma's », un restaurant cinq étoiles, et « Mister Parker's », un restaurant de 65 couverts avec un menu à prix fixe.
HISTOIRE	Construit dans les années cinquante en tant qu' « Holiday Inn » avant de devenir un hôtel et spa « Merv Griffin's Givenchy ». A rouvert ses portes en octobre 2004.
LE « PETIT PLUS »	Chic rétro pour baby-boomers américains.

Rauer Komfort

Ein Aufenthalt in freier Natur ist nicht für alle ein Vergnügen. Vor allem für jene, die enge Zelte ohne fließend warm und kalt Wasser, unförmige Schlafsäcke und Gemeinschaftsbäder fürchterlich finden und beim Campen von richtiger Bettwäsche und Gourmet-Verpflegung träumen. »El Capitan Canyon« lässt den Traum vom guten Leben in der Natur wahr werden. Früher ein ganz normaler, gut besuchter Campingplatz mitten in einer heiligen Indianerstätte und in Strandnähe, wurde daraus 2001 die Luxusversion »El Capitan Canyon«. Hundert Zedernholz-Hütten mit kleinen Terrassen liegen lauschig zwischen Eichen- und Mammutbäumen. In jeder der Hütten steht ein komfortables Bett mit weißer Baumwollwäsche und hübschen Quilt-Überwürfen. Die Holzhütten haben eigene Badezimmer, einige sind sogar mit Jacuzzis ausgestattet. Wer es noch ursprünglicher mag, kann in einem der 26 luftigen Safarizelte auf Holzplattformen übernachten. Die Gemeinschaftsbäder sind nur ein paar Schritte weiter weg. »El Capitan Canyon« liegt zehn Minuten von Santa Barbara, sodass man den Morgen mit Kajakfahrten auf dem Pazifik verbringen kann und den Nachmittag mit einer Shopping-Tour in der historischen spanischen Missionsstadt. Schön auch die Wanderwege, die sich quer durch die Berge des Resorts ziehen. Die Wanderkarte warnt vor Klapperschlangen und Berglöwen: Selbst auf einem Luxus-Campingplatz hat Mutter Natur das Sagen.

Buchtipp: »Geh zur Hölle, Welt« von Newton Thornburg. Der Kultthriller spielt in Santa Barbara.

Vivre à la dure, en douceur

Les joies de la nature ne font forcément pas le bonheur de tous, surtout quand on a une aversion pour les tentes minuscules, les cailloux sous les sacs de couchage, les latrines à ciel ouvert et l'absence d'eau courante. « El Capitan Canyon » est la réponse rêvée aux amoureux de la nature qui aiment leur confort et bien dîner. Cet ancien terrain de camping privé situé sur un vieux site cérémonial indien, à deux pas d'une magnifique plage du Pacifique, a été transformé par ses propriétaires en 2001 en « campement de luxe ». Cent charmants bungalows en cèdre avec une véranda nichent entre les chênes géants et les sycomores. À l'intérieur vous attendent un lit douillet recouvert d'un édredon et de draps blancs en coton, une vraie salle de bain et, pour certains, même un « jacuzzi ». Ceux qui préfèrent un séjour plus rustique opteront pour une des 26 spacieuses tentes safari en toile perchées sur une plate-forme en bois (avec des bains non loin). Comme Santa Barbara n'est qu'à dix minutes en voiture, vous pouvez alterner les plaisirs de la ville et du grand air, passer la matinée en kayak sur le Pacifique et l'après-midi à faire du lèche-vitrine dans le ravissant quartier colonial hispanique de la ville. Ou encore, faire une randonnée tranquille dans les montagnes environnantes. La carte des sentiers vous met en garde contre les serpents à sonnettes et les pumas, vous rappelant que, même dans un campement de luxe, la nature a toujours le dernier mot.

Livre à emporter : « Fin de fiesta à Santa Barbara » de Newton Thornburg. Un classique du polar situé à Santa Barbara dont l'atmosphère est particulièrement bien rendue.

ANREISE	Rund 195 km nördlich von Los Angeles und 27 km nordwestllich von Santa Barbara.	ACCÈS	À environ 195 km au nord de Los Angeles, et 27 km au nord-ouest de Santa Barbara.
PREISE	Hütten ab 110 €, Zelte ab 90 €.	PRIX	Bungalows à partir 110 €, tentes à partir de 90 €.
ZIMMER	100 Zedernholzhütten und 26 Safarizelte auf Holzplattformen.	CHAMBRES	100 bungalows en cèdre et 26 tentes safari en toile sur des plates-formes en bois.
KÜCHE	Sandwiches, Pizzen, Brot, Wein, Käse und andere Delikatessen im »Canyon Market« mit Tischen und Bänken.	RESTAURATION	Le « Canyon Market » propose sandwiches, pizzas, pains, vins, fromages et autres délices à manger sur place ou à emporter.
GESCHICHTE	Seit 1970 ein Campingplatz, 2000 mit Holzhütten zur Luxusversion ausgebaut.	HISTOIRE	Campement ouvert en 1970 ; de nouveaux bungalows ont été construits en 2000.
X-FAKTOR	Campen mit Komfort.	LE « PETIT PLUS »	Du camping avec tout le confort d'un hôtel.

Post Ranch Inn, Big Sur

Under a Grass Roof

At the Post Ranch Inn it is easy to disappear from sight. It sits back from the highway, on a mountain ridge overlooking the Pacific Ocean that is invisible to passers-by. Your room is in a cabin or cottage that has been especially designed by local architect Mickey Muennig to blend into and harmonize with the wild natural surroundings on the ranch's 98 acres. There are treehouses on 9 foot stilts (to protect the sensitive roots of the surrounding trees). Cylindrical cottages with mountain views. And for those who like to be, literally, covered by nature, there are five ocean-view cottages with sloped rooftops packed with sod that sprouts grass and wildflowers. Post Ranch Inn was built in the 1990s, after the eco-minded residents of the Big Sur area had passed stringent land-use and zoning rules. It demonstrates that a world class luxury spa resort – and the Post Ranch Inn has won almost every American travel magazine's accolade in this category – can be 100% ecologically sensitive, too. Which is a comforting thought to hold on to as you are lying – no, disappearing into – the massage table at the Post Ranch Inn's spa during your La Stone Massage.

Book to Pack: "Big Sur" by Jack Kerouac.
The Beat Generation author of "On The Road" writes about time spent in a Big Sur cabin.

Post Ranch Inn
Highway One, P.O. Box 219
Big Sur, CA 93920
USA
Tel. +1 831 667 2200
Fax +1 831 667 2824
Email: info@postranchinn.com
Website: www.postranchinn.com
Booking: www.great-escapes-hotels.com

DIRECTIONS	Off U.S. Highway 1, 150 miles (240 km) south of San Francisco.
RATES	From $525 to $1085 a night incl. breakfast buffet.
ROOMS	30 rooms, in architecturally unique buildings with an ecological bent.
FOOD	Sierra Mar, an award-winning, glass-enclosed restaurant. Breakfast, lunch and dinners of "New California Cuisine" and a 3,000 bottle wine cellar.
HISTORY	Purpose-built eco-resort. Opened in 1992.
X-FACTOR	Maximum luxury and privacy on the Big Sur coast.

Unter einem Dach aus Gras

Einfach mal abtauchen. Dafür eignet sich das »Post Ranch Inn« besonders gut. Das Gasthaus liegt hoch über dem Highway auf einer Bergkante und überblickt den Pazifik, den man beim Vorbeifahren von der Straße gar nicht sehen kann. Die Zimmer sind in einer der Hütten oder einem der Cottages der rund 40 Hektar großen Ranch untergebracht und fügen sich so harmonisch in die unberührte Landschaft ein, wie es ihr Architekt, Mickey Muennig, geplant hatte: Baumhütten stehen auf gut 2,5 Meter hohen Pfählen, um die empfindlichen Wurzeln der Bäume rundherum zu schonen, und zylinderförmige Cottages gewähren freie Sicht auf die Berge. Für Gäste, die Natur pur erleben möchten, gibt es fünf Cottages mit rasenbedeckten Schrägdächern, aus denen Gräser und Wildblumen sprießen. »Post Ranch Inn« wurde in den Neunzigern gebaut, nachdem die ökobewusste Gemeinde Big Sur strikte Raumnutzungsverordnungen verabschiedet hatte. Das Resultat ist ein schönes Beispiel dafür, dass auch ein erstklassiges Luxus-Spa – das »Post Ranch Inn« hat Auszeichnungen der meisten US-Reisezeitschriften erhalten – zu Hundert Prozent ökoverträglich sein kann. Das ist so beruhigend wie eine »La-Stone«-Massage im Spa des »Post Ranch Inn«.

Buchtipp: »Big Sur« von Jack Kerouac.
Der Beat-Generation-Autor von »Unterwegs« schreibt über ein Zeit in einer Hütte in Big Sur.

Sous un toit de verdure

Au « Post Ranch Inn », il est facile de se fondre dans la nature. L'hôtel est situé en retrait de la grande-route, sur une crête rocheuse qui domine le Pacifique tout en restant invisible pour les passants. Les structures ont été spécialement conçues par l'architecte local Mickey Muennig pour disparaître dans le paysage et s'harmoniser avec l'environnement naturel de ce ranch d'une quarantaine d'hectares. Il y a des cabanes perchées sur des pilotis de trois mètres (pour protéger les racines délicates des arbres environnants) ; des cottages circulaires avec vue sur les montagnes ; et pour ceux qui aiment être, littéralement, enfouis dans la végétation, cinq bungalows donnant sur la mer dont les toits inclinés sont plantés de gazons, d'herbes folles et de fleurs sauvages. Le « Post Ranch Inn » a été construit dans les années quatre-vingt-dix après que les habitants à la conscience écologiste de la région de Big Sur eurent adopté des lois strictes en matière d'utilisation des sols et de zonage. Cela prouve qu'un luxueux hôtel et spa de classe internationale (il a été acclamé par pratiquement toutes les revues américaines de voyage) peut être également totalement respectueux de la nature. Ce qui achèvera sans doute d'apaiser vos esprits tandis que vous serez allongé – non, que vous disparaîtrez – sur une table molletonnée pour votre massage à quatre mains.

Livre à emporter : « Big Sur » de Jack Kerouac.
L'auteur emblématique de la génération beatnik décrit ses séjours dans une cabane à Big Sur.

ANREISE	Neben dem US-Highway 1, 240 km südlich von San Francisco.
PREISE	Zwischen 420 € und 865 € pro Nacht inkl. Frühstücksbuffet.
ZIMMER	30 Zimmer in einzigartigen Häusern, die nach strikt ökologischen Grundsätzen gebaut wurden.
KÜCHE	Im »Sierra Mar« gibt's Frühstück, Mittag- und Abendessen mit neuer kalifornischen Küche. Das Restaurant mit riesigen Glaswänden hat einen Weinkeller mit 3000 Flaschen und wurde dafür mit einer Auszeichnung bedacht.
GESCHICHE	Als Öko-Resort gebaut und 1992 eröffnet.
X-FAKTOR	Luxus in der Abgeschiedenheit der Küste von Big Sur.

ACCÈS	Par le U.S. Highway 1, à 240 km au sud de San Francisco.
PRIX	De 420 € à 865 € la nuit, petit-déjeuner compris.
CHAMBRES	30 chambres, dans des bâtiments dont l'architecture respecte l'environnement.
RESTAURATION	Le « Sierra Mar », un restaurant primé entouré de parois de verre. « Nouvelle cuisine californienne » servie au petit-déjeuner, déjeuner et dîner. La cave à vins abrite plus de 3 000 bouteilles.
HISTOIRE	Hôtel écologique ouvert en 1992.
LE « PETIT PLUS »	Le summum du luxe et de l'intimité sur la côte de Big Sur.

Be Here, Now...
Wilbur Hot Springs, Wilbur Springs

Wilbur Hot Springs, Wilbur Springs

Be Here, Now

Nobody going to San Francisco wears flowers in their hair anymore (except, perhaps, if they are in a wedding party), and the Bay Area is no longer the hippie capital that it was in the 1970s. Nevertheless the social scene in San Francisco remains looser, more tolerant, and more relaxed than in other parts of the U.S. For example, there is the tradition of the Hot Springs Weekend. Newcomers to San Francisco soon discover this local ritual: you drive north for two hours, to Sonoma County, and check in to one of a handful of simple rustic bathing retreats that dot the area. Wilbur Hot Springs is perhaps the most famous of the bunch: a big old Victorian house with simple rooms, a bunkhouse, and a bathhouse where clothing is optional and the sulphurous water in the three pools ranges from hot to hottest (110 degrees Fahrenheit, or 43 Celsius). The retreat dates back to the 1860s, when bathing in hot springs waters for curative purposes became a fad in America. When the fad died out, the retreat languished for nearly a century, but found new life in the 1970s as a center for therapy and detox. Now it's a staple for San Franciscans of a certain age – New Age, that is – who come for the peace and quiet, the 1800 acre nature preserve, the yoga classes and the absence of room keys and electrical outlets. Things to bring (according to Wilbur's manual): a flashlight, a bathrobe, your own food (meals are self-cooked in a communal kitchen), a sense of humor. Oh, and don't forget to pack your karma.

Book to Pack: "Be Here Now" by Ram Dass.
Classic 1970s road-to-bliss manual.

Wilbur Hot Springs	
Wilbur Springs, CA 95987	
USA	
Tel. +1 530 473 2306	
Email: info@wilburhotsprings.com	
Website: www.wilburhotsprings.com	
Booking: www.great-escapes-hotels.com	

DIRECTIONS	Located in Colusa County, CA, about 80 miles (130 km) northwest of Sacramento Airport.
RATES	$75 for a bed in the bunk room; private rooms from $115.
ROOMS	One three-bedroom suite, 17 private guest rooms, and one communal bunk room with 11 beds.
FOOD	Bring and cook your own meals in the communal kitchen.
HISTORY	Established on the site of a failed copper mine in 1865 by Ezekial Wilbur; purchased and remodelled in the 1970s by Gestalt therapist Dr. Richard Miller.
X-FACTOR	Drop your clothes and cares in one of Northern California's oldest New Age hot springs retreats.

Provence in Kalifornien

Das Napa Valley gab sich lange geschmeichelt, wenn man es mit der französischen Provence verglich, und tat so, als läge ein Stück des Rhônetals direkt an der amerikanischen Pazifikküste. Doch in den letzten Jahren ist Napa reifer geworden und bekennt sich nun ohne Wenn und Aber zu seiner kalifornischen Identität. Noch immer findet man im Napa Valley ein paar Orte mit unverkennbar französischem Flair. Etwa das elegante Landhotel »Auberge du Soleil«, das einem französischen Château nachempfunden wurde. Auf dem 13 Hektar großen Privatgrundstück wachsen Weinreben und Olivenhaine, so als wäre man tatsächlich in der Provence. Die »Auberge du Soleil« liegt, mit tollem Ausblick auf Tal und Berge, mitten an einem lauschigen Hang, und Privatwege laden zu ausgiebigen Spaziergängen ein. Wunderschön auch die Blütenpracht: Im Frühjahr fallen Glyzinien blau über Gitter, und im Winter leuchten gelbe Senfblumen aus den Feldern. Bei seiner Eröffnung vor dreißig Jahren war die »Auberge« noch das einzige Luxusresort im Napa Valley. Trotz Konkurrenz ist es bis heute das stilvollste Haus der Region geblieben (Restaurant und Spa sind übrigens Spitzenklasse) und hat sich – als eines der ganz wenigen Hotels Amerikas – die Aufnahme bei »Relais & Châteaux« redlich verdient.

Buchtipp: »Mein Jahr in der Provence« von Peter Mayle.
Liebevoll-bissiger Bericht des britischen Autoren über das erste Jahr in der Provence.

La Provence en Californie

L'image romantique qu'on se fait de la vallée de Napa, c'est celle d'un petit fragment de la vallée du Rhône transplantée par les airs sur la côte Pacifique. Toutefois, ces dernières années, Napa a développé une identité propre typiquement californienne même s'il subsiste quelques poches où l'on peut encore se surprendre à commander son petit-déjeuner en français en se croyant dans un village de Provence. C'est particulièrement vrai à l'« Auberge du soleil ». Cette demeure grandiose, copie d'un château français, est entourée d'un domaine privé de treize hectares plantés de vignes et d'oliviers, sillonné de sentiers d'où l'on peut admirer les montagnes au loin. Venez au printemps, quand les treillis croulent sous la glycine, ou en hiver, quand les fleurs de moutarde jaune vif remplissent les champs. L'auberge fut le premier établissement de luxe à ouvrir dans la région il y a 30 ans et reste l'étalon or de Napa (forcément, c'est l'une des rares auberges américaines du groupe Relais & Châteaux). Des chambres spacieuses décorées avec goût à la française, un restaurant gastronomique de rang international avec un choix de plus de 1 300 vins (la cave la plus complète de Napa), un spa et un centre de remise en forme excellents... c'est un tel ravissement que vous risquez de ne pas sortir du domaine durant tout votre séjour.

Livre à emporter : « Une année en Provence » de Peter Mayle.
Le récit humoristique d'un Anglais expatrié dans un terroir bien français.

ANREISE	105 km nördlich vom internationalen Flughafen San Francisco.
PREISE	Zimmer ab 400 €; Privat-Cottages ab 2250 €.
ZIMMER	50 Einzel- und Doppelzimmer, zwei Privat-Cottages.
KÜCHE	Elegante und vielfältige kalifornische Küche; Tasting-Menüs.
GESCHICHTE	1985 eröffnet.
X-FAKTOR	Das erste Luxus-Resort im Weingebiet von Napa Valley ist bis heute der erstklassigste.

ACCÈS	Á 105 km au nord de l'aéroport international de San Francisco.
PRIX	Chambres à partir de 400 €, cottages privés à partir de 2250 €.
CHAMBRES	50 suites à une et deux chambres, deux cottages privés.
RESTAURATION	Le restaurant de l'auberge propose une cuisine éclectique californienne raffinée ; menu de dégustation.
HISTOIRE	Ouvert en 1985.
LE « PETIT PLUS »	La plus ancienne et la plus luxueuse des auberges au milieu des vignobles de la vallée de Napa.

The Ahwahnee, Yosemite National Park

Jaw-Dropping

The Yosemite Valley, a place of bare, dramatic, granite mountains and cliffs, of high waterfalls and giant Sequoia trees, has been stunning visitors with its grandeur for thousands of years. (The Miwok Indians called this place, "Ahwahnee", or "Place of the Gaping Mouth"). So compelling is the area's beauty that in 1864, during the worst battles of the American Civil War, President Abraham Lincoln took time out to sign the decree which set Yosemite aside as America's first nature preserve. The Ahwahnee lodge was constructed in 1927, within the boundaries of the park, to encourage well-heeled visitors to come to this remote and often desolate area. It is a grand hotel, in the opulent turn of the century style, with massive open public spaces (the hotel's Great Lounge is a 77 feet long, 51 feet wide cathedral of a room with 24-foot-high ceilings, ten floor-to-ceiling windows and a profusion of wrought-iron chandeliers). Perhaps the Ahwahnee's architects were so awed by the famous Yosemite landmarks visible from the hotel's location – the Half Dome, the Yosemite Falls, and Glacier Point – that they designed their interiors to match the scale of the great outdoors. In any case, this grand hotel (with grounds designed by Frederick Law Olmstead) has survived economic booms and busts, the wear and tear of decades, and the ever-present threat of fire in the forest (the Ahwahnee's "redwood" façade is actually poured concrete that has been painted to look like wood!) As the Ahwahnee nears its eightieth year, it has become as much of an icon as Yosemite's natural wonders.

Book to Pack: "The Yosemite" by John Muir.
Essays by the distinguished American naturalist responsible for the creation of Yosemite Park.

The Ahwahnee
Yosemite National Park, CA 95389
(for bookings):
Yosemite Central Reservations
6771 North Palm Avenue
Fresno, CA 93704
USA
Tel. +1 559 253 5635
Website: www.yosemitepark.com
Booking: www.great-escapes-hotels.com

DIRECTIONS	One mile (1.5 km) east of Yosemite Village, in Yosemite National Park.
RATES	Rooms and cottages from $379, suites from $480 to $936.
ROOMS	99 rooms and 24 cottages.
FOOD	Huge resort dining room serving traditional American food at breakfast, lunch and dinner.
HISTORY	Originally built in 1927 as a "modern luxury hotel" inside the Yosemite National Park. Landscaping by Frederick Law Olmstead. Remodeled in 2004.
X-FACTOR	A grand old American classic, surrounded by some of the continent's most heartstopping scenery.

Atemberaubend

Das Yosemite Valley mit seinen spektakulären Granitfelsen, in die Tiefe stürzenden Wasserfällen und riesigen Mammutbäumen lässt die Herzen der Besucher seit Jahrtausenden höher schlagen. Indianer des Miwok-Stammes nennen den Ort »Ahwahnee« oder »Offen stehender Mund«. Die Schönheit des Tales ist atemberaubend. Sogar Präsident Abraham Lincoln ließ sich von ihr einnehmen. Obschon mit dem amerikanischen Bürgerkrieg beschäftigt, unterzeichnete er ein Dekret, das aus Yosemite das erste Naturschutzgebiet der Vereinigten Staaten machen sollte. Die »Ahwahnee« Lodge wurde 1927 mitten im Nationalpark gebaut, um gutbetuchte Besucher in die einsame Gegend zu locken. Als großzügiges Grand Hotel konzipiert, spiegelt das Haus den opulenten Stil der letzten Jahrhundertwende wider. Die Hotelhalle erinnert an eine Kathedrale – 24 Meter lang, 16 Meter breit, 7,5 Meter hohe Decken, zehn raumhohe Fenster und überall schmiedeeiserne Lüster. Es scheint, als ob die Architekten von »Ahwahnee« den großartigen Sehenswürdigkeiten rund ums Haus, dem »Half Dome«, den »Yosemite Falls« und dem »Glacier Point«, mit ebenso grandiosen Räumlichkeiten begegnen wollten. Das Grand Hotel hat gute und schlechte Zeiten erlebt, Wind, Wetter und der ständigen Brandgefahr getrotzt. Die Fassade des Hauses ist deshalb auch nicht aus echtem Holz, sondern im Rot der Bäume angemalter Beton. Bald feiert die »Ahwahnee« Lodge ihren Achtzigsten und gehört mittlerweile zu den Sehenswürdigkeiten von Yosemite – genau wie die Naturwunder.

Buchtipp: »The Yosemite« von John Muir.
Essays vom angesehenen Umweltschützer, der sich für den Schutz des Yosemite-Parks einsetzte.
Buchtipp: »Der John Muir Trail« von Johann Schinabeck.
Beschreibt den beliebten 350 km langen Wanderweg, der nach dem Umweltschützer John Muir benannt wurde, zwischen dem Yosemite-Tal und dem Mount Whitney in Kalifornien.

Bouche bée

La vallée du Yosemite, avec ses spectaculaires massifs granitiques nus, ses falaises, ses cascades, ses séquoias géants, sidère ses visiteurs par sa splendeur depuis des millénaires. Les Indiens Miwok l'avaient baptisée « Ahwahnee », « lieu de la bouche bée ». Sa beauté est si envoûtante qu'en 1864, au cours des heures les plus sanglantes de la guerre de Sécession, Abraham Lincoln prit le temps de signer un décret faisant d'elle la première réserve naturelle du pays. Le « Ahwahnee » a été construit en 1927, en lisière du parc, afin d'attirer les touristes fortunés dans ce coin reculé et sauvage. C'est un grand hôtel dans le style opulent du début du siècle, avec des salles de réception ouvertes et spacieuses (le grand salon fait 24 mètres de long, 16 mètres de large, 7,5 mètres de haut, avec dix fenêtres allant du sol au plafond et une profusion de lustres en fer forgé). Ses architectes durent être si impressionnés par les monuments naturels célèbres visibles depuis le site – le « Half Dome », les « Yosemite Falls », le « Glacier Point » – qu'ils conçurent les intérieurs aux proportions du paysage. Les jardins furent dessinés par Frederick Law Olmstead. L'établissement a survécu aux aléas de l'économie, aux outrages du temps et à la menace omniprésente des incendies de forêt (la façade en « séquoia » est en fait en béton peint en trompe-l'œil de bois !).
Aujourd'hui, à l'aube de ses 80 ans, il est devenu un monument à part entière, au même titre que les merveilles naturelles qui l'entourent.

Livre à emporter : « Un été dans la Sierra » de John Muir.
Le célèbre naturaliste américain à l'origine de la création du parc raconte son voyage pour accompagner des moutons en transhumance.

ANREISE	1,5 km östlich von Yosemite Village im Yosemite-Nationalpark.
PREISE	Zimmer und Cottages ab 300 €; Suiten zwischen 385 € und 745 €
ZIMMER	99 Zimmer und 24 Cottages.
KÜCHE	Im riesigen Speisesaal der Lodge wird traditionell amerikanisches Frühstück, Mittag- und Abendessen serviert.
GESCHICHTE	1927 als modernes Luxushotel im Yosemite-Nationalpark gebaut. Landschaftsarchitekt: Frederick Law Olmstead. 2004 Renovierung.
X-FAKTOR	Amerikanischer Klassiker mitten in einer der spektakulärsten Landschaften des Kontinents.

ACCÈS	À 1,5 km à l'est de Yosemite Village, dans le parc national du Yosemite.
PRIX	Chambres et bungalows à partir de 300 €, suites entre 385 € et 745 €.
CHAMBRES	99 chambres et 24 bungalows.
RESTAURATION	Immense salle à manger où l'on sert une cuisine traditionnelle. Petits-déjeuners, déjeuners et dîners.
HISTOIRE	Construit en 1927 comme «hôtel moderne de luxe» dans le parc national du Yosemite. Jardins dessinés par Frederick Law Olmstead. Réaménagé en 2004.
LE « PETIT PLUS »	Un grand classique américain, au cœur de l'un des paysages les plus époustouflants du continent.

Dunton Hot Springs, Dolores

"Vild Vest"

Who buys an entire ghost town? Christoph Henkel, the heir to the German soap and chemical company fortune, came upon the ruins of what is now Dunton Hot Springs in the early 1990s, during a ski trip to nearby Telluride, Colorado. The ramshackle cabins and former saloon along the Dolores River in a breathtaking mountain valley had been a thriving gold miner's camp in the 1890s. Still, you had to have a lot of imagination to see the grand old rough and tumble days of Dunton in the ruins that remained. But Henkel did: he had grown up reading the fantasy Western tales of the German writer Karl May (which were indeed fantasies, since May never visited the U.S. in his life). As he walked through the ghost town, Henkel had a flash of inspiration. He bought the entire town for just over 1 million dollars, and began recreating his own version of May's "vild vest." As you first enter the lonely valley, the sight of Dunton's painstakingly weatherbeaten log cabins filled with museum-quality art and the luxury teepees outfitted with hot tubs may seem a bit too perfect, too cinematic (Henkel, also a film producer, has created a very high-end movie set). But any misgivings one might have about the Ralph Lauren-ness of it all quickly vanish, lulled away by the silence of the stunning valley, the million stars overhead, and by the heat of Dunton's abundant natural hot springs, which burble up in steamy pools amidst snow-dusted fields. At Dunton, foreign inspiration has revived an American classic.

Book to Pack: "Winnetou the Apache Knight" by Karl May. Fantasy novel of the American West by the famous German author.

Dunton Hot Springs

P.O. Box 818

52068 West Fork Road

Dolores, CO 81323

USA

Tel. +1 970 882 4800

Fax +1 970 882 7474

Email: info@duntonhotsprings.com

Website: www.duntonhotsprings.com

Booking: www.great-escapes-hotels.com

DIRECTIONS	About 30 miles (50 km) southeast of Telluride, Colorado airport.
RATES	From $250 to $400 per person per day, incl. all meals.
ROOMS	12 log cabins and three teepees.
FOOD	Local organic foods prepared by in-house gourmet chef, served in Dunton's original saloon.
HISTORY	Former mining camp town restored and transformed into exclusive resort.
X-FACTOR	Where else in the world can you sleep in a teepee that has a hot tub?

»Wild-West«-Fantasien

Auf die Idee, eine Geisterstadt zu kaufen, kommt man nicht einfach so. Doch Christoph Henkel, Erbe des gleichnamigen deutschen Seifen- und Chemikalienunternehmens, hatte in den Neunzigern beim Anblick der Ruinen von »Dunton Hot Springs« eine zündende Idee. Er entdeckte das ehemalige Goldminen-Camp, das um 1890 seine Blütezeit erlebte, während eines Skiurlaubs im nahen Telluride, Colorado. In seiner Fantasie machte er aus den zerfallenen Häusern (mit Saloon!) am Dolores River wieder den glorreichen Ort aus den Zeiten des Goldrauschs. Henkels Vorstellungskraft kommt nicht von ungefähr. Er wuchs mit den »Wild-West«-Geschichten von Karl May auf, der kein einziges Mal in den USA war und all seine Indianer- und Cowboygeschichten erfand. Christoph Henkel kaufte kurzerhand die alte Geisterstadt für etwas mehr als 1 Million Dollar und machte sich daran, seine Version von Karl Mays Wildem Westen umzusetzen. Heute stehen die Holzhütten in diesem einsamen, wunderschönen Tal immer noch verwittert da – aber luxuriös ausgestattet und voller museumsreifer Kunst. Die Szenerie zusammen mit den Luxus-Tipis mit eigenen Badewannen sieht aus wie ein Ralph-Lauren-Stillleben und mag fast zu perfekt, zu cineastisch wirken. Henkel, der auch als Filmproduzent tätig ist, hat hier aber nur auf den ersten Blick eine einzige, große Filmkulisse erschaffen. Die Stille im atemberaubend schönen Tal, die leuchtenden Sterne am dunklen Himmel und die dampfenden heißen Quellen, die sich im Schnee zu Becken sammeln, können nicht mal im Film so zauberhaft sein.

Buchtipp: »Winnetou« von Karl May.
»Wild-West«-Fantasien des berühmten deutschen Autors.

« L'ouest sôfache »

Qui irait s'offrir toute une ville fantôme ? Christoph Henkel, héritier d'un empire allemand de savons et de produits chimiques, est tombé sur les ruines de « Dunton Hot Springs » au début des années quatre-vingt-dix, alors qu'il skiait non loin à Telluride dans le Colorado. Vers 1890, ces cabanes branlantes et l'ancien saloon bordant le Dolores abritaient une colonie prospère de chercheurs d'or. Il fallait quand même pas mal d'imagination pour visualiser la grande époque du « Far West » dans les vestiges délabrés. Mais Henkel avait grandi en lisant les westerns fabuleux du romancier allemand Karl May (qui n'a jamais mis les pieds en Amérique !). En se promenant dans la ville désertée, il eut une vision. Il la racheta pour un million de dollars et s'attela à recréer « l'ouest sôfache » de May. En pénétrant dans la vallée isolée, on peut trouver que les cabanes minutieusement patinées par le temps remplies d'art de qualité et les tipis de luxe équipés de jacuzzis sont un peu trop parfaits et théâtraux (également producteur de cinéma, Henkel a créé un plateau de cinéma haut de gamme). Mais le chic genre Ralph Lauren s'efface rapidement devant le silence, la splendeur du paysage, les millions d'étoiles dans le ciel et la chaleur des abondantes sources chaudes qui gargouillent dans des bassins fumants au milieu des prés saupoudrés de neige. À Dunton, une inspiration venue d'ailleurs fait revivre un classique américain.

Livre à emporter: « Winnetou, l'homme de la prairie » de Karl May.
Roman sur l'Ouest américain par le célèbre auteur allemand.

ANREISE	Zirka 50 km südöstlich vom Flughafen Telluride in Colorado.
PREISE	Zwischen 200 € und 320 € pro Person, inkl. aller Mahlzeiten.
ZIMMER	12 Log-Cabins und drei Tipis.
KÜCHE	Bio-Gourmet-Küche im ehemaligen »Saloon«.
GESCHICHTE	Ehemaliges Minen-Camp, in den Neunzigern zu einem exklusiven Resort renoviert und umgebaut.
X-FAKTOR	Wo sonst auf der Welt gibt es Tipis mit Badewannen?

ACCÈS	À environ 50 km au sud-est de l'aéroport de Telluride, dans le Colorado.
PRIX	Entre 200 € et 320 € par personne et par jour, en pension complète.
CHAMBRES	12 cabanes en rondins de bois et trois tipis.
RESTAURATION	Plats bios avec des ingrédients locaux préparés par le grand chef maison, servis dans le « saloon ».
HISTOIRE	Ancienne colonie de chercheurs d'or restaurée et convertie en complexe hôtelier de luxe.
LE « PETIT PLUS »	Existe-t-il un autre endroit au monde où vous pouvez dormir dans un tipi équipé d'un jacuzzi ?

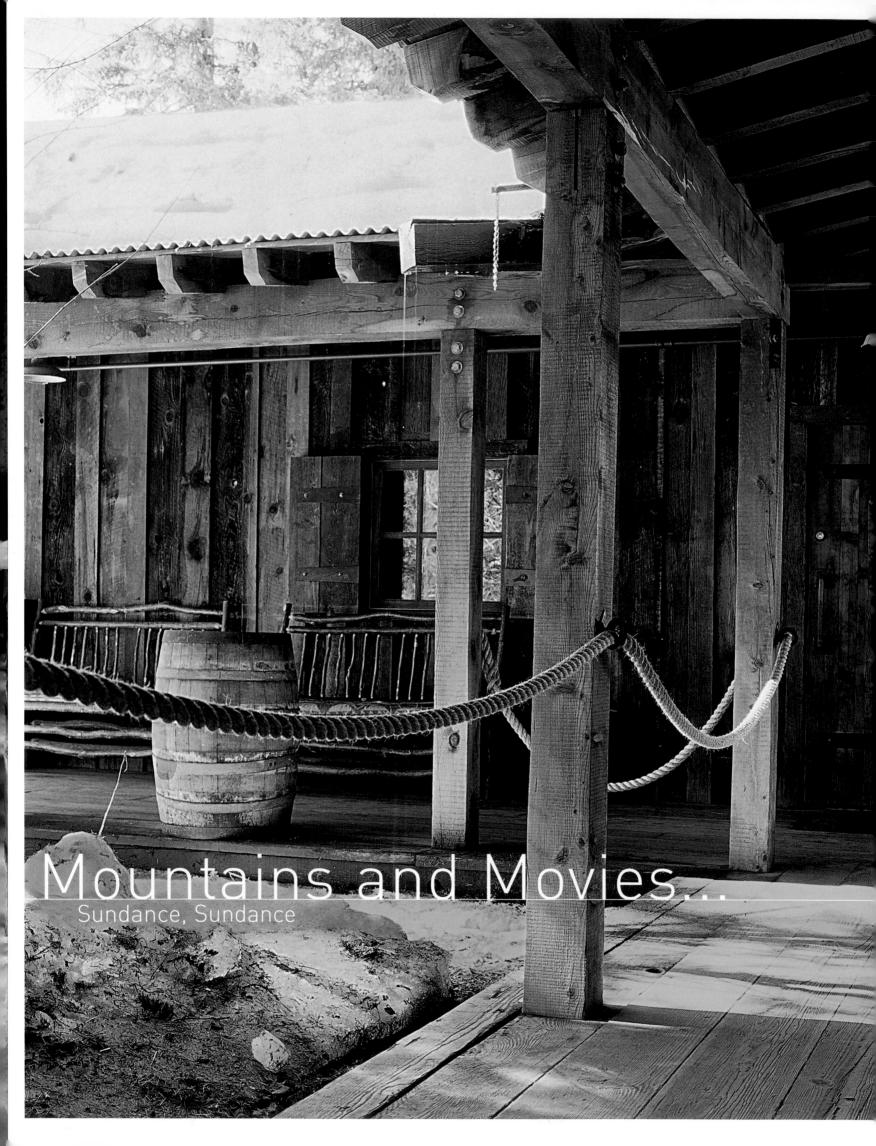

Mountains and Movies...
Sundance, Sundance

Sundance, Sundance

Mountains and Movies

Some of the best getaway havens owe their existence to the extraordinary vision of a single person. Thoreau's Walden Pond is famous because of the poet's need to experience solitude and harmony with nature. If Thoreau had been rich and had cared to share his solitude with the public, he might have come up with Sundance, the arts community and resort nestled in the Utah mountains. Sundance is the creation of Robert Redford, the movie star and director who soared to fame in the 1970s in the movie about the American outlaws, Butch Cassidy and the Sundance Kid. Redford, a bit of an outlaw himself, turned his back on the chic Hollywood scene and used his earnings to buy nearly 25,000 acres of virgin land in the Utah foothills for a family hideaway. But by the 1980s, his idea of a private retreat had evolved into something else – an arts community, built in total harmony with the environment (no structures rise above the tree line). At Sundance, cottages are made of natural materials, wood and stone, and decorated in Native American motifs. The buildings fade into the exhilarating landscape; at Sundance the land is the star. You can ski here, of course, and hike and do all the mountain resort things; but you can also make pottery, go to concerts, watch the latest independent films, and, in the spa, enjoy an organic footbath while surrounded by the music of Navajo Indians. "Creativity is at the core of Sundance culture," says Redford of his one-man's-dream retreat. "It is our contribution to a better world."

Books to pack: "The Outlaw Trail: A History of Butch Cassidy and his Wild Bunch" by Charles Kelly.
The true story of the famous American outlaw will immerse you in the culture of the old Utah West.

Sundance RR3 Box A-1 Sundance, UT 84604 USA Tel. +1 801 225 4100 Fax +1 801 226 1937 Email: reservations@sundance-utah.com Website: www.sundanceresort.com Booking: www.great-escapes-hotels.com	**DIRECTIONS** Located about 50 miles (80 km) southeast of Salt Lake City airport. **RATES** From $225 for a basic cottage, up to $1825 for a 5 bedroom house. **ROOMS** 95 guest cottages and twelve rental houses. **FOOD** Restaurants include the Tree Room (gourmet dinners), the Foundry Grill (casual Western cooking) and the Owl Bar, a restored 1890s interior moved here from Wyoming. **HISTORY** Originally the family retreat of film star cum environmentalist Robert Redford; the resort opened in 1988. **X-FACTOR** Culture, art, and cutting edge cinema, plus stunning snowcapped mountains.

Berge und Filme

Manche der schönsten Paradiese auf Erden haben ihre Existenz einem Visionär zu verdanken. »Walden Pond«, ein Naturschutzgebiet in Massachusetts, ist das Werk des Dichters und Pazifisten Henry D. Thoreau, der sich im 19. Jahrhundert von der Zivilisation zurückzog, um in Einklang mit der Natur zu leben. Eine ähnliche Entstehungsgeschichte hat Sundance in Utah. Der Künstler- und Ferienort wurde vom Filmstar und Regisseur Robert Redford gegründet. Redford hatte den Ort 1969 während der Dreharbeiten zu »Butch Cassidy und Sundance Kid« entdeckt. Der Film, der ihn zum Star machte, handelte von zwei Western-Banditen. Und genauso wenig wie sich die Filmhelden ans Gesetz hielten, beugte sich Redford den Regeln Hollywoods. Er kehrte der Filmstadt den Rücken und kaufte in den Bergen von Utah gut 10.000 Hektar unberührtes Land. Dort plante er eine Ferienresidenz für sich und seine Familie. In den Achtzigern entwickelte sich aus dem privaten Rückzugsort ein ökologisches Künstler-Resort. Kein Gebäude ist höher als die Bäume, die Cottages mit Indianer-Motiven sind aus Naturmaterialien wie Holz und Stein. Das Resort fügt sich in die traumhafte Landschaft ein und überlässt den großen Auftritt der Natur. Selbstverständlich kann man hier Ski laufen und wandern, wie es sich für einen richtigen Bergort gehört. Man kann aber auch töpfern, Konzerte besuchen, den neuesten Independent-Film anschauen, sich im Spa mit einem biologischen Fußbad verwöhnen lassen und dazu Navajo-Musik lauschen.

Buchtipp: »The Outlaw Trail: A History of Butch Cassidy and his Wild Bunch« von Charles Kelly.
Die wahre Geschichte eines berühmt-berüchtigten Banditen vor dem Hintergrund der amerikanischen Western-Kultur.

Les sommets du cinéma

Certains des meilleurs refuges doivent leur existence à la vision extraordinaire d'un seul homme. La cabane de Thoreau à « Walden Pond » est née de son besoin de solitude et d'harmonie avec la nature. S'il avait été riche et avait souhaité partager sa solitude avec le public, ce grand poète aurait peut-être choisi « Sundance », une communauté d'artistes nichée dans les montagnes de l'Utah. « Sundance » est l'œuvre de Robert Redford, star et réalisateur de cinéma, qui a accédé à la célébrité dans les années soixante-dix grâce à un film sur les hors-la-loi américains « Butch Cassidy et Sundance Kid ». Redford, un peu hors-la-loi lui-même, a tourné le dos au glamour hollywoodien et cassé sa tirelire pour acheter 10 000 hectares de terres vierges au pied des montagnes de l'Utah et s'y réfugier avec sa famille. Toutefois, dès les années quatre-vingt, son concept d'un refuge familial avait évolué en une communauté d'artistes, construite en complète harmonie avec l'environnement (aucun bâtiment ne dépasse la cime des arbres). Toutes les maisons sont construites avec des matériaux naturels, de la pierre et du bois, et ornées de motifs indiens. Elles se fondent dans un paysage revigorant. À « Sundance », la star, c'est la nature. Naturellement, on peut y skier, faire des randonnées et tout ce qu'on fait dans une station de montagne. Mais on peut également pratiquer la poterie, aller au concert, voir les derniers films indépendants, et, dans le spa, goûter à un bain de pied organique en écoutant de la musique navajo. « La créativité est au cœur de la culture de Sundance », déclare Redford de sa retraite de rêve. « C'est notre contribution à un monde meilleur ».

Livres à emporter : « Les mémoires de Butch Cassidy » de Martin Roger.
L'histoire vraie du célèbre hors-la-loi racontée par un auteur de polars.

ANREISE	Rund 80 km südöstlich vom Flughäfen Salt Lake City.	ACCÈS	À 80 km au sud-est de l'aéroport de Salt Lake City.
PREISE	Ab 180 € für ein einfaches Cottage, bis zu 1475 € für ein Haus mit fünf Schlafzimmern.	PRIX	À partir de 180 € pour un chalet de base, jusqu'à 1475 € pour une maison individuelle avec 5 chambres à coucher.
ZIMMER	95 Gäste-Cottages und zwölf Häuser.	CHAMBRES	95 chalets et douze maisons à louer.
KÜCHE	Der »Tree Room« mit Gourmetmenüs im Kerzenlicht und der »Foundry Grill« mit Spezialitäten aus dem amerikanischen Westen. Die »Owl Bar« stammt aus den 1890ern und wurde von Wyoming nach Sundance transportiert.	RESTAURATION	Le « Tree Room » (cuisine gastronomique dans un cadre romantique), et le « Foundry Grill » (cuisine simple de l'Ouest américain); on peut prendre un verre au « Owl Bar », dont la décoration datant des années 1890 a été restaurée et apportée du Wyoming.
GESCHICHTE	Ursprünglich die Ferienresidenz von Filmstar und Umweltschützer Robert Redford; seit 1988 ein Resort.	HISTOIRE	Initialement retraite familiale de l'acteur écologiste Robert Redford, la station a ouvert ses portes en 1988.
X-FAKTOR	Kultur, Kunst und angesagtes Kino; atemberaubend schöne Berglandschaft.	LE « PETIT PLUS »	Culture, art et cinéma d'avant-garde.

Amangani, Jackson Hole

Wild West, High Style

In the 19th century, the high wide valley of Jackson Hole, Wyoming probably boasted more bison and elk than people. Fur trappers and Native Americans passed through this remote area with its thrilling view of the snowcapped and jagged Grand Teton Mountains, the youngest range in the Rockies. Today's Jackson Hole is a world away from those old Wild West days – the hunters and trappers are history now, replaced by well-heeled skiers who rub elbows with celebs and other assorted Hollywood royalty.

Still, the Amangani resort retains, in its design and ambience, something of the spirit of those old frontier days. Like all the outposts of the famous Aman chain, it incorporates the culture of its place. The Amangani structure doesn't rise up to disturb the view of the mountains and big sky; instead, the three story building is cut into the hillside, and clings to the contours of the East Gros Ventre Butte, melding with the landscape. Western materials are used throughout – from the Oklahoma sandstone of its exterior, to the Pacific redwood furniture and sconces, the woven cowhide and faux-wolf fur chairs in the suites. Call it Western minimalist. It's an Aman, so of course there's a good spa, but more energetic guests may want to head to the Amangani's library, with its collection of Native American and Western literature, and borrow a book. Take it with you to the outdoor heated infinity pool, and read of bygone days surrounded by a stunning view of the mountains and valleys where the buffalo once roamed.

Books to pack: "The Big Sky" and "The Way West" by Alfred B. Guthrie.
Epic adventure stories of America's vast frontierlands.

Amangani
1535 North East Butte Road
Jackson Hole, WY 83001
USA
Tel. +1 307 734 7333
Fax +1 307 734 7332
Email: amangani@amanresorts.com
Website: www.amanresorts.com
Booking: www.great-escapes-hotels.com

DIRECTIONS	Located near Jackson Hole, Wyoming, about 25 miles (40 km) from Jackson Hole airport.
RATES	Suites starting at $525 per night.
ROOMS	40 suites, including 29 suites, six deluxe suites, four Amangani suites and the Grand Teton suite.
FOOD	Breakfast, lunch and dinner at The Grill, a 65-seat dining room.
HISTORY	Opened in 1998.
X-FACTOR	Admire the Grand Tetons from the heated 113 foot (35 metre) long infinity pool.

Der Wilde Westen ganz komfortabel

Im 19. Jahrhundert gab es im weiten Hochtal von Jackson Hole in Wyoming wahrscheinlich mehr Bisons und Elche als Menschen. Einzig Pelzjäger und Indianer durchquerten die gottverlassene, wunderschöne Gegend der Grand Teton Mountains, die jüngste Bergkette der Rockies. Jäger und Trapper gibt es hier nicht mehr – der Wilde Westen ist längst Vergangenheit. Ersetzt wurden sie durch eine gutbetuchte Schickeria, die hier gemeinsam mit bekannten Persönlichkeiten und Hollywood-Stars ihren Skiurlaub genießt. Das Amangani-Resort hat etwas vom Geist des Wilden Westens in die heutige Zeit hinübergerettet. Wie in allen Resorts der Aman-Gruppe wird das lokale kulturelle Erbe gehegt und gepflegt. Die Anlage kuschelt sich sanft in die Landschaft ein, die Konturen des dreistöckigen Gebäudes führen entlang der Kuppe des »East Gros Ventre« und lassen den Blick auf die Berge und den weiten Himmel frei. Auch in der Materialwahl bleibt das Resort lokal verwurzelt: Von den Außenwänden aus Sandstein aus Oklahoma über Möbel und Wandleuchter aus Pazifik-Rotholz bis hin zu den mit Kuhfell- oder falschem Wolfspelz bezogenen Stühlen in den Suiten – alles ist typisch für den Westen. Am treffendsten kann man die Ausstattung wohl mit Western-Minimalimus bezeichnen. Zu den Annehmlichkeiten des Resorts gehört selbstverständlich auch ein Top-Spa. Wer sich nicht nur vom Wohlfühl-Programm einlullen lassen will, findet in der Bibliothek eine interessante Auswahl an Indianer- und Wild-West-Literatur. Besonders gut in den alten Zeiten schwelgen lässt sich am geheizten Outdoor-Infinity-Pool. Von dort kann man ab und zu den Blick über die atemberaubend schönen Berge und Täler schweifen lassen.

Buchtipps: »Der weite Himmel« und »Der Weg nach Westen« von Alfred B. Guthrie.
Epische Abenteuergeschichte mit Fortsetzung aus dem Wilden Westen.

Le Far West, version luxe

Au 19ᵉ siècle, la grande vallée de Jackson Hole, dans le Wyoming, comptait sans doute plus de bisons et d'élans que d'habitants humains. Seuls les trappeurs et les Indiens traversaient cette région isolée dominée par les sommets déchiquetés et perpétuellement enneigés du Grand Téton, la plus jeune chaîne de montagnes des Rocheuses. Aujourd'hui, Jackson Hole est bien loin des mystères de l'Ouest, les chasseurs et trappeurs ont cédé la place aux skieurs rupins qui côtoient les célébrités et autres sommités du gratin hollywoodien.

Néanmoins, l'Amangani conserve, par son décor et son atmosphère, quelque chose de l'esprit de la conquête de l'Ouest. Comme toutes les antennes de la célèbre chaîne hôtelière Aman, il intègre la culture du lieu. Le bâtiment ne dépasse pas trois étages pour ne pas déranger la vue sur les montagnes et l'immensité du ciel. Il semble taillé dans le flanc rocheux et s'accrocher à la crête de l'« East Gros Ventre » Butte, se fondant dans le paysage. Partout, on a utilisé des matériaux de l'Ouest américain : grès de l'Oklahoma à l'extérieur ; meubles et appliques en séquoia du Pacifique à l'intérieur ; cuirs de vache tressés et fauteuils tapissés en faux loup dans les suites. On peut parler de minimalisme western. Comme dans tous les hôtels Aman, le spa est à la hauteur de la situation mais les plus énergiques préféreront peut-être passer par la bibliothèque, choisir un livre dans sa collection d'ouvrages sur les Indiens et le Far West, et l'emporter dans la piscine chauffée à ciel ouvert pour se plonger dans les récits du bon vieux temps devant un panorama époustouflant de pics et de vallées où paissaient autrefois les bisons.

Livre à emporter : « Oregon-Express » de Alfred B. Guthrie.
Aventures épiques dans le Grand Ouest au 19ᵉ siècle, suite de « The Big Sky »

ANREISE	Rund 40 km vom Flughafen in Jackson Hole, Wyoming.
PREISE	Suiten ab 425 € pro Nacht.
ZIMMER	40 Suiten, davon 29 Suiten, sechs Deluxe-Suiten, vier Amangani-Suiten und die Grand-Teton-Suite.
KÜCHE	Frühstück, Mittag- und Abendessen im »The Grill« mit 65 Sitzplätzen.
GESCHICHTE	1998 eröffnet.
X-FAKTOR	Bad im geheizten Infinity-Pool mit Blick auf den Grand Teton.

ACCÈS	Situé près de Jackson Hole, dans le Wyoming, à environ 40 km de l'aéroport de Jackson Hole.
PRIX	Suites à partir de 425 € la nuit.
CHAMBRES	40 suites, réparties en 29 suites simples, six suites de luxe, quatre suites Amangani et la suite Grand Téton.
RESTAURATION	Petit-déjeuner, déjeuner et dîner servis au « Grill », une salle à manger de 65 couverts.
HISTOIRE	Ouvert en 1998.
LE « PETIT PLUS »	Admirer le Grand Téton depuis la piscine de trente-cinq mètres de long, chauffée et en plein air.

Europe

Africa

Asia

Photo Credits | Fotonachweis
Crédits photographiques

South America

432–559

All 15 hotels are exclusively photographed by the photographer Tuca Reinés, Sao Paulo, www.tucareines.com.br for the book published by TASCHEN.

North America

560–717

All 22 hotels are exclusively photographed by the photographer Don Freeman, New York, www.donfreemanphoto.com for the book published by TASCHEN.

Photo Credits | Fotonachweis
Crédits photographiques

© 2007 TASCHEN GmbH
Hohenzollernring 53, D-50672 Köln
www.taschen.com

To stay informed about upcoming TASCHEN titles, please request our
magazine at www.taschen.com/magazine or write to TASCHEN,
Hohenzollernring 53, D-50672 Cologne, Germany, contact@taschen.com,
Fax: +49-221-254919. We will be happy to send you a free copy of our
magazine which is filled with information about all of our books.

CONCEPT AND LAYOUT:	Angelika Taschen, Berlin
PROJECT MANAGER:	Stephanie Bischoff, Cologne
LITHOGRAPH MANAGER:	Thomas Grell, Cologne
TEXT:	Shelley-Maree Cassidy, New Zealand (Europe and Africa); Christiane Reiter, Hamburg (Asia and South America); Daisann McLane, New York (North America)
FRENCH TRANSLATION:	Delphine Nègre-Bouvet, Paris (Europe); Philippe Safavi, Paris (North America); Michèle Schreyer, Cologne (Asia and South America); Thérèse Chatelain – Südkamp, Cologne (Asia and South America); Stéphanie Tabone for LocTeam, S.L., Barcelona (Africa)
GERMAN TRANSLATION:	Claudia Egdorf, Düsseldorf (Europe); Gabriele-Sabine Gugetzer, Hamburg (Europe); Simone Ott Caduff, California (North America); Sylvia Still for LocTeam, S. L., Barcelona (Africa)
ENGLISH TRANSLATION:	Cathy Lara, Berlin (Asia); Sophie Lovell, Berlin (Asia); Michael Hulse, Warwick (South America)
DESIGN:	Lambert und Lambert, Düsseldorf
PRINTED IN	China
ISBN	978-3-8365-0133-0